THE GENTILE BIAS
AND OTHER ESSAYS

SUPPLEMENTS TO
NOVUM TESTAMENTUM

VOLUME LIV

LEIDEN / E. J. BRILL / 1980

KENNETH WILLIS CLARK

THE GENTILE BIAS

AND OTHER ESSAYS

SELECTED BY

JOHN LAWRENCE SHARPE III

WITH A FOREWORD BY HUGH ANDERSON

LEIDEN / E. J. BRILL / 1980

340799

ISBN 90 04 06127 4

PRINTED IN THE NETHERLANDS

TO
ADC & JAS

CONTENTS

ACKNOWLEDGEMENTS

The editor gratefully acknowledges the permission to reprint granted by the publisher and editors of the books and journals in which the articles of Professor Kenneth W. Clark first appeared: to Matthew Black, editor of *New Testament Studies,* and to Cambridge University Press for permission to reprint "Worship in the Jerusalem Temple after A.D. 70"; to the editors, W. D. Davies and David Daube, and to Cambridge University Press for permission to reprint "The Effect of Recent Textual Criticism upon New Testament Studies" which appeared in *The Background of the New Testament and its Eschatology: Studies in Honor of C. H. Dodd;* to Joseph A. Fitzmyer, S.J., editor of the *Journal of Biblical Literature,* for permission to reprint "The Meaning of ἐνεργέω and καταργέω in the New Testament," "Realized Eschatology," "The Gentile Bias in Matthew," and "The Theological Relevance of Textual Variation in Current Criticism of the Greek New Testament"; to the American School of Oriental Research for permission to reprint "The Posture of the Ancient Scribe" from *The Biblical Archaeologist;* to W. C. van Unnik and J. N. Sevenster, editors of *Studia Paulina, Festschrift for Johannis de Zwaan,* for permission to reprint "Textual Criticism and Doctrine"; to the editors of *The Bulletin of the John Rylands Library* for permission to reprint "The Making of the Twentieth-Century New Testament"; to Allen K. Wikgren, editor of *Early Christian Origins, Festschrift for Harold R. Willoughby,* for permission to reprint "The Sins of Hermas"; to Kurt Aland, editor of *Studia Evangelica,* for permission to reprint "Observations on the Erasmian Notes in Codex 2"; to the editorial staff and to the publisher E. J. Brill for permission to reprint "The Text of the Gospel of John in Third-Century Egypt" from *Novum Testmentum;* to the editor J. Cobert Rylaarsdam and to the University of Chicago Press for permission to reprint "Today's Problems with the Critical Text of the New Testament" from *Transitions in Biblical Scholarship;* to J. K. Elliott, editor of *Studies in New Testament Language and Text: Essays in Honor of George D. Kilpatrick* for permission to reprint "The Meaning of [κατα] κυριεύειν"; to the editors, Eugene Howard Barth and Ronald Edwin Cocroft, and to the publisher E. J. Brill for permission to reprint "The Meaning of αρα" from the *Festschrift to Honor F. Wilbur Gingrich, Lexicographer, Scholar, Teacher, and committed Christian Layman;* and to editor David Edward Aune, and to E. J. Brill, publisher of *Studies in New Testament and Early Christian Literature: Essays in Honor of Allen P. Wikgren* for permission to reprint "The Israel of God."

FOREWORD

By Hugh Anderson

In the course of a long and distinguished teaching career at Duke University as well as through scholarly contacts in various parts of the world, Professor Kenneth Willis Clark made very many friends. That the altogether pleasant task of introducing this volume should have fallen to me I can only attribute to the leadings of a kindly Providence that pointed to one who had benefited more than most from association with Kenneth Clark. I knew him as the most helpful of colleagues at Duke from 1957 to 1966, and have known him always since as wise counselor and warm friend.

Not only Professor Clark's former students, a number of whom are themselves now in important teaching and related posts, but the scholarly world generally will welcome this representative selection of his papers. The articles assembled here span a period of over thirty years and cover an extensive range of subject matter, the former sure testimony to an unflagging zeal for scholarship, strong in the evening of his academic pilgrimage as in the morning and daytime, the latter to his comprehensive grasp of both larger issues in the field of New Testament studies and of significant items of detail.

Professor Clark's reputation is founded mainly on his outstanding and authoritative work as textual critic, and it is good now to have some important samples of his enterprise in that area under one cover, though even these are but a small part of his total contribution. On the occasion of Kenneth Clark's receiving a D. D. degree from the University of Glasgow, Professor William Barclay observed in his laureation that he had probably perused more manuscripts of the New Testament than any of his contemporaries. When one thinks of Kenneth Clark's unremitting pursuit of manuscripts, one also thinks back by association to the earlier devoted labors of such as J. J. Griesbach and Caspar René Gregory. He has not been, however, a "remote" textual critic, confined in the cavernous recesses of his speciality and never surfacing to behold the light or to breathe the air of common day—witness his concern for the theological implications of text-critical insights and for their application to appraisal of modern versions of the New Testament (see "The Theological Relevance of Textual Variation in Current Criticism of the Greek New Testament").

As his essays clearly reveal, there are other dimensions to K. W. Clark's scholarship than this text-critical work. No less weighty and always judicious and well-balanced are his contributions as historical critic, exegete and linguist. I should say that the great merit of his exercises in these areas is first that they are written with a clarity and precision that by no means always characterizes the *genre*, and second that in an age when too many have been prone to leap too quickly from the texts of the New Testament to a rather subjective psychologizing, philosophizing or theologizing, they call us back to the cruciality of a sound and solid historical and linguistic study, undertaken with as much honesty and objectively as possible.

The articles printed here fall broadly, in regard to content, into three main groups: 1. Historical-exegetical; 2. Text-critical; 3. Linguistic. Let me draw attention to some salient features in each category.

1. The most frequently cited of all Clark's papers, that on "Realized Eschatology," properly occupies a place between groups 1 and 3, insofar as it is primarily an investigation of the meaning of the Greek verbs ἐγγίζειν and φθάνειν. But in conjunction with J. Y. Campbell's earlier article on the same topic, it had searching implications for the wider understanding of Jesus' eschatological ministry and message, went far toward overcoming C. H. Dodd's notion of "realized eschatology," and pointed toward the recent consensus, which in his later years Dodd himself joined, that we must do justice to the futuristic element in Jesus' proclamation and should speak at most of "self-realizing eschatology."

While not everyone will agree with the ideas on Paul's view of Law, circumcision, Judaism and Christianity presented in "The Israel of God," it does summon us to a greater exactitude in our use of terms like Jew, Gentile, Christian, in relation to the first century A.D., and in this highly controversial territory its conclusion merits serious scrutiny, namely that Paul did not yield to anyone in his set loyalty to the best he knew in Judaism, nor weaned men away from both Judaism and Hellenism to form a new religion, but allowed his Jewish converts to stay within Judaism and drew his Gentile converts into Judaism, the "true" Judaism.

"The Gentile Bias in Matthew," first published in 1947, anticipates recent redaction studies, and in arguing that "the Jewish paricularism in the earlier part of Matthew is overshadowed by the main theme of the Gospel which is better presented in the Great Commission," and so in highlighting the "universalist motif," it offers a needed corrective, as I see it, to the persistent tendency to overstress Matthew's "Jewishness."

K. W. Clark's readiness to question established or traditional tenets of scholarship is admirably illustrated by his paper on "Worship in the Jerusalem Temple after A.D. 70," in which he seeks to overthrow the widely accepted notion that the practice of the cultus was totally discontinued in Jerusalem from the close of the Jewish War. While the case he conducts, with considerable erudition, be it said, might seem to some to savor too much of *argumentum e silentio*, it should at least give us pause before making sweeping statements about the absolute cessation of all religious activities in the Temple between A.D. 70 and 135.

The inclusion of the essay on "The Sins of Hermas" is to be welcomed as a salutary reminder that New Testament research may not be restricted to or terminated with the Canon of Scripture.

2. The articles on textual criticism speak eloquently for themselves of the writer's expertise in his specialization. They are written with the customary lucidity and the complexities are handled with a deft touch which facilitates communication to the non-expert. This is true whether K. W. Clark is discussing specific recent papyrus manuscript discoveries, as in "The Text of the Gospel of John in Third-Century Egypt," or in drawing threads together and assessing (with a clear analytical eye) the contemporary status of textual criticism, as in "The Effect of Recent Textual Criticism upon New Testament Studies" or "Today's Problems with the Critical Text of the New Testament." In particular the latter splendidly exemplifies the author's honesty in the quest for objectivity, of which we have spoken, while at the same time witnessing to his acknowledgement of the inescapability of the subjective judgment in textual investigation (as in interpretation generally): "A disciplined subjectivity is a legitimate critical instrument, especially when we do acknowledge our use of it. Nevertheless, it should be recognized that it can never represent the final judgment. Eclectic emendation is always a tentative proposal, subject to weightier overarching evidence wherever such evidence can be discerned. Because of its subjective character, eclectic emendation cannot escape bias, however, inadvertent."

3. The fact that the articles on linguistic matters appear to deal with "small things," like the Greek enclitic ἄρα ("The Meaning of αρα") is no real measure of their importance. They not only reveal the author's sensitivity to the nuances of *Koinē*, but also indirectly uphold two principles we neglect to our cost: first, that a feeling for the ancient language and for the inner attitude or demeanor of those who use it is an indispensable prerequisite of sound exegesis; second, that it is incumbent upon the translator of the New Testament to allow his translation to live within the first-century Christian experience. It is this latter principle that informs

the essay on "The Meaning of ἐνεργέω and καταργέω in the New Testament." There it is maintained, *inter alia,* that the renderings of ἐνεργέω in Galatians ii.8, in the King James Version and the Revised Standard Version ("wrought effectually in Peter ... was mighty in me" and "worked in Peter ... worked for me," respectively) are both modern and humanistic under-translations, which scarcely do justice to the first-century's strong and perennial inclination toward supernatural imagery and belief. And I for one am almost persuaded by K. W. Clark's alternative suggestion "that presents a vigorous imagery at home in the first-century Christian movement": "For he who infused the supernatural spirit for Peter in order that he might authoritatively preach among the Jews, infused me too with that same spirit, so that I might as authoritatively preach among the pagans." At any rate the implied maxim that even the most modern of translations must seek to be faithful to the *Zeitgeist* of early Christianity is worthy of all consideration.

The essays in these pages are a tribute to a brand of scholarship in which larger understanding of complex problems of history and interpretation is rooted and grounded in a meticulous care for the so-called "small things," and which I believe regrettably we have seen diminish in our time. That almost without exception they have stood and continue to stand the test of time very well indeed marks out Kenneth Willis Clark as one who has stood above the fads and fancies that have tended to dominate theology and New Testament interpretation of late. All in all the volume may be regarded as *monumentum aere perennius.*

New College
The University of Edinburgh

THE GENTILE BIAS IN MATTHEW

IT IS commonly held that the Gospel of Matthew was written by a converted Jew. In proof of this are usually noted such features as the genealogy, the blocks of teaching material, the many quotations from Jewish scripture, the eschatological passages, the Jewish particularism, Semitic words and idioms, and particularly the use of "kingdom of Heaven" instead of "kingdom of God." It then becomes necessary to explain the gentile bias of the Gospel as a secondary trait, which crops forth in the story of the virgin birth, the heightening of miracle,[1] the rejection of Israel (e.g. 21 43), the denunciation of Pharisees (Ch. 23) and Sadducees (e.g., 16 6), and the Great Commission.

In this particular connection, we seldom are reminded that the gentile Luke also presents a genealogy, that Luke and even the pagan Epictetus were also much interested in the type of teaching materials employed in Matthew, that all Christians — both Jewish and gentile — had long since become accustomed to scriptural proof texts and prophecies (whether from the LXX or the Hebrew text) as also to the eschatological background of Christian belief. Furthermore, Jewish particularism in the earlier part of Matthew is overshadowed by the main theme of the Gospel which is better presented in the Great Commission. As for Semitic terms and rabbinic avoidance of the divine name, the usual generalities are subject to refutation by detailed analysis. In short, the oft repeated argument for Jewish authorship seems more traditional than rational, and may profitably be reviewed especially in the light of the possibility that no part of it rules out a gentile authorship.

[1] See M. S. Enslin, *Christian Beginnings* (New York, 1938), pp. 395–6.

But as to the gentile bias in the gospel, always remembered yet relegated to secondary importance, there is real difficulty in ascribing it to a Jew. Many a Jew in Syria had been hellenized, but a Jewish Christian of about 90 A.D. would hardly be found writing a gospel whose theme is the definite and final rejection of Israel by her God. It is sometimes suggested that a convert from Judaism would thus react vehemently against the religion to which he had previously held. But this is quite subjective and merely speculative; Paul illustrates a less vehement reaction of one who still insisted that God had not repudiated His people (Rom 11 1). Furthermore, at the time of the writing of Matthew a Jew did not feel the need to renounce Judaism in order to confess belief in Jesus Christ. Such a renunciation is more natural from the viewpoint of a gentile "Matthew."

The Matthean thesis is not the same as the earlier message of Paul, that gentiles also may be saved by inclusion in the new Israel; nor is it yet like the later message of Marcion that Jews and gentiles have different gods and separate destinies. It is instead the message that Christianity, now predominantly gentile, has displaced Judaism with God as the true Israel. "The children of the kingdom will be cast out" (8 12); "in his name will the gentiles trust" (12 21). "The kingdom of God will be taken away from you, and given to a people producing the fruits of the kingdom" (21 43). "Go and make disciples of all the gentile peoples (τὰ ἔθνη) .... teaching them to obey all the commands I have laid on you."

This gentile bias is the primary theme in Matthew. The Jews as a people are no longer the object of God's salvation. They have rejected and killed God's son (21 39)[2]; now God has rejected them and shut them out of the kingdom, transferring his favor to Christian believers as the true Israel. This theme is repeatedly illustrated, in an impressive succession of stories (peculiar to Matthew): the Two Sons (21 28–32), the Vineyard Tenants (21 33–43), the Wedding Feast (22 1–14), the Ten Virgins (25 1–13),

---

[2] This story is also told by Mark and Luke, but without the Matthean climax of 21 43; the accusation is repeated in 27 4–5, another passage peculiar to Matthew.

the Talents (25 14–30)[3], and the Judgment by the Son of Man (25 31–46).

The gentile bias of this primary theme in Matthew rises to a climax as the author declares that the Great Commandment is the epitome of the Law and the Prophets; in Mt 22 40 there is no scribe, as in Mk and Lk, to agree with this extreme conclusion. Now it is declared that the true Messiah need not, indeed cannot, be a descendent of David (22 41–46). Then follows the denunciation of the Pharisaic representatives of Judaism and the lament over Jerusalem whose children would not accept God's proffered salvation (23 37–39). Next comes the dire prediction of the destruction of the very Temple of Judaism (but in 12 6 the Christian Messiah has already been declared greater than the Temple).

This is the context in which we must understand the eschatological discourse of Mt 24. Although originally developed by Jewish Christians, and early recorded by Paul and Mark, such apocalyptic imagery has been fully learned and accepted by gentile Christians as well. The "Little Apocalypse" is adopted by the gentile Luke as well as by "Matthew." It is idle, therefore, to contend that such a passage reflects a Jewish mind at work. On the contrary, not only could a gentile mind produce Mt 24 (as well as Lk 21), but its meaning in the Matthean context clearly reflects the gentile bias of one who turns the coming Judgment against Judaism itself. The faithful slave of 24 45 represents the gentile Christian who stands ready for the imminent coming of his Lord; while the wicked slave, unimpressed by the imminence of his Lord's return, represents recalcitrant Judaism condemned in wailing and gnashing of teeth to the lot of the "hypocrites" (24 51). This word is peculiar to Matthew, and surely reflects Ch. 23.

The Matthean picture of judgment and rejection is not presented as a warning to Judaism to repent. The author believes that the warning has already been sufficient, and penitence is

---

[3] Matthew adds to this story, as compared with Luke, the casting out of the profitless slave into outer darkness where there will be wailing and gnashing of teeth — a phrase applied to Judaism in 24 51 also.

no longer to be expected. Judaism as such has definitely rejected Jesus as God's Messiah, and God has finally rejected Judaism. This gentile bias is the primary thesis in Matthew, and such a message would be natural only from the bias of a gentile author.

With the present-day rejection of Matthew the tax-collector as author of the First Gospel, the remnant of that ancient ascription which still sees a Jew as author of the gospel may also merit careful scrutiny. It is commonly repeated that a Jewish author is indicated by the Matthean quotations of numerous scriptural passages. Westcott and Hort list 123 such "quotations" in Matthew, but it is seldom noted that they also list 109 in Luke's gospel and 133 in Acts. In addition to the scriptural quotations drawn from Mk or Q, "Matthew" used about 40 quotations while Luke used about 50. Unless we argue from these data that Luke also was a Jew, it is not logical to contend that this calls for a Jewish author for Matthew. Although "Matthew" is more deliberate in pointing to fulfilled prophecy, a similar significance is implicit in Luke, as it is also in other gentile Christian writings. Such an application of the Jewish scriptures to validate the Christian development was a common practice among contemporary Christian writers—gentile as well as Jewish.

But it may be urged that "Matthew" sometimes used the original Hebrew rather than the LXX. On this point, we may note first the conclusions in which agreement has been reached. "Matthew" usually reflects the LXX. His own peculiar material, especially, shows use of the LXX. He even alters Markan quotations in the direction of the LXX. So much can be safely accepted. Beyond this point, various commentators have found certain quotations which vary from the LXX text, and which seem to some to be closer to the Hebrew text.[4] But in the brief lists of such citations it is not often that two commentators agree upon the same quotations as having a Hebrew base, so elusive are the criteria. It is not even certain as to the particular scriptural passage or passages which the evangelist may have

---

[4] I am indebted to Dr. Howard Carroll, of High Point (N.C.) College, for a careful study of O.T. quotations cited by various scholars as possibly based on the Hebrew.

had in mind. We cannot, then, be sure which passage or passages should serve as our base when seeking to determine Hebrew or LXX influence. Furthermore, we have to consult only the Masoretic text, with little knowledge of the earlier form or forms of the Hebrew. A typical conclusion to this matter is that in Robinson's recent commentary.[5] Concerning the few debatable quotations in Matthew, he concludes that sometimes "we have a completely independent rendering of the Hebrew text;" or again, that we have "either an independent translation from the M.T. or from some Hebrew text which differs from that which has become traditional." But such phrases are meaningless under analysis, for the supposed Hebrew base is completely hypothetical and the independence of rendering may obscure a LXX origin as easily as a Hebrew. Robinson further observes that the gospel author "himself used a Greek version by preference." Bacon likewise concludes that the evangelist "is always dependent on the LXX."[6] To consent to this conclusion is to recognize that the scriptural quotations employed in Mt point neither to any use of the Hebrew text nor to a Jewish author.

In the matter of language there are a few selected terms in the Gospel of Matthew which are worth notice here. The author is said to reveal a traditional reverence in avoiding the divine name. It is obvious that "kingdom of Heaven" is characteristic of Matthew, especially when it is deliberately substituted for Mark's "kingdom of God." But Mark is a Jew, though he feels no irreverence in writing θεός. Paul too is a Jew who often writes "kingdom of God," and constantly writes θεός. This suggests that the reverence reflected in the ancient term for *Jahweh* was not violated in primitive Christian times when a Jew wrote or spoke the name θεός. Furthermore, "Matthew" did write "kingdom of God" in his gospel, in four instances.* Commentators have proposed special reasons why he did this, but the fact that he did refutes our usual theory. As for the term θεός, "Matthew" has written it in his gospel scores of times.

---

[5] Theodore H. Robinson, *The Gospel of Matthew* (Moffatt Commentary) New York, 1928; p. xvi.

[6] Benjamin W. Bacon. *Studies in Matthew* (New York, 1930), p. 477.

* 12.28; 19.24; 21.31; 21.43.

Perhaps we can discover a reason for the preference of Matthew for the phrase "kingdom of Heaven," other than that he liked it or had made it a habit, but it is not reasonable to continue to declare that it was because he, as a Jew, would have felt irreverent in writing the divine name.

Another term of special interest is "phylactery" in 23 5. George Fox has recently published a valuable note on this term in which a useful clue may be found.[7] He has observed that the Hebrew ṭōṭaphōth (Ex 13 16; Deut 6 8, 11 18) is translated only by ἀσάλευτον in the LXX. In the Syriac Peshitta and in the Targum it is rendered tephillîn. But in Mt 23 5 the tephillîn are referred to as φυλακτήρια. From these data Fox reasons that the evangelist attributes gentile superstition to the Pharisees trusting in the magic of an amulet, instead of the more reverent understanding of tephillîn. Olmstead believes that Jesus himself used a term other than tephillîn, some term that meant "amulet," and that Jesus thus criticised the Pharisees.[8] But the context clearly shows that originally ostentation rather than misuse of the tephillîn, was the basis of this criticism. In any case, although many Jews may have missed the deeper meaning in the use of their tephillîn, "Matthew's" unique use of the term φυλακτήρια reflects an author of gentile mind.

Another term worth noting is the name for the devil. Only the Semitic term σατανᾶς is used by Paul (eight times)[9] and Mark (five times). The gentile Luke uses σατανᾶς five times (once from Mk), and διάβολος five times (twice changing Mk). Matthew has σατανᾶς four times (three times from Mk), διάβολος six times (once changing Mk), ὁ πονηρός once (changing Mk), and ὁ πειράζων once. These terms may have been interchangeable with all Christians, but the fact that two earlier Jewish-Christian writers, Paul and Mark, use only the Semitic form, without exception, again suggests that "Matthew" like Luke reveals a gentile bias.

---

[7] G. George Fox, "The Matthean Misrepresentation of Tephillîn" (*Journal of Near Eastern Studies* 1 [1942] 373–7).

[8] A. T. Olmstead, *Jesus in the Light of History* (1942), p. 182.

[9] The term διάβολος alone occurs in Ephesians, twice.

With reference to various Semitic words in Matthew, it seems conclusive that the author did not even understand the vernacular of the Jews. He avoids the use of Mark's βοανηργές (3 17) and ταλειθά κούμ (5 41) by omitting them; also of κορβάν (7 11) and βαρτίμαιος (10 46) and ραββουνεί (10 51) and even Ἀββά (14 36) by using Greek instead. He twice hellenizes Mark's Ἰσκαριώθ. (Mk 3 19, 14 10). He does not understand the term *hosanna* (Mt 21 9), nor the name *Golgotha* which he attempts to translate (27 33). He does explain the meaning of "Jesus" and "Emmanuel," perhaps unaided; however, as Bacon observes, "it is hard to imagine a Christian *milieu* without sufficient linguistic knowledge" for this. Perhaps a Jewish author might do as poorly with the colloquial Aramaic, but Mark has surely shown a somewhat better understanding of it.[10]

It is possible that we have been too easily persuaded that the arguments we have often repeated really support our traditional view that the author of Matthew was a Jew. We have attempted here to point out that the customary arguments beg the question of Jewish authorship. It might be added that interest in numerological patterns so often observed in Mt[11], or in ethical precepts, is by no means alien to gentile contemporaries of "Matthew."

All commentators have agreed that the Gospel of Matthew incorporates both Judaistic and Hellenistic elements. They differ as to the proper explanation for this. E. F. Scott, who refrains from stating that the author was a Jew, observes that he was "not a partisan." In his gospel, "the Jewish coloring belongs to the sources, not to the work itself. Moreover there is much in it that suggests the atmosphere of a Gentile, rather than a Jewish, church."[12]

Perhaps we can attempt a still more definite hypothesis to explain the facts. "Matthew" was strongly partisan, favoring

[10] Even Mark is awkward with ταλειθά κούμ (5 41) and ὁ υἱὸς τιμαίου βαρτίμαιος (10 46) and Ἀββά ὁ πατήρ (14 36), all of which are avoided in Matthew.

[11] See the introductions of Moffatt (p. 257) and Enslin (p. 390).

[12] E. F. Scott, *Literature of the New Testament* (New York, 1936), pp. 75, 67.

the gentile and renouncing the Jew. He was a gentile Christian who wrote his gospel in Syria, where Gentile Christianity threatened to dominate even in the days of Paul. He was persuaded that the Christian gospel, originally delivered to the Jews, had been rejected by them as a people; that God had now turned his back upon Judaism and chosen the largely gentile Christianity. The two strains in his gospel reflect these two stages in God's plan to save his chosen people. But the assurance that the gentiles have displaced the Jews is the basic message and the gentile bias of Matthew.

WORSHIP IN THE JERUSALEM
TEMPLE AFTER A.D. 70

I

One of the best known facts of ancient history is the destruction of the Jerusalem Temple in A.D. 70. Yet another, and related, historical datum, although known, has been greatly slighted: the destruction of Jerusalem and its Temple in A.D. 135. Between the First Revolt and the Second Revolt there lies a history of the Jewish State of sixty-five years which has come to be treated as something less than an epilogue. This period in the State's continued existence is an important lacuna that requires to be filled in, and to that end we here raise a single question: 'Did Jews worship on the holy mountain until the *final* destruction in A.D. 135?'

It has long been the historian's habit to speak (e.g. S. G. F. Brandon recently)[1] of 'the overthrow of Israel as a national State' whose 'existence terminated in A.D. 70'. If by this is meant autonomous existence, such must be understood to have terminated 133 years earlier when Pompey subjugated the independent Maccabean State.[2] But if the reference is to an end of the subject State, then it is not the year 70 but the year 135 in which this came about. Historical information is more abundant up to the First Revolt and only sparse beyond that point to the Second Revolt, but history cannot afford the imbalance of circumstantial recording.

Even the meagre information we do possess about the Second Revolt is quite sufficient to portray no mean power opposing the Romans in 132–5. Dio Cassius describes the conflict as 'a war of no slight importance nor of brief duration' (69, 12, 1), for which 'Hadrian sent against them his best generals, first of whom was Julius Severus, dispatched from Britain where he was governor,... who did not venture to attack his opponents in the open... in view of their numbers' (69, 13, 2–3). The casualties among the Roman legions were heavy,[3] and Dio reports 580,000 Jews slain in the fighting so that 'nearly all of Judaea was desolated' (69, 14, 1–2). Eusebius emphatically states that these were 'no small wars' (*H.E.* IV, 5, 2), and the 'military aid' (IV, 6, 1) sent in by the emperor consisted of many of his best legions from as far off as Mauretania.[4] Despite the power of the Roman Empire, the Judaeans were able to win a brief independence and, as in Maccabean times, began to

---

[1] S. G. F. Brandon, *The Fall of Jerusalem and the Christian Church* (1951), xvii and 166.
[2] Cf. Appian, *Syr.* 50; Jos. *War*, I, 150–4.
[3] Dio Cassius, *Rom. Hist.* 69, 14, 3; Fronto, *Parth.*
[4] See F. Gregorovius, *The Emperor Hadrian* (1898), pp. 151 f.

strike their own currency. The peak of the conflict came after two years, in the long siege of a 'strong citadel' near Jerusalem.[1] Indeed, Appian (*Syr.* 50) states that once again Jerusalem itself was destroyed, and many a later historian has repeated this,[2] some averring that it was at this time that the site of the Temple was ploughed up.

This is by no means the picture of a virtually non-existent State whose end had come sixty-five years earlier. The records about the Second Revolt are few, fragmentary and brief, but those that survive indicate a fierce story comparable to that of the First Revolt as detailed by Josephus. Years ago, Rendel Harris observed that this 'greatest of all such disasters...is not written as large in history as it occurred in fact; there was no Josephus in Hadrian's time...to publish an almost daily bulletin of horrors. We should think less of the year A.D. 70 as a turning-point in history', he wrote, 'if providence had not provided us with a chronicler'[3]—or, better still, if there had been a similar chronicler about the year A.D. 135. But the complete historical record repeals the dogma that the Jewish State ended in A.D. 70. Therefore, our first point would be this: the history of the Jewish State ended in A.D. 135, and not in A.D. 70, so that there is an additional history of sixty-five years which must some day be written and understood more adequately.

Within the general history of the Jewish State between A.D. 70 and 135, the question of the sacrificial cult has increasingly impressed itself upon the writer as requiring renewed consideration. This question seems not to have been seriously discussed for the past century. Perhaps the first to consider the possibility of continued sacrifice after A.D. 70 was Prudentius Maranus in the eighteenth century, who concluded that private sacrifice outside of Jerusalem continued until the time of the Emperor Julian.[4] A series of three scholars over a century—Jaabez,[5] Kreuzenach,[6] and Hirsch Chajes[7]—agreed that at least the paschal lamb continued to be offered on a renewed altar on the original sanctified site until the final destruction by Hadrian. This position seems to us to be the most reasonable interpretation of all the data.[8] Another scholar, Albert Schwegler, went much further in holding that the full Levitical cultus was restored.[9] However, in 1848 the opinions of all these scholars were opposed by a young scholar in Breslau, Bernhard Friedmann, in a dissertation under Dr Heinrich Graetz who together argued that all sacri-

---

[1] The unlocated fortress of Beththera (Eus. *H.E.* IV, 6, 3).

[2] Gregorovius (*ibid.* p. 153 n. 1) lists a number of such sources.

[3] Rendel Harris, 'Hadrian's Decree of Expulsion of the Jews from Jerusalem', *H.T.R.* XIX (1926), 198. See also Gregorovius, *ibid.* p. 151.

[4] Prudentius Maranus, *Ausg. der Apologeten*, LXXV. This view was embraced also by Semisch.

[5] Jaabez, שאילת יעבץ (Altona, 1739).

[6] Jost, ed., *Israelitische Annalen* (1840), no. 26.

[7] Hirsch Chajes, דרכי הוראה (Zolkiew, 1842).

[8] Both this view and that of Maranus could be accepted in combination.

[9] Albert Schwegler, *Nachapostolisches Zeitalter* (Tübingen, 1846), pp. 308–9.

fice ceased in A.D. 70.[1] Then through much of the year 1849 Friedmann carried on a debate with Friedenthal, also of Breslau, in the pages of the *Literaturblatt des Orients*.[2] Friedenthal's final contention was that the paschal lamb continued to be sacrificed on the sacred altar, as long as the genuine site was known. The question was once again raised by Derenbourg in 1867 who sought to refute the rabbinic passages frequently offered as evidence of continued sacrifice.[3] So for more than a century, the problem was active and successive scholars produced variant theories as to the continuation of the sacrificial cult after A.D. 70.[4]

Logically, the first argument is the *a priori* assumption that such worship continued. If we had no record one way or the other, it would be inconceivable that Jews would make no effort to return to Temple worship at the end of the First Revolt. To be satisfied with the view that worship ceased altogether in A.D. 70, one must prove to oneself that circumstances presented an absolute barrier to such worship. As long and as often as the Jew in ancient times was able to continue Temple worship, he must (as history shows) adhere to it. The Temple had suffered repeated destructions, by the Babylonians in 586,[5] and again by the Syrians in 168,[6] and was once again desecrated by the Romans in 63 B.C.[7] After each occasion worship was renewed, although in the case of Syria a proscription of worship was overcome only by three desperate years of war. As late as A.D. 70 there was no disposition in Jewish orthodoxy to discard voluntarily the traditional Temple worship. The attitude of Essenes and Therapeutai adverse to animal sacrifice was certainly not normative. The earliest Christians (e.g. Peter, John, Paul) shared the orthodox participation in Temple worship. Only one factor could bring the Jews to cease such worship and that would be the physical prevention imposed upon them. We shall indicate below how this one essential obstruction was interposed in A.D. 135 and not before; but until such a condition developed, the *a priori* argument carries considerable force.

A second argument to be considered lies in the close parallel between the period 70–135 and the exilic period. In general terms, to describe the one is to describe the other. The Jewish State was finally reduced by a dominant world empire after a long and bitter conflict. The fortress of Jerusalem was destroyed and much of its wall thrown down. The Temple itself was destroyed

---

[1] Friedmann and Graetz, 'Die angebliche Fortdauer des jüdischen Opfercultus nach der Zerstörung des zweiten Tempels', *Theologische Jahrbücher*, VII (Tübingen, 1848), 338–71. Friedmann gives an account of the history of criticism relating to this issue.

[2] Fürst, ed., *Literaturblatt des Orients*, x (Leipzig, 1849): Friedenthal's argument is found in cols. 328–32, 492–5, 524–8, 573–6, 702–4, whereas Friedmann's is in cols. 401–5, 433–8, 465–9, 934–7.

[3] J. Derenbourg, *Essai sur l'histoire et la géographie de la Palestine* (Paris, 1867), 'Notes additionelles', note XIV 'Le sacrifice après la destruction du temple' (pp. 480–3).

[4] Quite recently, Louis Finkelstein has argued that Titus promised restoration of the Temple but because of Samaritan and Nationalist opposition the promise was never fulfilled. Cf. *Akiba* (1936), pp. 216–34.

[5] II Kings xxv. 8–10.   [6] I Macc. i. 20–3, 39, 45 f., 54; ii. 8, 12; iii. 45, 50 f.

[7] Jos. *War*, I, 148 f.; Appian, *Syr.* 50.

and burned and its sacred objects carried off.[1] The population was decimated and the military strength broken. Financial resources for restoration or maintenance were meagre, but the conqueror pronounced no edict against the continuation of religious worship. Differences there were between the two occasions but basically the situation was the same. Both times the consequences of military defeat offered serious obstacles to continued worship in the Temple.

Yet it does appear that in the exilic period Palestinian Jews resumed their regular Temple worship.[2] In the first place, there is evidence that destruction in 586 had not been complete and that some remnant of the holy place survived. In the first chapter of Haggai reference is made to the necessity of renewing the wooden panel with timber from the neighbouring hills. Before the new Temple was built Zechariah (vii. 3) attests to the activity of 'the priests of the house of the Lord' and to offerings presented in the Temple (vii. 2). Similarly, his contemporary Haggai refers (i. 4, 9) to the dilapidated condition of the house of the Lord[3] in which nevertheless sacrifices have been offered (ii. 14). Even before these two exiles reached Jerusalem, Ezra (i. 4) represents Cyrus as encouraging contributions for renovation of 'the house of God which is in Jerusalem'.[4] Not only did the damaged Temple stand throughout the exilic era, but actual worship there is reported by Ezra (vi. 3) in the decree of Cyrus in 538. Much earlier, indeed soon after the Babylonians had departed, Jeremiah (xli. 5) tells of eighty worshippers from the north who brought 'cereal offerings and incense to present at the Temple of the Lord'. Mitchell (*ICC* on Haggai ii. 3) alludes to continued Temple worship in observing that the task of renovation was great, 'even if the ancient site had been sufficiently cleared to permit the reconstruction of the altar and the resumption of sacrifice'. Oesterley too believes that 'the holy site itself still remained, and to set up an altar again would easily be accomplished'.[5] He arrives at the conclusion that 'the altar had been used for offering sacrifices during the whole period of the Exile'.[6] This conclusion appears to be manifestly logical and frequently supported and therefore need not here be fully debated but only briefly recalled.[7]

The reasons that point to continued Temple worship during the exilic era

---

[1] On the destruction of the Temple in 586 B.C., see II Kings xxv. 8–10; Jer. xxxix. 8; lii. 13; Jos. *War*, v, 391, 405, 411. On the later destruction in A.D. 70, see Jos. *War*, VI, 271–5.

[2] The period between temples was seventy years (586–516 B.C.), closely equivalent to the sixty-five year period between the destructions of the First and Second Revolts.

[3] See also Haggai i. 2, 14; ii. 3, 7.   [4] See also Ezra iii. 8 f.; v. 15.

[5] Oesterley, *History of Israel* (1932), II, 56.

[6] *Ibid.* p. 82. See also p. 94: 'During the whole of the exilic period the priests in Palestine had been officiating in the Temple.' Again (p. 94): '...they found the Temple still standing, but in a dilapidated state...sacrifices were being offered...'; and (p. 92): '...it is unreasonable to suppose that during the, approximately, half-century which followed, these people would have refrained from using the traditional place of worship in their midst'.

[7] E.g. Martin Noth, *History of Israel* (1958), p. 305: '...religious ceremonies had continued to be maintained'.

apply equally well to the period of 70–135. The circumstances were similar, the religious motivation the same, the opportunity was present. After A.D. 70 a considerable Jewish population remained in and about Jerusalem, the Romans issued no edict of proscription forbidding Temple worship, the centrality of this worship had motivated the desperate defence. Furthermore, Oesterley's argument for the Exile is again relevant after A.D. 70: 'the holy site itself still remained, and to set up an altar again would easily be accomplished...priests were in Jerusalem for carrying out whatever was possible in the customary forms of worship'.[1] It is difficult to compare the destruction wrought upon the Temple in 586 B.C. and A.D. 70, since we are informed only that on both occasions walls were destroyed and sections were burned. Historians themselves have confused the two occasions so that it is sometimes difficult to know to which occasion to assign the record. Dio Cassius writes simply of 'a part of the Temple being set on fire' in A.D. 70 (65, 6, 3). Although Josephus paints a scene of fiery horror in Book VI (272), specifying the burning of chambers containing money, vestments and sacred treasures (282), his exaggeration is evident when later (387–91) he reports that the priest Jesus and the treasurer Phineas delivered the priestly vestments and some of the sacred treasures to the Romans. Again, Josephus reports in the same Book VI (271, 322) the death of numbers of priests, and yet it is clear that many priests survived the First Revolt. Another obstacle to the Temple worship after 70 was the official transference of the Temple tax from Jerusalem to Rome,[2] but the decree merely increased impoverishment and did not necessarily destroy determination to continue the offering of the sacrifices. Such Temple worship as may have continued would have been carried on with only a minimum of restoration of the holy premises, and in less grandeur of ritualistic style. Such circumstances had been imposed during the Exile and could well be endured again after A.D. 70.

It is an important factor, further, that when the Romans completed the conquest of Jerusalem in A.D. 70 the official attitude toward the Jews was surprisingly lenient. No measures of reprisal or suppression were taken. Mommsen reminds us that 'no hindrances were put in the way of the Jews exercising their religious customs either in Palestine or elsewhere'.[3] The legions were withdrawn and only a small garrison force was stationed in this Roman province after A.D. 73, the customary Tenth Legion according to Josephus (*War*, VII, 5); and even this force was withdrawn in the time of Trajan to engage in the Parthian War.[4] Under Domitian (A.D. 86), two *alae* and four cohorts or about 2500 men were stationed in Judaea.[5] Following the cessation of hostilities Jews in increasing numbers moved into Judaea and

---

[1] Oesterley, *ibid.* p. 56 (this is said with reference to the exilic period).
[2] See Jos. *War*, VII, 218; Dio Cassius LXVI, 7.
[3] T. Mommsen, *Provinces of the Roman Empire* (1899), II, 238; cf. Eus. *H.E.* III, 17.
[4] F. Gregorovius, *The Emperor Hadrian* (1898), pp. 19, 113.
[5] *Corpus Inscriptionum Latinarum*, III, p. 857, Dipl. xiv.

Jerusalem, and Jewish pilgrims continued to come to the Temple with their offerings. Seven synagogues survived in the city to serve the need of the Jerusalem community.[1] Traditional religious rites and ceremonies were persistent, and would have been observed as fully as possible. Only when the Temple worship was threatened by Hadrian's design to establish a Temple of Jupiter on the site did revolt again break out, and one may reason that such a threat to the Temple cult must have been absent up until that time (about 130 or 132).

Some would hold that the Romans agreed to the restoration of the Jewish Temple. Graetz believes that 'the Jews made the re-erection of the Temple ...a condition of their laying down arms', but it is unreasonable to hold that the Jews were in any position to impose conditions upon Titus. The idea rests upon Talmudic passages and upon the Epistle of Barnabas (xvi. 1–9): 'they who destroyed his Temple shall again build it up'. A variant report is that the Samaritans opposed this Roman intention, so that Hadrian prescribed a shift in the location of the Temple—which in turn was resisted by the Jews.[2] Several Christian writers, apparently following one another, report that the Jews rebelled in the time of Hadrian and began to restore the Temple structure, and thus provoked Hadrian to wage war against them.[3] Still another form of the idea is that the Jews were permitted to restore the Temple themselves. Schürer holds that 'the intention to carry on this work was certainly entertained' but 'whether during these troubled years of war the rebuilding may actually have been begun must be left undecided'.[4] Finkelstein cites rabbinic references persuading him that 'the promise to undertake the building was made by Trajan. Nothing less than such a promise could possibly justify the establishment of a Trajan Day.'[5] George Adam Smith and W. Robertson Smith find that 'there is even some evidence that the restoration of the Temple was contemplated or commenced', that is, by the Romans in their original plan for rebuilding the city. But none of these contentions is necessary to our view that Jews continued to worship on the Temple mount, although it is quite possible that limited restoration of the Temple facilities may have been made gradually over the years by the Jews. The statements that Hadrian again destroyed the Temple may also have an independent truth, with reference to a dilapidated and repaired Temple that survived the attack of Titus.[6] The Mishnah (Taanith IV, 6) speaks of two destructions of the Temple on Thammuz 17 when it was levelled with the plough. This appears to be another instance of confusing the two accounts, or rather conflating the

---

[1] F.-M. Abel, *Histoire de la Palestine* (1952), II, 48; H. Vincent et Abel, *Jérusalem* (1926), II, 877 f. See Epiph. *De mens. et pond.* 14.

[2] Cf. Genesis R lxiv. 7 (p. 710). The text is quoted in English in Finkelstein, *Akiba*, pp. 313 f.

[3] Chrysostom. *Orat. adv. Judaeos*, v, 10; Georgius Cedrenus, *Historiarum Compendium* (ed. Bekker), I, 437; Nicephorus Callistus, *Eccl. Hist.* III, 24, Dio 69, 12.

[4] Schürer, I, 2, p. 302.   [5] L. Finkelstein, *Akiba* (1936), pp. 313 f.

[6] Jerome, *Zach.* 8, 18, 19; *Chronicon Paschale* (ed. Dindorf), I, 474.

two. In either case, the phrase must be understood figuratively as expressing extreme devastation, for an ancient plough would be a futile instrument indeed to attempt to move among the great stone blocks and paving stones upon the Temple mount. Destroyed indeed was the Holy Place in A.D. 70 but not entirely nor finally. The sacred altar with its surroundings must have been a poor thing, but a holy place nonetheless where propitiation might still be made for divine mercy and blessing.

II

If at this point we are prepared to accept the possibility that the sacrificial cult in Jerusalem did not altogether cease in A.D. 70, we may the more fairly assess the numerous passages that may be offered in support. Such are to be found in the New Testament, and in patristic and rabbinic writings. These are not new citations, but in the past it has been customary to reject them singly as each is encountered, by the following circular argument: since there was no sacrifice offered after A.D. 70 such passages as refer to sacrifice cannot have a literal relevance to actual sacrifice; and since therefore these passages cannot be used as evidence of sacrifice, there is found to be no such evidence.[1] Reason would call upon us to break this false circle, by first of all recognizing the possibility at least that sacrifice continued in some modest form. With tentative assent we may reassess the weight of familiar testimony, in the light of the foregoing argument.

First of all, it may be observed that when the Gospels refer in the account of Jesus to the Temple and its sacrificial cult, although they are composed after A.D. 70 there is no embarrassment and no disclaimer nor any reference to an invalid or an inactive altar.[2] Several Christian documents appeared during Domitian's reign, which refer to the sacrificial cult with normal and respectful attitude. Chief among them is Hebrews,[3] whose exaltation of Christ tends to obscure its implied commendation (and attestation?) of the active cult. There is no reason why the author must choose the priestly figure and the sacrificial rite for his purpose, unless the priest and the sacrifice were considered valid and noble. Although Christ is presented to Christians as the eternal High Priest, the imagery is drawn from the traditional Jewish cult and no comment whatever is made as to cessation thereof. In fact the effectiveness of the reasoning depends upon the acknowleged status of priest and sacrifice; as in viii. 4: 'now if he were on earth, he would not be a priest at all, since there are priests who offer gifts according to the law'. Although the

---

[1] Jews sometimes take pride in the abolition of sacrifice in A.D. 70, as evidence of superior religious insight. Abolition in A.D. 135 offers the same opportunity for pride, and yet it is doubtful that the cessation of sacrifice would have occurred so early apart from the political catastrophe. Christians also usually interpret the destruction by Titus as confirmation of the true worship 'in spirit and in truth'. Such a prejudice presents an obstacle to historical objectivity.

[2] The same thing is true of the Acts account of Paul (xxi. 26; xxiv. 17 f.).

[3] Note esp. Heb. v. 1–4; vii. 1–x. 22. The same respectful usage of the sacrificial imagery is found in Eph. v. 2; I Pet. ii. 5; Rev. xi. 1 and xiv. 17 f., all in the final decade of the first century.

Christian writer believes in the superiority of his own new covenant with God, nevertheless he acknowledges the existence still of an inferior Jewish rite. 'The priests go continually into the outer tent, performing their ritual duties' (ix. 6); 'gifts and sacrifices are offered which cannot perfect the conscience' (ix. 9); 'and every priest stands daily at his service, offering repeatedly the same sacrifices' (x. 11). Note the reasoning in x. 1 f. 'The law...can never, by the same sacrifices which are continually offered year after year, make perfect those who draw near. Otherwise, would they not have ceased to be offered?' And this document was written in the reign of Domitian, many years after the destruction by Titus!

Clement of Rome was another Christian contemporary, whose epistle to the Corinthians provides evidence in agreement with Hebrews. At about the same time he wrote: 'To the High Priest his proper ministrations are allotted, and to the priests the proper place has been appointed, and on Levites the proper services have been imposed. The layman is bound by the ordinances for the laity (xl. 5).... Not in every place are the daily sacrifices offered... but only in Jerusalem; and there also the offering is not made in every place, but before the shrine, at the altar' (xli. 2). These early Christians write naturally and without embarrassment of the contemporary Temple worship, however objectionable the idea may be to a twentieth-century Christian. It is even reasonable to consider that Christians might have participated in the sacrificial cult still within the Jewish framework, when Clement reminds the Corinthians (xl. 2) that 'he commanded us to celebrate sacrifices and services...' (τάς τε προσφοράς καὶ λειτουργίας ἐπιτελεῖσθαι).[1] Of course, there are passages in Clement and elsewhere which declare that the true sacrifice is a contrite spirit, a generous hand, a penitent heart, a sincere prayer. But this 'high religion' has for centuries been part of the sacrificial cult, rather than hostile to it; and therefore to proclaim it is not to attest the abandonment of sacrifice.

It is particularly surprising to find the Jewish contemporary, Josephus, also in agreement with Hebrews and I Clement. In the *Antiquities* (III, 224–36), about A.D. 94, he describes at length the sacrificial cult as though nothing has happened to alter the customary procedure. A few years later, he becomes explicit in addressing Apion: 'For them [the people of Rome] we offer perpetual sacrifices; and not only do we perform these ceremonies daily, at the expense of the whole Jewish community, but...we jointly accord to the emperors alone this signal honour which we pay to no other individual' (II, 77). Again, he calmly states: 'We have but one Temple for the one God.... The priests are continually engaged in his worship' (II, 193–8). In his account of the War he spared no emphasis in describing the desolation of the Temple mount, and yet here he does not even think to explain how the cult was restored to effective operation. Thackeray (Loeb) sees the problem and

---

[1] For all the detail of his classic commentary, Lightfoot is evasive at such points.

records the usual view in a futile footnote: 'The present and future tenses
...are noteworthy in a work written after A.D. 70, which brought the Temple
cult to an end.' But this is shutting one's eyes tight not to see the unwelcome
evidence for the continuation of the cult. Since the verb tenses are acknowledged to be noteworthy, their witness should not be shrugged off but rather
duly noted and credited.

Early in the second century another document gives similar testimony.
II Esdras purports to describe events of the sixth century B.C., but really has
an eye to the condition of Judaea after A.D. 70. Esdras sorrowfully speaks of 'the
desolation of Zion' (iii. 2) and 'the degradation of your sanctuary' (xii. 48).
But shortly thereafter a Christian introduction to the book was added, whose
thesis is (as in the Gospel of Matthew) that God will retract the glory given to
Israel and instead will give 'the Kingdom of Jerusalem' to the Christians.[1]
Concerning the Temple sacrifice God speaks to the Jews (i. 31): 'When you
make offerings to me, I will turn my face away from you....' Oesterley
(apparently because of the 'A.D. 70 dogma') thinks that 'this reads as though
the writer were writing before...A.D. 70', but passes it off as a reminiscence of
Isaiah i. 13, 14 (which really has no relevance). But this testimony should be
taken more seriously, as evidence for a date prior to A.D. 135 until which time
sacrifice continued. Oesterley also observed that 'the reference to sacrifices
and feasts suggests a converted Jew rather than a Gentile Christian as the
writer'. But this suggestion loses force when the Temple is surprisingly trans-
ferred to Christians (ii. 11): 'I will give to these [the Christians] the ever-
lasting dwellings which I had prepared for those others [the Jews].'

In the Christian writings of the early second century, the figurative use of
the sacrificial imagery is frequent. This usage does not offer direct evidence
that the Temple sacrifice continues; still less that Christians even occasionally
might participate. By this date, the tension between Judaism and Christianity is high and there is the tendency toward distinctive procedures. Yet
despite this development there is not evident as yet any Christian hostility to
the traditional sacrificial cult. The *Didaché* (ch. xiii) carries out a full parallel
citing the Mosaic offerings of the Temple as obligations upon Christians, the
only difference being that the offerings go to the Christian prophets, 'for
they are your high priests'.[2] Barnabas dares to use the cultic scapegoat and
heifer for the elucidation of the work of Jesus. Ignatius frequently describes
the Christian community in terms of the Temple Court (θυσιαστήριον).[3] The
purity of the Christian 'sacrifice' is defined in traditional Jewish terms in the
Didaché (xiv. 1–3) and even by Hermas.[4] It is fully apparent that Christians
are comfortably at home in the cultic tradition, even as late as the early
second century. No one of these authors reports that the Temple is abandoned

---

[1] See the same idea in Bar. iv. 6–8: 'the covenant...is ours'.
[2] Cf. also *Did.* xiv. 1–3.
[3] Ignatius, *Eph.* v. 2; *Mag.* vii. 2; *Trall.* vii. 2; *Rom.* ii. 2; *Philad.* 4.
[4] Hermas, *Mand.* x, iii, 2; *Sim.* v, iii, 8; *Sim.* VIII, ii, 5.

and the cult extinct, or should be. We do read in Barnabas ii. 6, referring to sacrifices and oblations, 'these things he abolished'; but the meaning revealed by the context is that for Christians the old Mosaic law is displaced by 'the new law of our Lord Jesus Christ'. Furthermore, Barnabas is here praising the purity of worship by quoting Isaiah and Jeremiah whose remarks did not at all imply abolition of the cult in their time. The famous chapter xvi, though it may refer to the Roman intention to rebuild the Jewish Temple (xvi. 3–4), is primarily the exaltation of the spiritual 'Temple of God' (esp. xvi. 6–7); but there is no word of the actual Temple's end. That these Christian writers might be expected to seize the opportunity, if the cult were inactive, to moralize explicitly on God's favour toward Christianity, is shown by the fact that later Christian writers did exactly this thing. Therefore it may be concluded that their reticence in the early second century is indirect evidence that Jews continued in some fashion to sacrifice on the holy site until the Second Revolt.

In seeking a conclusion to the problem of continued Temple worship after A.D. 70, one of the major sources has been the Talmud. Scholars of the past have directed our attention to numerous rabbinic sayings which may cast light upon the problem. Foremost among these is the instruction of Gamaliel II (*fl.* A.D. 100) to his slave:[1] 'Go out and roast us the Passover offering on the perforated grill'; then ensues detailed discussion on the correct procedure. Some interpret this as evidence that the sacrificial cult was still operative, but Derenbourg (*Essai*, p. 480) points out that Gamaliel then resided in Jamnia which might relate his testimony to provincial areas only. Another passage from the Mishnah (Rosh hashana, ch. III), finds rabbis after A.D. 70 discussing the proclamation of the New Moon and the blowing of the Shofar. This convinces Friedenthal (col. 703) 'daß selbst nach der Tempelzerstörung das Paschalamm geopfert wurde, weshalb für Individuen, die dieses Opfer brachten...'.

A passage in Eduyot (VIII, 6) raises a significant question, relating to the need of a Temple for valid sacrifice. It records that R. Joshua held that one can sacrifice without a Temple, that is, without a house for the spirit of God.[2] Such a question would relate to the possibility of provincial sacrifice, but also to the validity of offerings on the Temple mount if a Holy of Holies were not present in some form. The same text states that R. Eliezer had heard that while the Temple was being erected, curtains or screens were used for privacy. These curious points are relevant to our thesis, that sacrifice in the traditional sanctuary may not have ceased suddenly and completely before A.D. 135. The Mechilta, on Exodus xviii. 27, gives the assurance than when 'one of the water-drinkers made a sacrifice, at once a mysterious voice from the Holy of

---

[1] Pesachim 75a. Some would attribute this passage to Gamaliel I.

[2] Note the use of Mt Gerizim by the Samaritans to the present day, for many centuries without a Temple.

Holies declared: He who accepted the sacrifices of Israel in the desert receives them now too'. M. Geiger[1] assigns this to the post-70 period and Derenbourg (p. 482) agrees but insists that it is an isolated instance of one Jew who risked the venture under the eyes of the Romans. We have suggested above that this would be no great risk in view of the leniency of the Legion. In modern times historians tend to be quite prosaic and systematic; yet we should be prepared for the unpredictable and resilient ways of religious conviction and practice. It is to be recognized that there are many Talmudic references to the ruined Temple and to the cessation of sacrifices, and when reading such passages it is habitual for the mind to spring to the year 70, but if one should find release from such a habit it is usually found possible to apply the year 135 equally well.

An explicit instance of Jewish sacrifice in the Temple in the time of Hadrian is reported in a unique Hebrew document discovered in Nablus in Palestine about 1900, and published in 1901–3 by Adler and Séligsohn.[2] Based upon the fourteenth-century chronicle of Aboul-Fath, this 'New Samaritan Chronicle' includes the account of a Jewish pilgrim to Jerusalem who brings a pair of pigeons for sacrifice, in the High-priesthood of Amram (A.D. 120–30). His Samaritan hosts in Bira substitute rats for the pigeons so that the Temple is polluted. The Temple authorities arrest the two culprits and condemn them to hard labour in the Temple court. The account further speaks of the later visit of Hadrian and his burning of the Temple. The historical basis of the chronicle must be acknowledged, although the story of the Jewish pilgrim has a romantic flavour. This story is accepted as authentic by William Seston, the Master of Conferences at the University of Strasbourg, writing in 1933.[3] The story affords this much evidence, at the very least: that the Samaritan chronicler saw no historical difficulty in this realistic account of the Temple activity shortly before the destruction by Hadrian in A.D. 135. Since the chronicle is a unique copy in an obscure location, in a Hebrew text whose publication fifty-seven years ago has been little noticed, its testimony to Temple worship in Jerusalem about A.D. 125 has rarely been considered.

That the sacrificial cult in Jerusalem did not survive beyond A.D. 135 is certain. This came about because the power of the victorious Romans enabled them to force abandonment of the Temple. Not only was the consecrated structure destroyed; it was supplanted, for the first time in history. Not only

---

[1] M. Geiger, Urschrift, p. 152.

[2] Elkan N. Adler and M. Séligsohn, Revue des Études juives, vols. XLIV–XLVI (1901–3); for our special story see vol. XLV (1902), pp. 80 f.

[3] William Seston, Revue des Études anciennes, XXXV (1933), 205–12; esp. 210. His French text, in translation, is as follows: 'Between 120 and 130, a Jew presented in the Temple for sacrifice a box containing, he said, two pigeons. There came from the box two rats which some Samaritans had slipped in while he slept; the priest, in anger, wanted to put the Jew to death; but he accused the Samaritans and the leaders of the Jewish community tried them for their capricious deed and sentenced them to a laborious life as slaves in the Temple court. The offence was serious, for the Jewish sacrifice had been turned to derision and the Temple contaminated by the impure animals.'

were Jews excluded from worship there henceforth, but gentiles were admitted to the new Temple of Jupiter. The new gentile cult prevented the restoration of the old Jewish cult. Similar action by the Syrians in 168 B.C. would surely have brought about the cessation of animal sacrifice in Judaism at that time, at least in Jerusalem, if the Maccabean revolt had failed to recover autonomy for the Jews. Still another illustration of this determinative factor is seen in the closing of the Temple of Onias in Leontopolis about A.D. 73.[1] Although no structure replaced it, this Temple was locked and barricaded and proscription of worship there was enforced by a military guard. Such circumstances as these did not accompany the destruction of the Jerusalem Temple in A.D. 70. The prohibitory conditions of A.D. 135 were unique in the history of the Jewish cult, and only such insurmountable obstacles could explain the final cessation of sacrifice in A.D. 135. What may have been possible before 135 is reflected in Trypho's remark to Justin after that date. When Justin asks (xlvi. 2) 'whether it is possible to keep all the institutions of Moses at the present time', Trypho replies: 'no, for we are aware... that it is not possible to slay a passover-sheep elsewhere than in Jerusalem', and now, he implies, such is no longer possible. There is also the implication in his response that the impossibility has come about recently, and it is here suggested that this occurred in A.D. 135, at the real end of the nation's history.

[1] Jos. *War*, VII, 420–36.

THE ISRAEL OF GOD

From gentile to Jew to Christian : was this the course of conviction and affiliation for a gentile convert to "Christianity" in the first century ? This question may be raised with Paul of Tarsus, the Jewish-Christian who deliberately assumed the special role of "Christian" evangelist to gentiles. He distinguished his role and its attendant theological problems from the comparable role of Peter, another Jewish-Christian who particularly addressed his appeal to Jews. The inquiry that we here make of Paul might be formulated thus : From a theological standpoint, was it required of a gentile to become a Jew in the process of becoming a "Christian" ? A variant formulation might take this form : When the Jew, Paul, converted a gentile to "Christianity" did the convert thus become a Jewish proselyte ? What was the mind of Paul on this theological question ? The response is involved in the general milieu of gentile-Jewish-Christian relationships in the first generation of Christian origins. In the attempt to understand Paul's mind on such a question one is led to the related inquiry : Who is a Jew ?

It has been maintained by many that in Paul's missionary enterprise the convert as a gentile might come directly to Christ; that is, he need never assume a state of allegiance to Judaism. This would mean that in the mind of Paul, within the first Christian generation, there was a third religious entity; such as came to be called in the second century a "third race". Independent of the cults of gentiles, and separate from Judaism, there would be converts from both who would completely withdraw in order to enter upon the "Christian" Way, separated from both. This view has been attributed by many to Paul, and yet even in our advanced stage of exegetical criticism there is reason to challenge the view and to press for renewed analysis of Paul's own contention, as bearing upon the issue here raised.

They were Jewish missionaries, Paul and Barnabas, who were quite prepared to receive gentiles into their religious community without circumcision, although the dominant Jewish position was insistence upon the rite as traditionally practiced. Obviously the

Jewish leaders considered that Paul's converts were moving from gentile religion to Judaism. That Paul discounted the need for circumcision does not mean that Paul excused the gentile "Christian" from membership within Judaism. Foakes-Jackson did so interpret Paul's charge to the Galatians (5.2) : "... if you receive circumcision, Christ will be of no advantage to you." He attributes to Paul the warning that "if they became Jewish proselytes, they would be more attracted to the fulfilment of the external precepts of the Law ..."[1]

But this is not the position that Paul took. He did make his position quite clear and we may well rely upon his own words, in his epistles and as reported by Luke. Whereas Paul did renounce the requirement for a *physical* circumcision for the Gentile convert, he argued vigorously and at length for the retention of that traditional characteristic of Judaism, circumcision, correctly understood. A convert must accept circumcision; that is, the "true" circumcision. He urges : "If a man who is uncircumcised keeps the precepts of the law, will not his uncircumcision be regarded as circumcision?" (Rom 2.26). "He is a Jew who is one inwardly, and real circumcision is a matter of the heart, spiritual and not literal" (Rom 2.29). Paul's declaration is applicable both to the born Jew and to the gentile convert whose spiritual circumcision satisfies the law and qualifies him for membership *within Judaism*. In the Colossian letter (2.11), Paul adheres to the "circumcision made without hands ... the circumcision of Christ," a rite performed once-for-all signifying for the gentile convert the true mark of Judaism as found in the Law of Moses.

What greater or clearer qualification for the gentile convert to be acceptable within Judaism could there be, than to be recognized as in the line of Abraham, Isaac and Jacob? So Paul argues that the man of faith is a spiritual descendant of Abraham, who was "the father of all who believe without being circumcised," as well as "the father of the circumcised who ... follow the example of the faith which our father Abraham had" (Rom 4.11f.). "He is the father of us all" (Rom 4.16). This was later reflected in the Epistle of Barnabas (13.7), where God speaks : "I have made thee, Abraham, the father of the gentiles who believe in God in uncircumcision." By this reasoning, Paul brought his gentile converts within Judaism as "the household of faith" (Gal 6.10), for "in Christ Jesus the blessing of Abraham

---

[1] F.J. Foakes-Jackson, *The Life of St. Paul* (New York, 1926), p. 245.

might come upon the gentiles" (Gal 3.14). "If you are Christ's, then you are Abraham's offspring, heirs according to promise" (Gal 3.29).

Furthermore, the gentile convert is also a descendant of Isaac, child of the "free woman" rather than of Hagar the slave. Through "our forefather Isaac ... God's purpose of election might continue" (Rom 9.11). A "Christian's" lineage, whether a Jew or a gentile, was traceable also through Jacob. Paul applied God's discrimination (Mal. 1.2-3) to the first-century "Christian," Jew or gentile : "I have loved Jacob but I have hated Esau" (Rom 9.13). The convert Luke declares that Mary's son "will reign over the house of Jacob" (Luke 1.33). The triple ascription to Abraham, Isaac and Jacob was a definite earmark of the Jews' religion. Yahweh had declared even to Moses (Ex. 3.6) : "I am the God of your fathers, the God of Abraham and of Isaac and of Jacob" (quoted by Luke in Acts 7.32). The same expression is attributed to Peter, when speaking of God's glorification of Jesus (Acts 3.13). Paul's colleague Luke envisions Abraham and Isaac and Jacob "in the kingdom of God" (Luke 13.28f.; cf. Matt. 8.11) where they will sit at table with "Christians." To demonstrate belief in the resurrection, Luke declares that the God of Abraham and Isaac and Jacob is "the God of the living" (Luke 20.37f.; cf. Matt. 22.32). Paul's recourse to each of the patriarchs in the "Christian's" lineage is summed up and often repeated by Luke, as well as by Matthew, in this characteristic triple formula of Judaism. This lineage of the "Christian", be he Jew or gentile, continues to be the earmark of the family of Judaism.

Another indication that Paul's gentile convert was received into Judaism is the administration of baptism, a Jewish rite. It is recognized that several interpretations of the baptismal rite were applied to different religious occasions in Judaism. In my judgment, both proselyte baptism for gentiles and messianic baptism for both Jews and gentiles offer the most appropriate explanations, but among the alternative interpretations all are Jewish. Daube points out that "leading Hillelites ... did consider a male convert fully Jewish as soon as he was baptized."[1] The initial summons to baptism by John the Baptizer was certainly in the Jewish context, whatever explanation of it one may accept. Accordingly, Paul later alludes to the rite as common among "all of us who have been baptized into Christ Jesus" (Rom 6.3), the anointed Messiah of Judaism's expectation. "For

---

[1] David Daube, *The New Testament and Rabbinic Judaism* (London, 1956), p. 109.

by one Spirit we were all baptized into one body — Jews or Greeks"
(I Cor 12.13). We are not surprised that Paul sees a deeper theological
sense in the rite : "We were baptized into his death, we were interred
therefore with him ... as the Messiah was resurrected ... we too might
walk in newness of life" (Rom 6.3f.). Indeed, Paul represents the
spiritual ἀνάστασις as having already been experienced : "You were
buried with him in baptism, you were also raised with him through
faith, in the ἐνέργεια of God" (Col 2.12), a once-for-all ἀνάστασις.
Underlying Paul's heightened interpretation lies the traditional baptismal rite of Judaism, applied to the gentile "Christian" (cf. Acts
19.5).

A further religious requirement characteristic of Judaism was
applied to the gentile "Christian;" namely, dietary observance.
Whereas a gentile convert was excused from much of the detailed
requirement of Torah, the old "Noachian" laws must be observed :
"You shall not eat flesh with its life, that is, its blood" (Gen. 9.4;
cf Deut. 12.16). This was the exceptional demand customarily imposed
upon the gentile convert to Judaism, and it was retained within
the early "Christian" cult. "It has seemed good ... to lay upon you ...
these necessary things : that you abstain ... from blood and from
what is strangled" (Acts 15.28f.; 21.25). Paul and the leaders in
Jerusalem found agreement in this long practiced approach of Judaism.
It included the further prohibition of flesh which had been sacrificed
on a gentile altar, as a specific violation of the blood-life proscription
(I Cor 10.28f.). In this traditional respect the gentile "Christian"
was called upon to observe the minimum of dietary requirement
within Judaism. As to minor details, Jewish and gentile "Christians"
ate together in the Antioch community, where Peter initially assumed
the liberal posture of living "like a gentile and not like a Jew" (Gal.
2.14).

Central to the Jewish religion, in Paul's thought, was the concept
of "justification" or approval by God, and this he proclaimed to both
Jew and Gentile. For the Jew, Paul found the true example in Abraham (long before the Mosaic formulation) who believed God's promise
"and it was reckoned to him as righteousness" (Rom 4.3). Therefore,
Paul insists, God's approval of the Jew depends upon belief, trust
or faith in God; rather than upon works, or the performance of the
manifold precepts of Torah. Paul reminds the Roman "Christians"
that "David pronounces [Psa. 32.1-2] a blessing upon the man to
whom God reckons righteousness apart from works" (Rom. 4.6).

This very same conception Paul applied to any gentile convert :
"Is this blessing pronounced only upon the circumcised, or also upon
the uncircumcised?" (4.9). The example of Abraham supplies the
answer that the gentile is included in the blessing. "God is one; and
he will justify the circumcised on the ground of their faith and the
uncircumcised because of their faith" (Rom. 3.30). Paul's gentile
convert as a "Christian" thus entered Judaism on the same terms
as his Jewish convert enjoyed who was already in Judaism and remained so. "Are we Jews any better off? No, ... both Jews and
Greeks are under the power of sin ... and no human being will be
justified ... by works of the law ... But now the righteousness of
God has been manifested apart from law ... through faith in Jesus
Christ for all who believe" (Rom. 3.9, 20-22). "It is evident that no
man is justified before God by the law" (Gal. 3.11). "Israel who pursued
the righteousness which is based on law did not succeed in fulfilling
that law ... because they did not pursue it though faith" (Rom 9:31f.).
"Gentiles who did not pursue righteousness have attained it ... through
faith" (Rom. 9.30). "The promise may ... be guaranteed to all [Abra-
ham's] descendants — not only to the adherents of the law but also
to those who share the faith of Abraham" (Rom. 4.16). "The promise
to Abraham and his descendants," both Jew and gentile, "did not
come through the law but through the righteousness of faith" (Rom.
4.13). The evidence is abundant that, in Paul's interpretation, the
religious experience of a new convert from the gentile community
coincided with that of a new convert who was already Jewish, both
on an equal footing within Judaism.

Additional evidence of the Jewishness of Paul's gentile converts
is noted in their consistent association with the synagogue. Some
gentile converts had already become Jewish when Paul proclaimed
his gospel of freedom in the synagogues, and therefore must have
already satisfied the requirements imposed by the Jewish community.
In the synagogue at Pisidian Antioch, Paul adressed both the "sons
of the family of Abraham, and those among you that fear God"
(Acts 13.26). "And when the meeting of the synagogue broke up,
many Jews and devout converts to Judaism followed Paul and Barnabas" (Acts 13.43). In Corinth, Paul "argued in the synagogue
every sabbath, and persuaded Jews and Greeks" (Acts 18.4). It would
be easy to cite a score of passages to confirm that throughout Paul's
"Christian" career he retained his connection with the synagogue.
This is not contrary to his sense of special responsibility for the con-

version of gentiles. His long experience in Corinth is reported neither as a break with the synagogue nor with Judaism. When Paul removed "to the house of a man named Titius Justus, a worshiper of God ... next door to the synagogue," no less a Jewish pesonage than the ruler of the synagogue along with the family were his converts and supporters (Acts 18.7f.). Shortly thereafter, in Ephesus, we find Paul again speaking in the synagogue (Acts 18.19; 19.8). Once again, circumstances impelled him to withdraw to "the hall of Tyrannus ... for two years" (Acts 19.9f.). But this episode does not imply any break with Judaism on Paul's part, for we soon find him "hastening to be at Jerusalem, if possible, on the day of Pentecost" (Acts 20.16). After arrival, "he purified himself ... and went into the temple" (Acts 21.26) still conducting himself very much the sincere and devout Jew. In his missionary activity he is not seeking to build a separate and new cult apart from Judaism. His converts to "Christianity," including gentiles, stand within the "true" Judaism.

Some scholars have held that a clear split occurred in Corinth, when Paul announced : "From now on I will go to the gentiles." Subsequently, so they may maintain, a chiefly gentile ἐκκλησία stands opposed to the Jewish synagogue. But Paul's conduct until the end makes clear that he considered his own movement and all its members, both Jewish and gentile, as part of his life-long Jewish religion. The ἐκκλησία was a "Christian" assembly within Judaism governed by its traditional elders (Acts 14.23). Paul often called it the ἐκκλησία τοῦ θεοῦ[1] — a term which may have distinguished it from orthodox synagogues although it does not imply an extra-Jewish institution. The Thessalonian letteɪs are addressed to "the ἐκκλησία in God the Father," clearly referring to the God of Judaism. The observance of the Jewish sabbath continued among the "Christian" believers, for Jew and gentile alike, and Paul's own visits in the synagogues are reported often as taking place on the sabbath.[2]

Many other characteristics of Judaism persist in the mind and the practice of Paul, the Jewish missionary. As a self-professed Pharisee, he found authority in the Sacred Scriptures and adhered to a monotheistic belief. He still worshipped in the Temple, observed its purificatory rites and offered sacrifice, observed the religious festivals and contributed alms. His declaration to the Corinthians is not sur-

---

[1] I Cor. 1.2; 10.32; 11.16, 22; 15.9; II Cor. 1.1; Gal. 1.13; I Thess. 2.14; II Thess. 1.4.
[2] Acts 13.14,27,44; 15.21; 18.4.

prising : "God's temple is holy" (I Cor. 3.17). He reminds them of the priestly participation in the sacrifices : "Those who are employed in the temple service get their food from the temple, and those who serve at the altar share in the sacrificial offerings" (I Cor. 9.13; cf. 10.18). Near the end of his career, as Luke reports, Paul defends his Jewishness : "I went up to worship at Jerusalem" (Acts 24.11). "They found me purified in the temple" (Acts 24.18; cf. 21.26). The temple was for him a worthy concept to apply to the believer's personal purity, especially in Corinth : "You are God's temple and ... God's Spirit dwells in you" (I Cor. 3.16; cf. 6.19 and II Cor 6.16). In Paul's *apologia* before Felix, he recounted : "After some years I came to bring to my nation alms and offerings" (Acts 24.17). However this may be interpreted, at least it was an attitude faithful to Judaism, as was also his "priestly service of the gospel of God, so that the offering of the gentiles may be acceptable, sanctified by the Holy Spirit" (Rom. 15.16). So also in the Jewish concept of animal sacrifice Paul saw a worthy imagery for the crucifixion of Jesus : "Christ our paschal lamb has been sacrificed" (I Cor. 5.7). In later years, "Christians" retained this imagery after the destruction of the temple and the renunciation of sacrifice. Still another simile Paul drew from Jewish ritual : "Cleanse out the old leaven, that you may be fresh dough, as you really are unleavened" (I Cor. 5.7). Other rituals he touches upon out of long habit, when writing to the Colossians : "Let no one pass judgment on you in questions of food and drink or with regard to a festival or a new moon or a sabbath" (2.16). Indeed, the entire "law is holy" (Rom. 7.12), deserving of the correct interpretation and a reverent attitude.

Although Paul thought of himself especially as a missionary *for* gentiles, he was certainly a missionary *within* Judaism. He was not an alienated Jew, as some would describe him; though his was a modified Judaism : "According to the Way, which they call a sect, I worship the God of our fathers ... neither against the law of the Jews, nor against the temple ... have I offended at all" (Acts 24.14 and 25.8). Although his religious posture has been subject to debate among Jews, anciently and lately, Paul yielded to no one in his deliberate fidelity to the best he knew in Judaism. He was not drawing men out of Judaism or Hellenism so as to form a new religion. His Jewish converts remained within Judaism and his gentile converts were drawn into Judaism, the "true" Judaism. To the last he insisted :

"I myself am an Israelite, a descendant of Abraham," and his converts were considered to be among God's people (Rom. 11.1).

The first question we have considered has been : In the thought of Paul, must a gentile become a Jew in order to become a Christian? It has seemed to us that Paul in his own words has given this answer : When a gentile was converted to the "Christian" belief, he thereby in that same change became a Jew, a "true" Jew. But this understanding proposes a new and a different question for Paul : Who *is* a Jew, and who is not a Jew? Once again, we may appeal to Paul's own words for his answer. "Not all who are descended from Israel belong to Israel, and not all are children of Abraham because they are his descendants" (Rom. 9.6f.). "It is not the children of the flesh who are the children of God, but the children of the promise;" that is, the descendants of Abraham through Isaac (Rom. 9.8). "He is a Jew who is one inwardly, and real circumcision is a matter of the heart, spiritual and not literal" (Rom. 2.29). This does not exclude the traditional rite of circumcision for Jews, but does make essential for Jews "the righteousness of faith" (Rom. 4.13). Paul often applied here Habakkuk 2.4 : "He who through faith is righteous shall live" (Rom. 1.17; Gal. 3.11; cf. Rom. 3.21f.; Phil. 3.9). Paul becomes quite explicit in identifying God's people : "A man is not justified by works of the law but through faith in Jesus Christ" (Gal. 2.16). The same affirmations which open the door for the gentile convert, also disqualify many a Jew who rests his fate upon "works of law." Alluding to the freedom from physical circumcision, symbolic of the law, Paul gives his benediction upon the "true" Jews : "Peace and mercy be upon all who walk by this rule, upon the Israel of God" (Gal. 6.16).[1]

In modern times the identity of the Jew has been a political and sociological problem, and a variety of identifications have been proposed. Jean-Paul Sartre is quoted as saying that "a Jew is a man whom other men call a Jew." Some would hold that whoever calls himself a Jew is one, even as Paul more than once claimed for himself [2] whereas some disputed his right to such a status. Various criteria have been proposed : descent from Jewish forebears, Jewish parents

---

[1] The sect of the Essenes of Qumram considered themselves to be "the true Israel", as noted by Dupont-Sommer in *The Essene Writings from Qumran*, trans. G. Vermez (Oxford, 1962), p. 42.

[2] Acts 21.39; 22.3; 24.14; 25.8; Rom. 11.1; Gal. 2.15; cf. Rom. 2.17.

(especially the mother), observance of Torah, practice of rites, dietary requirements, participation in synagogue worship, national citizenship in Israel, or even (as attributed to Ben Gurion in our time) belief in Psalm 15. First-century Judaism did not maintain a membership roll. Within Judaism there was a great variety of distinctive attitudes, as is shown by the numerous sects (Pharisees, Sadducees, Essenes, Zealots, Ebionites, Therapeutai, Hellenists, Christians, etc.) and by the varied personalities (Philo, John the Baptist, Jesus, Paul, Steven, Shammai, Hillel, Josephus, etc.). It was against such a background that Paul of Tarsus proclaimed his key to the identity of the Jew in his time : "He is a Jew who is one inwardly, and real circumcision is a matter of the heart, spiritual and not literal" (Rom. 2.29). "We ourselves, who are Jews by birth ... even we have believed in Christ Jesus, in order to be justified by faith in Christ" (Gal. 2.15f.).

The same definition of a Jew which Paul applied to those born in Judaism, he applied also to the gentile convert. The pertinent and relevant question was not : Must a gentile become a Jew in order to be a Christian? It was Paul's basic assumption that his gentile converts entered his own Judaism. His question, rather, was : Who is a Jew? Paul applied the same identification to both Jew and gentile : "He is a Jew who is one inwardly" who follows "the example of the faith which our father Abraham had." "Gentiles have attained righteousness through faith;" Paul's God has reckoned them as righteous, justified by God along with Jewish converts to the "Christian" faith. "By one Spirit we were all baptized into one body — Jews or Greeks ... — and all were made to drink of one Spirit" (I Cor. 12.13). During Paul's lifetime, all differences between "Christian" and Jew were issues to be resolved *within* Judaism. Within Judaism Paul's Jewish and gentiles converts to faith in Jesus as the Messiah, reckoned by God's grace to be righteous through their faith rather than their works, all became (in Paul's interpretation) the true circumcision, "the Israel of God."

THE SINS OF
HERMAS

I

Recently a Christian leader undertook to answer the question,
"What is a . . . bishop?" In his answer he stated, "He is not a
'holy man' in the accepted meaning of the term."[1] It may not be
clear how the term is accepted today, but the disclaimer was
obviously intended to disarm the common Christian reader; and
yet the Christian historian and theologian is aware that from the
beginning Christianity demanded holiness not only from official
leaders but from every professing member.

The immediate background for this Christian demand in the
first century is represented in the admonition of Ben Sira (Ecclus.
21:1): "My child, have you sinned? Sin so longer, and offer
petition for your previous sins." The *Discipline Scroll* of Qumran
(iii, 9-11) similarly enjoins the novitiate to "direct his steps so as to
walk perfectly in all God's ways . . . Let him not swerve either to
the right or to the left, nor transgress a single one of God's words."[2]
Again, about the turn of the era, the Wisdom of Solomon (15:2 f.)
confidently insists: "We will not sin, for we know that we are
accounted yours. For to know you is perfect uprightness."

Such typical expressions in late Judaism remind us of the principle
of perfectionism proclaimed by Jesus (Matt. 5:48): "You are to be
perfect, as your heavenly Father is."[3] Paul habitually addressed
the Christian believers throughout his correspondence as "saints"

[1] T. Otto Nall, *Together* (March, 1958), p. 13.

[2] Translation of G. Vermès, *Discoveries in the Judean Desert* (New York, 1956).

[3] Cf. also Luke 6:36. Quotations from the English New Testament follow the
Revised Standard Version.

or "holy persons." [4] When we come to the generation of Hermas of Rome we find the Christian literature sprinkled with similar phrases. For example, in Hebrews: "Holy brothers, who share in a heavenly call . . ."(3:1);" . . . the love which you showed . . . in serving the saints" (6:10). And in I Peter (quoting Lev. 19:2): "You shall be holy, for I am holy" (1:16); "You are a chosen race, a royal priesthood, a holy nation . . . " (2:9); "Whoever has suffered in the flesh has ceased from sin, so as to live for the rest of the time in the flesh no longer by human passions but by the will of God" (4:1 f.). Ignatius reminds the Ephesians (14:2), "No man who professes faith sins," and in I John it is repeatedly urged, "No one who abides in him sins; no one who sins has either seen him or known him" (3:6); "No one born of God commits sin . . . he cannot sin because he is born of God" (3:9); "We know that anyone born of God does not sin" (5:18).

These are familiar passages but they are here recalled for three reasons: first, because the ideal of the perfect life has disappeared from contemporary Christian society; second, because in the current theological fashion the emphasis on universal sin has eclipsed the ideal of the sinless life; and third, because the experience and message of Hermas can be understood only when we revive the sense of Christian perfection which prevailed in his day.

Hermas was indoctrinated in this belief, as he reports in Similitude V (1:5) where the Shepherd charges him, "Do nothing evil in your life . . . let no evil desire arise in your heart . . . refrain from every wicked act . . ." [5] In Vision IV (2:5) the Church has set the goal to "serve the Lord blamelessly for the rest of the days of your life." [6] Again, in the fourth Mandate (1:11) the Shepherd directs that "he who has sinned sin no more," and later in the same Mandate (3:1 f.) Hermas reveals such instruction also from others: "I have heard, sir, from some teachers that there is no second repentance beyond the one given when we went down into the water and received remission of our previous sins." Such teachers as Hermas refers to were in accord with the conviction of the author of Hebrews that "it is impossible to restore again to repentance those who have once been enlightened" (6:4); "For if we sin

---

[4] E.g. Rom. 1:7; I Cor. 1:2; II Cor. 1:1; Phil. 1:1; Col. 1:2; II Thess. 1:10; Philem. 5.

[5] Quotations from the Apostolic Fathers are based on the Loeb edition, ed. by K. Lake (London, and New York, 1913), with occasional and minor independent revision.

[6] Cf. also I Clem. 40:4.

deliberately after receiving the knowledge of the truth, there no longer remains a sacrifice for sins, but a fearful prospect of judgment" (10:26).[7] This teaching was confirmed by the Shepherd in reply: "You have heard correctly, for that is so. For he who has received remission of sin ought never to sin again but to live in purity." Once more, in Sim. IX (18:1 f.) the Shepherd pronounces, "He who has knowledge of God is bound no more to do wickedly but to do good . . . those who have knowledge of God . . . and do wickedly . . . shall die for ever."

Many have held that Hermas had little support in this stern doctrine, but actually it appears frequently in the literature, both canonical and apocryphal. That we should find in dialectic contrast the realistic recognition that Christians do sin, does not invalidate the evidence that salvation was understood to depend not upon a favorable balance in the "book of life" but upon a clean page. A life of purity was thought to be quite possible and was indeed expected. The contemporaries of Hermas are not given to "Pauline pessimism" or capitulation to moral failure.[8] Hermas, as a typical Christian sinner, is not typical of all Christians; rather, his condition of post-baptismal guilt presents a special problem that applies to some Christians but not to most. The ideal picture is drawn in Sim. IX (29) where the white mountain shelters "innocent babes . . . no evil enters their heart, nor have they known what wickedness is, but have ever remained in innocence . . . all the days of their lives." Some moderns explain that such a life of purity was a more reasonable expectation in a day when the *eschaton* was imminent, but the early Christian could have had no illusion that the sinless life was easy even for a limited time. Hermas himself was conscious of failure and stricken with terror when he exclaimed (Vis. I, 2:1): "If this sin is recorded against me, how shall I be saved?"

It is against such a background that Hermas developed his distressing sense of guilt. The particular sins charged against him constitute the subject of our inquiry here, but we can entertain no doubt that he was concerned about his guilt. In the subconscious state of his first vision, he reports, "I . . . knelt down and began to pray to the Lord and to confess my sins" (I, 5:3). Again, in Vis. III (1:5 f.), in a similar state, he records, "I knelt down and confessed my sins again to the Lord, as I had also done before. And she (the personified Church) came . . . and listened to me praying

---

[7] See also Mand. IV (3:6-7).

[8] Sim. IX (23:4) has the formal expression, "Man who is mortal and full of sin," which refers to the general condition of the unregenerate, who are called upon to emulate God in his mercy.

and confessing my sins to the Lord." The occasion of the third vision was more than a year after that of the first, and therefore these two reports would not alone reflect habitual preoccupation with his sense of guilt, but on the later occasion the Lady upbraids him for persisting on the subject of his sins. In Mand. IV (2:3) Hermas bluntly admits, "I am a sinner . . . my sins are many and various." In Sim. VII (1 f.) an instructive interchange takes place when Hermas asks the Shepherd of Repentance to dismiss from his home the Shepherd of Punishment who has been tormenting him excessively, but the Angel of Repentance responds, "You must be afflicted . . . your sins are many. . . . " This at least is clear, that Hermas the Christian, who had once been baptized and cleansed of sin, was now again charged with sin and personally confessed his renewed state of guilt. This "plot" to the story is expressed emphatically in Vis. I (2:4): "It is an evil and mad purpose for a revered spirit and one already approved, if a man desire an evil deed, and especially if it be Hermas the temperate."

II

What specifically were the sins of Hermas? The answer to this is difficult because his own report is often inconsistent and confusing, but the attempt to find the answer may yield useful insights not only biographical but psychological and theological as well. First of all, in Vis. I, Hermas sees the admired Rhoda in heaven, who explains to him, "I was taken up to accuse you of your sins before the Lord." Here at the outset the term "sins" is plural and undefined, and furthermore she assures him that she has not as yet made any charges—and the apocalypse never again refers to this function of hers. Nevertheless, she informs Hermas, "God . . . is angry with you because you sinned against me." This he denies as a false charge, insisting that he always respected her as a sister, indeed even as a goddess,[9] and never went so far as to speak a suggestive word to her. This refutation she appears to accept as the truth, for she then shifts to an allegation of a wicked desire in the heart (her knowledge of which is not explained).[10] To this Hermas makes no response, although earlier in the reported vision he did refer to her as "that woman I had desired." However, in the actual encounter he had insisted that his only thought was innocent as he reflected

[9] Instead of "goddess," Codex A reads "daughter," and the Ethiopic reads "lady."

[10] Cf. Matt. 5:28, paralleled in the Talmud (e.g., Shabbath 64a and Berakoth 24a). Cf. Epictetus *Discourses* II.xviii.15.

in his heart how admirable her beauty and character as befitting a good wife. The possible psychological subleties here are elusive, and yet it may be that Hermas would have the reader understand that this was the basis of the charge of an evil design. Some have taken the episode to imply his psychological infidelity. When Rhoda asks if in a good man an evil desire is not equivalent to an evil deed, Hermas makes no response as she goes on to affirm that it is so.[11]

At a later moment he finds himself in the presence of the old woman who personifies the Church, when she insists with finality, " . . . the thought did enter your heart concerning her. It is such a design as this which brings sin on the servants of God" (2:4). But Hermas himself makes no confession on this point and admits no evil action or intent. Although Rhoda has as yet laid no charge before the Lord, nevertheless she declares that his sin against her is the cause of God's anger. When the vision has passed, the shaken Hermas is in despair, considering that this sin had been recorded against him; but to him it is a false allegation for which he admits no guilt and of which he has not been convicted, though he makes no further defense of his innocence and no remonstrance against being falsely charged.

But if we are to understand that Hermas was held guilty of the evil thought, it should be remembered that this sin must be of long standing. A long interval had elapsed during which Hermas married and had a grown family. Since his encounter with Rhoda at the river Tiber she had died, and "after some time" he saw her in a vision in heaven. The psychologist might ponder whether he first became aware of his attitude toward her when he served as her slave in younger years, or when "after many years" he courteously helped her from the river, or even later when she appeared in his first vision. In the light of this psychological perplexity, a nice point to clarify is whether this sinful thought *originated* before or after his baptism; if before, his sense of guilt must be associated with its continuance or recurrence in some post-baptismal time. It will be granted that Hermas was not concerned with such refinement of theory; nevertheless certain theological implications are present in the situation. At the last, Rhoda's very charge—expressed gently and without reproach—strikes him with surprise and incredulity. It is made to appear that only God knew of his subconscious and secret desire, even without any formal accusation by Rhoda. Consequently, this allegation does not explain any sense of guilt in Hermas himself, to satisfy the "plot" of the story. Before the first

[11] Cf. Matt. 5:27; Mand. XII (2:3); Epictetus *Diss*. II.xviii.15-19.

vision closes the Church denies that such a sin has made God angry with Hermas (3:1).

Another passage in Mand. IV (1:1 f.) also may have reference to the personal sin of Hermas, where the Shepherd instructs him, "Guard purity and let not any thought come into your heart about another man's wife, or about fornication or any such wicked thing; for by doing this you do great sin. But if you always remember your own wife you will never sin."[12] We are not told whether Rhoda, who had owned him as slave, had been married at any time, nor are we informed as to whether Hermas became married during or after his period of slavery. The Shepherd's Mandate does not fit exactly the biographical account of Hermas, but seems to be a general rule which developed out of his personal problem.[13] In the same fourth Mandate (1:4 f.) Hermas inquires of the Shepherd, "If a man have a wife faithful in the Lord, and he find her out in some adultery, does the husband sin if he lives with her?" We note that the wife is "faithful in the Lord," that is, a Christian; that the conversation discusses not her sin but only that of her Christian husband. Here the Shepherd propounds the principle, "So long as he is ignorant, he does not sin. . . ."[14]

This principle is but lightly affirmed in our document, as it appears obliquely in only two other places. In Sim. V (7:2 f.) the Shepherd declares the unity of flesh and spirit and denounces the belief that the flesh may be defiled with impunity. When Hermas points out that a man (perhaps himself?) may have acted in ignorance prior to the Shepherd's teaching, the latter concedes that God can forgive him. Again, in Sim. IX (18:1-2) the Shepherd instructs that knowledge of God makes a man all the more subject to his punishment. A contemporary apology, the Preaching of Peter (Frag. VIII),[15] gives similar comfort: "Whatsoever any of

---

[12] Cf. Exod. 20:17 and Deut. 5:21. Tertullian's slur upon Hermas was quite undeserved (*De Pudicitia* 10 and 20).

[13] A point of special interest emerges from the Shepherd's further words (Mand. IV,1:2): "For if this desire enter your heart you will sin." The clear meaning of the future verb is not that you do sin in the thought but rather that the evil thought is parent to the overt deed which is sin. The idea has a parallel in the teaching of Jesus that whereas hate may lead to killing, both the overt deed and the incipient thought are equally sinful. But there is the subtle implication in Hermas that the evil thought is sin not of itself but rather because it is potential of the overt sin. So also Vis. I (2:4), whereas both senses are present in Mand. IV (1:1).

[14] The same idea is expressed in positive form in Jas. 4:17.

[15] See Clem. Alex. *Strom.* vi.6,48; J. N. Reagan, *The Preaching of Peter* (Chicago, 1923).

you did in ignorance, not knowing God aright, if he, having learned to know, repent, all his sins will be forgiven him." Although these passages are similar in pointing out that ignorance makes a critical difference in the sight of God, it must be noted that they do not support the exact principle declared by the Shepherd in Mand. IV; for whereas they state that God is lenient to forgive a sin committed in ignorance, the Shepherd has said that the husband's ignorant conduct is not even to be counted as a sin. Furthermore, Sim. IX and the Preaching of Peter speak of general knowledge of God, whereas Sim. V and Mand. IV refer to explicit knowledge of fact. If the Shepherd's Mandate represents the position of Hermas, then the latter's ignorance of evil might make further claim to innocence in the case of Rhoda.

III

The next allegation of sin made against Hermas is expressed also in the first Vision. This time the charge is made by the Church in the person of the old woman. When he complains to her of Rhoda's accusation, she explains, "But it is not for this that God is angry with you, but to lead you to convert your family (οἶκος) which has sinned against the Lord, and against you, their parents." The modern reader may breathe a sigh of relief here in the interest of Hermas, because so slight a sin replaces one so heinous. A lack of domestic responsibility is not found among the sins commonly listed in the generation of Hermas. That it is here considered a sin is indicated by the transfer of God's imputed anger from the sin of evil desire to the sin of domestic negligence. Furthermore, we shall find that this new charge is equally serious, equally persistent throughout the document, and equally intricate in this apocalyptic report.

To placate God, Hermas is called upon to "convert" (ἐπιστρέφειν) his family or household. The English term "convert" conveys the thought that his family still are heathen and that he is to make them Christians. However, the context of the apocalypse shows that this is not the case, but rather that the reference is to the need for post-baptismal correction and reform. Their reform is the personalizing of the universal message of the book.[16] The household here referred to means only his own offspring, sons and daughters, called interchangeably ὁ οἶκος or τὰ τέκνα or occasionally τὸ σπέρμα.[17] In only three instances the double term "children and household" appears, as though Hermas' moral responsibility might extend more

16 See Vis. I (1:9; II (2:4 f.).
17 See Vis. I. (3:1-2); II (2:2).

widely.[18] His own children must have been numerous, since they are referred to as "all your children" (τοῖς τέκνοις σοὺ πᾶσιν, Vis. II, 2:3) or "all your household" (ὅλου τοῦ οἴκου σου, Vis. I, 1:9 and Sim. VII, 3 Latin). It would seem that these children are grown and morally responsible persons, who were previously converted to the Christian life as adults and have subsequently built up a shameful record of sinfulness.

Yet it is accounted as a sin of Hermas, engendering the wrath of the Lord against *him*, that his adult Christian offspring have sinned (ἀνομήσαντα, Vis. I, 3:1). The Church's accusation is: "You have not been instructing your family, and have allowed them to become terribly corrupt" (*Ibid.*). Their sin is said to be against the Lord and against the parents. What is meant by sinning against the parents is not made clear, and yet such an explanation is especially needed when we find no reference to the responsibility of the mother and only condemnation of the negligence of the father. Hermas is placed in the peculiar position of being responsible to God for sins committed against himself by his undisciplined children.

The nameless wife of Hermas plays only a minor part in the problem of his divine condemnation. She is mentioned only in Vis. II (2:3 f.) as his companion (σύμβιος) who sins with an uncontrolled tongue. It is not said whether this means gossip, grumbling, guile, abuse, or even blasphemy. Far too much has been imagined as to her bad character, despite the fact that the brief reference is really quite favorable to her. Hermas is to deliver the Church's message to all his children and his wife, and when she shall have heard it she will control her tongue and obtain mercy.[19] She is, however, quite unimportant to the "plot" and there is no explanation as to why Hermas is directed to consider her as a sister in the future. Perhaps we may judge from Mand. IV (4) that here also it is proposed to Hermas that he go beyond the normal requirement of morality.[20]

What are the sins of the children of Hermas, which fall upon the latter's shoulders? Two are specifically mentioned, double-minded-

---

[18] See Mand. XII (3:6); Sim. V (3:9); Sim. VII (6). Some have proposed that the term οἶκος here means the larger "flock" of Christians, but this is an improbable meaning for the synonyms τὰ τέκνα and τὸ σπέρμα.

[19] Codex Aleph here reads, " . . . you will obtain mercy."

[20] Mand. IV (4) contains the Shepherd's advice that remarriage is not a sin, and yet if the widower "remain single he gains . . . great glory with the Lord." Unlike Paul's objective (I Cor. 7:28 f.), it is here to "preserve purity and holiness." This idea of supererogatory conduct is mentioned again by Hermas in Sim. V (3:3): "If you do anything good, beyond the commandment of God, you will gain for yourself greater glory." See also 2:7 and 3:7 f.

ness and blasphemy, the latter of which should be considered fatal. They are mentioned in the general setting of persecution and apostasy (Vis. II, 2:2, 4, 7 f.).[21] Elsewhere it is implied that their sin is constituted of many daily evils which can be overcome only by "the daily righteous word" (ὁ λόγος ὁ καθημερινὸς ὁ δίκαιος), like the persistent strokes of the smith (Vis. I, 3:2). Although the sins of these Christian children may be many and varied and unidentified, the total result is fearfully impressive: "Your seed, Hermas, have offended God, and blasphemed the Lord, and through their great wickedness have betrayed their parents . . . they have added to their sins (ἁμαρτίαις) licentious acts (ἀσελγείας) and a mass of iniquity (πονηρίας), and so their sins (ἀνομίαι) have been made complete" (Vis. II, 2:2). The psychologist would say today that Hermas must have been greatly concerned about the sins of his children, for this theme is repeated with emphasis in Vis. I and Vis. II, and again especially in Sim. VII (2 f.) where it is the "glorious angel"[22] (rather than God) who is "enraged at their deeds" of "great iniquity and sin," and yet the burden of guilt is laid upon Hermas as "the head of the whole household."

Despite their evil record, including blasphemy, the Church assures Hermas that "if they repent with all their heart, they will be inscribed in the books of life with the holy people" (Vis. I, 3:2). In Sim. VII (2) the Shepherd extends release to Hermas himself: "When, therefore, they repent, and have been purified, then the Angel of Punishment will depart from you." But the reader is perplexed when Hermas remonstrates (4), "They have repented with all their heart," and the Shepherd responds, "I already know that they have." Yet relief cannot come to Hermas immediately, he explains, because now the repentant ones must undergo affliction and self-imposed torture for a time.[23] In Vis. III (7:5 f.) the Church explains that the rejected "stones" may repent but they are less worthy even "after they have been tormented and fulfilled the days of their sins," i. e., a day's torment for a day's sin. Then when Hermas comments (Sim. VI, 4:2) that the penalty should be sevenfold, the Shepherd's explanation is that a single hour of torment has the "power" of thirty days, or one day the power of a year.[24]

[21] See Vis. III (7) for the double-minded "stones" in the tower allegory.

[22] Probably the same "glorious angel" referred to in Sim. IX (1:3), who sent the Shepherd to dwell with Hermas. In Vis. V (2) he is called the "most reverend angel."

[23] See also Mand. IV (2:2).

[24] One hour to a month means a ratio of 1 to 720, unless only twelve daylight hours are in mind. One day to a year means probably 1 to 360, assuming a pure lunar year.

The afflictions for sin are administered by another shepherd, the Angel of Punishment, and Hermas asks what the different punishments are. It is to be observed that although he is himself under the Angel of Punishment he has not experienced these afflictions. He is informed that such tortures are suffered in this life, and that they include losses, poverty, sickness, shiftlessness and failure, and insults by inferior persons. After these afflictions, men are turned over to the Angel of Repentance for instruction (Sim. VI, 3:4-6).[25]

In Sim. VII (4) the Shepherd says that it is the repentant children who must do penance and suffer affliction for their own sins.[26] But he has just declared (2) that the "glorious angel," enraged at their deeds, has required that Hermas be afflicted. Indeed, it is implied that it is *his* affliction that will bring about their repentance. Similarly, in Mand. XII (3:6), the salvation of his children and household is said to be dependent on *his* obedience to the mandates. Yet again, in Sim. VII (5), the Shepherd observes, "It is advantageous for you and for your house, to suffer affliction now," as though all must share the affliction. The "glorious angel" has directed (1) that Hermas be placed in the charge of the Shepherd of Punishment to be tested and afflicted although, so the Shepherd says (2), his own sins are "not so great as that [he] should be handed over to this angel." "You must be afflicted," says the Shepherd (1), because the "glorious angel" has ordered it so, but (6) "I will ask the Angel of Punishment to afflict you more lightly." Again, it is promised (6) that the affliction will last only a short time, after which he will be "restored" to his household.[27] In the light of so many inconsistent and even contradictory remarks, it is extremely difficult to secure any positive impression as to the real guilt of Hermas in the matter of his responsibility as head of the household.

It is therefore not surprising that Hermas himself should disregard the charge of guilt by proxy and challenge the Shepherd to reveal any personal charge. Even after all the story about Rhoda and the account of his evil children, Hermas still innocently inquires (Sim. VII, 1), "What have I done so wicked?" The Shepherd admits

25 The series of afflictions is given in connection with the parable of the well-fed sheep committed to the Shepherd of Punishment. Perhaps, therefore, these afflictions should be understood as especially applicable to those who live in luxury.

26 In Sim. X (2:4) the principle is stated, " . . . each one . . . is guilty of his own blood."

27 Some have drawn a biographical datum from this statement, that Hermas was a prisoner under arrest, but the natural meaning is that he will be delivered from the charge of the Angel of Punishment. We must remember that the imagery throughout is visionary and symbolical.

that his sins would not justify committing him to the Angel of Punishment but reiterates that his family has been sinful. To this Hermas again protests (3), "Even if they have done such things . . . what have I done?" Apparently he has not been impressed by the explanation of the Church in his first Vision (3:1) : "Because of their sins and iniquities you have been corrupted in daily matters"; nor by her words in the second Vision (3:1) : "You neglected them and became entangled in their evil deeds."

A more direct allegation is reflected in her instruction to him in Vis. II (3:1) : "You are no longer to bear malice against your children . . . for malice produces death."[28] But when Hermas later asks in Sim. VII "What have I done?", the Shepherd seems to grant that there is no serious charge directly against Hermas himself, for he replies (3) : "They cannot be punished in any other way, than if you, the head of the house, be afflicted. For when you are afflicted, they also will necessarily be afflicted, but while you fare well, they cannot suffer any affliction." The Shepherd promises in Sim. VII (2) that repentance by his children will release him from the punishing angel. Furthermore, the Church has praised him (Vis. II, 3:2, in a phrase from Heb. 3:12) for not having fallen away from the living God, but remaining in simplicity and continence.[29] That Hermas has been constant in such virtues is again implied in Sim. VII (6) : "Only continue in your humility and service to the Lord with a pure heart." Charges of neglect and malice have been mentioned but not sustained, and certainly not explained; while the impression remains that his afflictions are vicarious. As in the case of Rhoda, so also in the case of his family responsibilities it becomes a difficult and intricate matter to place at his own door some explicit and personal sin, with consistent and persuasive evidence.

IV

A third possible accusation against Hermas educed by critics from his apocalypse is that his mind has been set on prosperity and luxury. It is true that much is said about the sin of the wealthy, and also true that Hermas himself is said to have been wealthy

---

[28] The malicious are represented by the cracked stones in the tower vision (Vis. III,6:3). Cf. Sim. IX (23:4) : the term μνησικακεῖν has often been translated "to bear a grudge" but this seems less suitable to the context than "to bear malice," called here a demonic "heresy." Malice as a moral attitude is considered one of the worst of sins (cf. Mand. VIII,3 f.).

[29] The virtues of simplicity and innocence are commended in Mand. II (1 and 7). In Vis. I (2:4) these virtues are attributed to Hermas by the Church.

formerly (Vis. III, 6:7). Although he is wealthy no longer,[30] his constant concern with the sins of business and riches clings to him so as to persuade some that this is part of his struggle with guilt. A prelude to this theme appears in the very first of the visions, and it is Rhoda herself who first sounds the note. When speaking of his evil designs, she seems to have him in mind as she points out that evil designs bring death and captivity, "especially to those who obtain this world for themselves and glory in their wealth" rather than in "the good things which are to come" (1:8).

The theme of wealth is emphasized in the vision of the tower (Vis. III, 6:5-7), where the round, white stones are Christians who have both faith and wealth but whose business interests which misguide them (ψυχαγαγῶν) cause them to apostatize under persecution.[31] Their only hope lies in renunciation of their wealth, lest they renounce their Lord. "This you must understand," says the Church, "from your own previous experience." One may question here whether Hermas' financial decline has been due to his acceptance of the principle of renunciation or to misfortune.[32] The advice of the Shepherd to Hermas in Sim. IV (5) is to "abstain from much business and you will do no sin. For those who do much business also sin much, being engrossed in their business, and serving their Lord in nothing." It is further suggested to him (7) that "if anyone be occupied with but a single business, he can serve the Lord also."[33] The Shepherd alludes to the lies told by Hermas in doing business (Mand. III, 5), and Hermas condemns himself (3) as one who never in all his life has spoken a true word. I have "always spoken deceitfully with all men."[34] The man preoccupied with business, says the Shepherd (Mand. V, 2:1-2), is especially susceptible to ill temper which subverts his tranquillity and out of nothing produces bitterness, "because of daily business or of food or of some trifle, or about some friend, or about giving or receiving."

When Hermas asks (Mand. VIII, 3 f.) what are the vices to

[30] We take the participle ἔχων in Sim. I (4) as expressing a general condition rather than as a statement of fact pertaining to Hermas.

[31] In Sim. VIII (8) the half-dry, half-green sticks represent "those who are concerned with business and do not cleave to the saints." Sim. VIII (9) also speaks of the faithful rich, represented by the sticks two-thirds dry, who chose to mingle with the heathen. Cf. also Mand. X (1:4-5); Sim. I (10).

[32] The principle of renunciation is repeated in Sim. IX (31:1-2). Some would understand that Hermas' property has been confiscated.

[33] Among the sins associated with acquisitiveness are also covetousness, robbery and theft (Mand. VIII,5).

[34] Furthermore, says Hermas naively, "I gave out that my lie was true." Besides, "men believed my word."

avoid, the Shepherd includes evil luxury and much eating and extravagance of wealth (πολυτελείας πλούτου) among "the wickedest of all in the life of men." In Mand. XII (2:1) the Shepherd ranks adultery as the primary lust, after which in second place comes "extravagance of wealth, and much needless food and drink, and many other foolish luxuries" which "bring the servants of God to death." There is a special shepherd, the Angel of Luxury and Deceit (Sim. VI, 2), who engenders evil desires that lead to death or corruption. Death comes to the worldly who have also blasphemed against the Lord,[35] but for the corrupt not guilty of blasphemy repentance is still possible.[36] The latter pass, in their restoration, from the Shepherd of Luxury to the Shepherd of Punishment and finally to the Shepherd of Repentance. Their punishment matches their sin, turning luxury into poverty and business losses. Estimated by the force they exert on one's experience, every day of luxury is balanced by a year of poverty (at least in the memory).[37]

Further, it is possible to interpret the Shepherd as speaking of degrees of wealth. Several times he uses the heightened term πολυτέλεια to describe extravagance of wealth and food,[38] and it is especially significant that this term is employed when speaking figuratively about the joy of spiritual wealth in righteousness.[39] It is not made clear whether all wealth, greater or less, is condemned, although it is explicit stated that limited business activity need not controvert the demands of the Christian life (Sim. IV, 7-8). Some guidance is given by the Church (Vis. III, 9:2-4) when she instructs, "Do not take for yourselves a superabundant share of what God has created, but give also a part to those who lack . . . lack of sharing is harmful to you who are rich, and do not share with the poor."[40] The Shepherd also directs (Sim. I, 6) that you must "make no further preparations for yourself beyond a sufficient competence." This context is one of inspiring description commending spiritual wealth acquired in the heavenly city. How much

[35] Cf. Jas. 2:5-7.

[36] A similar thought is expressed in Sim. IX (19), where hypocrites from the "bare mountain" fare better than the hopeless apostates and blasphemers from the "black mountain."

[37] Cf. Sim. VI (5:3). It appears paradoxical that morally poverty is preferable to wealth and yet poverty is considered punishment for the sin of wealth. Furthermore, poverty is at once both the punishment and the corrective for the evil of wealth.

[38] Mand. VI (2:5); VIII (3); XII (2:1).

[39] Sim. I (10-11).

[40] Cf. Did. 4:6-8; Sim. X (4:3).

of all this belongs to the personal experience of Hermas? Since he
no longer indulges in luxuries, a degree of covetousness at most may
persist. Yet he shows himself to be a man of sensitive conscience
whose religious concern seems greater than his attention to business
interests that fall within permissible limits. As to the evils of prosperity, he seems to stand outside as an onlooker inquiring into
general principles that define the sinless life. It is certain that the
general instructions in Sim. I (8 f.) are given in the plural : "Instead
of lands purchase afflicted souls . . . look after widows and or-
phans."[41] "For this reason did the Master make you rich."

Thus we are prepared for the teaching of the parable of the elm
and the vine (Sim. II). The moral is that they are necessary to one
another, for the fruitless elm (the poor man) that supports the vine
(the rich man) increases its yield and the fruitful vine thus bears
also for the elm. This is a realistic recognition, at least, that we have
with us always both poor and rich—if not an approval of such an
economy. Yet the rich man is here assumed to be "poor as touching
the Lord" and the poor man is "rich in intercession and confession."[42] The surprising conclusion is an uncommon beatitude (10) :
"Blessed are those who have wealth, who understand that their
riches derive from the Lord." So the Shepherd has come round to
an approval of those who have wealth and faith, who do not
neglect to use their wealth in charity (a neglect with which Hermas
has not been charged). When finally we again recall that Hermas
no longer possesses wealth (Vis. III, 6:7), any personal charge
against him on this point seems very weak indeed.

V

Perhaps Hermas has commited the sin of double-mindedness or
doubt. Such an attitude is certainly treated as a sin and is dealt
with throughout the document.[43] The special homily on the subject
is in Mand. IX, which begins with the urging of the Shepherd,
"Remove from yourself doubt . . . for any man of doubt, unless he
repent, shall hardly be saved." In this context doubt is the antithesis
of faith and it defeats the Christian's petitions to God. Earlier a
young man appears to Hermas in a vision (Vis. III, 10:9) and
pointedly responds to him thus : "You are all made foolish by your
doubt." He explains to him (11:2-3) that the Church had appeared

41 Cf. Jas. 1:27.
42 Cf. Jas. 2:5.
43 I Clem. 11:2 and 23:2 f.; II Clem. 11:2,5 and 19:2 also allude to this
evil.

as an old woman "because your [pl.] spirit is old . . . and has no power through your enervation and doubt . . . weakened by the occupations of this life." A further reference to the connection between his business and his doubt may be implied in the allegory of the sticks (Sim. VIII, 8-9), where the half-green sticks are those doubters "who are concerned with business and do not cleave to the saints." Again, in the allegory of the stones (Vis. III, 7:1), the stones that roll beyond the road into the rough ground are doubting converts who "leave their true road . . . and err and wander miserably." Indeed, in Mand. X (1:1), it is said that doubt is sister to grief and ill temper.[44]

Another allegory is that of the twelve mountains (Sim. IX, 21), the fourth of which bears many herbs whose tops are green but whose roots are dry. These signify the double-minded, who profess their faith but possess no lasting conviction. Double-mindedness is "of the devil," says the Shepherd (Mand. IX, 11), and is an "earthly spirit" without power, as opposed to the power of faith which is from the Lord above. False prophets victimize the doubter who consults them (Mand. XI, 1-2). Here again we must ask, to what extent do these generalizations refer to Hermas and his sense of sin? The Church (Vis. II, 2:4) has pointed to the double-mindedness of his children, but the Shepherd charges him squarely (Sim. VI, 1:2): "Why are you double-minded concerning the mandates?" This question seems to mean (1:4) that Hermas is not confident that he can obey the mandates and so avoid future sin.[45]

But the doubt that is most vividly pictured is that of wavering in the face of persecution. While traveling on the public road, Hermas hears the ominous admonition of the Shepherd (Vis. IV, 1:4): "Do not be double-minded, Hermas." After he has encountered the gigantic beast and has safely passed by, he meets the Church, who now assures him (2:4): "You have escaped great tribulation through your faith, and because you were not double-minded" in the face of persecution. She had commended and assured him once before (Vis. II, 3:2): "You are saved by not 'having broken away from the living God,'[46] and by your simplicity." In our document, simplicity ($\dot{\alpha}\pi\lambda\acute{o}\tau\eta s$) is the antithesis of double-mindedness, and therefore to attribute simplicity to Hermas is to clear him of that sin as a temptation to apostasy. If Hermas was actually guilty of doubt, it must have been an attitude undefined and general. He

[44] In Mand. V (2:1), ill temper or bitterness ($\dot{o}\xi\upsilon\chi o\lambda\acute{\iota}a$) is said to lead astray the vain and double-minded.

[45] Cf. Mand. XII (3:4-4:5).

[46] Cf. Heb. 3:12, which is also a reference to apostasy.

neither confesses nor affirms this sin, but on the contrary is praised for its opposing virtue.

Double-mindedness is for some the forerunner of apostasy and irrevocable condemnation. When the Church finishes reading to him (Vis. I, 4:2) she asks: "Did my reading please you?" Hermas replies, " . . . the first part was hard and difficult," and this is the part he has just described (3:3) as "frightful, such as a man cannot bear." The Lady declares that this "first part was for the heathen and the apostates."[47] So also in the third Vision (6:1) she explains that the broken stones cast far away from the tower are the hypocritical "sons of wickedness," having no salvation. Also, in the parable of the sheep (Sim. VI, 2:3), those that "you see joyful and skipping . . . have been torn away from God completely . . ."; in the parable of the sticks (Sim. VIII, 6:4), the wholly dry sticks are apostates and blasphemers; and in the parable of the twelve mountains (Sim. IX, 19:1), the black mountain yields apostates and blasphemers. Indeed, often in the apocalypse the critical evil that brings final condemnation is blasphemy. For the joyous, skipping sheep "there is no repentance of life because they have added to their sins and blasphemed against the name of God." The dry sticks are blasphemers who "have finally perished to God." As for Hermas, he is nowhere charged with the ultimate sin of apostasy and blasphemy. The Church has said to him (Vis. II, 2:2), "Your children . . . have blasphemed the Lord," and yet his offspring are not finally rejected. Hermas himself certainly goes no further than doubt, and his doubt is not uncertainty of faith but rather a wavering confidence in his ability to fulfill obediently the mandates of the Shepherd.

VI

The purpose of this exploration has not been to exonerate Hermas of sin. He explicitly confesses guilt, at least in a general manner. Our examination of the treatment given the dominant sins in the apocalypse, especially those sins which many have charged to Hermas, has had two objectives: to judge the extent to which Hermas has been personally involved, and to expose to view certain theological implications. This is really a study of the Christian life in one special family, in the formative generation at the beginning of the second century. The sins of immorality, materialism, doubt and apostasy were clearly the foremost sins of that time, not only in the Shepherd of Hermas but in all the contemporary

---

[47] Cf. Vis. II (1:8).

Christian literature. But on the basis of this apocalypse, it is difficult to fix these sins clearly and explicitly on Hermas. His role in the document is as a foil, against which to expound these sins to his fellow Christians. While the message emerges from his personal experience, the apocalypse does not succeed in making Hermas the personal example of the sinner. Furthermore, it does not succeed in any attempt at a clear explanation of these sins, or of their sure consequences. The general principle which Hermas would teach is quite clear, but the definition of that principle remains vague and inconsistent.

There remains the impression that Hermas was a historical figure, and there is still the picture of a representative Christian family with its moral problems in a time of undefined theology. But we may not be persuaded that Hermas personally experienced all the problems and all the major sins which are discussed. His personality in the document is a composite one, in which the sins of his contemporaries are compounded.

Finally, let us make a few theological observations. First, Hermas is concerned about the sinless life here and now. The purity of the Christian society eclipses the eschatological view. Second, Hermas sees remission of sin as dependent upon the Christian's conduct and attitude within society.[48] This leads T. F. Torrance to object that Hermas knows nothing of "justification by grace alone."[49] But this judgment overlooks the fact that Hermas is discussing post-baptismal guilt. Certainly Hermas would have been heretical if he had postulated a second act of God, to recover the failure of a first act of grace. In the particular problem of Hermas, it must be man (the believer-sinner) who will undertake to appropriate anew the divine grace which has been once received but forfeited. The problem of post-baptismal sin was new and unique with Christians of his own day, a theological problem encountered here for the first time within the young Christian movement. Therefore this new problem required a new answer rather than mere repetition of the first principle of justification through grace. The revelation of Hermas teaches a limited extension of God's grace, for it is concerned not with twice-born men but with thrice-born men.[50]

[48] Cf. Bar. 19:10.

[49] T. F. Torrance, *The Doctrine of Grace in the Apostolic Fathers* (Edinburgh, 1948), p. 118.

[50] It should not be overlooked that Tertullian's earlier view is similar to the revelation of Hermas. In *De Poenitentia* 7, he observes, that baptized Christians should "know nothing of repentance, and require none of it"; yet God, "although the gate of forgiveness has been shut and fastened up with the bar of baptism, has permitted it still to stand somewhat open . . . but never more."

It has become usual to disparage Hermas as a theologian,[51] and certainly he is not systematic. Yet there is reason to contend that critics have failed to perceive the finesse with which he handles intricate and undefined theological problems in a formative day. We conclude that the biographical setting is authentic though the data are artificially compounded, that the visions are credible though they are sometimes inconsistent (as visions can well be), and that the theology is at once formative and sharply penetrating. Hermas personally is less sinful and more brilliant than critics have been wont to see.

[51] For example, Torrance repeats such an estimate in these words: "He was possessed of little Christian penetration, and certainly not much skill in the exposition. . . ."

"REALIZED ESCHATOLOGY"

IN 1936 appeared Charles H. Dodd's *Parables of the Kingdom*, based upon his Shaffer Lectures at Yale University in the spring of 1935. Therein, Dodd sought to establish his view that the ministry of Jesus is represented in the Gospels as "realized eschatology" (p. 51). He maintained that "in some way the Kingdom of God has come with Jesus himself" (p. 45). "The *eschaton* has moved fom the . . . sphere of expectation into that of realized experience" (p. 50). This contention was based primarily upon statements attributed to Jesus, wherein he declared — according to Dodd's translation — "The Kingdom of God has come upon you." The key verses in this argument are seven similar Synoptic references containing the statement, ἤγγικεν ἡ βασιλεία τοῦ Θεοῦ; and a Q reference in Mt 12 28 = Lk 11 20, ἔφθασεν ἐφ᾽ ὑμᾶς ἡ βασιλεία τοῦ Θεοῦ. These two statements are the chief pillars upon which Dodd begins to construct his argument. The key words by which their translation must be determined are ἐγγίζειν and φθάνειν; consequently, it is of vital importance to Dodd's theory of "realized eschatology" to examine closely the usage of these verbs, and to inquire whether they do in fact permit the translation urged by Dodd.

Extensive search among the papyri has verified the observation of Moulton and Milligan regarding ἐγγίζειν that "this verb is not so common as we might have expected." In a nonliterary papyrus of A.D. 217 a certain Aurelius Ptolemaeus presented a petition to the deputy-epistrategus Aurelius Severus, concerning his son's eligibility to become an ephebus. He wrote, "It is the custom . . . that those who are for the time being amphodogrammateis of the city should, as the contest of each year approaches (ἐνγίζοντος τοῦ ἐκάστου ἔτους ἀγῶνος),

publish a list of those who are about to become ephebi, in order
that each one may assume the status of ephebus at the proper
season" (*P. Oxy.*, 1202, 8–9). There can be no doubt that
Grenfell and Hunt, and later Moulton and Milligan, have here
translated ἐγγίζειν properly. The context requires the root
meaning, "to draw near."

We find among the Amherst papyri, now in the Pierpont
Morgan collection, the largest extant portion of the Greek text
of the *Ascension of Isaiah*, probably written in the second century. In one passage therein the writer uses ἐγγίζειν three
times as follows: "there shall be many signs and wonders in those
days, and at his approach (ἐν τῷ ἐγγίζειν αὐτ[ό]ν) his disciples
shall forsake the prophecy of his twelve apostles and the faith
and their love and their purity, and there shall be many heresies
at his approach (ἐν τῷ ἐγγίζειν αὐτόν), . . . and there shall
be many slanders and much vain glory at the approach of the
Lord (ἐν τῷ ἐγγίζειν τὸν κν̄)" (*P. Amh.*, I, xi, 4, 11; xii, 7).
In this messianic prophecy, as Grenfell and Hunt themselves
translate it, it is obvious that these unhappy conditions are expected to exist when he *draws near*, not after he *has come*.

Similarly there are decisive instances of usage in the LXX,
where ἐγγίζειν was used to translate a number of Hebrew and
Aramaic forms with such meanings as "to draw near, to approach,
to await, to hope for, to look eagerly for, to reach, to touch, to
strike."[1] None of these Hebrew terms refers to the actual progress of the experience involved, but rather to the anticipation
or, at most, the initial contact therewith. This is clearly illustrated in such a passage as Gen 33 3, relating that Jacob "went
on ahead of them, bowing seven times to the earth until he drew
near to his brother (ἕως τοῦ ἐγγίσαι τοῦ ἀδελφοῦ). Then Esau
ran to meet him . . ." Can any context make the meaning of
ἐγγίζειν more unequivocal? Still another such instance may
be cited in Ps 88 3, where the poet originally used the Hebrew

---

[1] Brown, Driver and Briggs, *Hebrew and English Lexicon of the Old Testament*, Oxford, 1907. By far the most frequent verbs translated by ἐγγίζειν
(109 times out of 127) are the synonyms נגשׁ and קרב, both meaning "to draw
near, to approach." The verbs נגע and מצא, which Dodd especially cites, are
found only eight times.

עָנִי in his complaint, "For my being was filled with evils, and my life drew near to Hades (ἡ ζωή μου τῷ ᾅδῃ ἤγγισε)." The poet is not describing his death and departure from this earth, which did not actually ensue — to say nothing of his actual arrival in Hades. Literally a hundred decisive illustrations can be exhibited from the LXX to demonstrate that in the pre-Christian centuries, as well as in the papyri of the second and third centuries A.D., ἐγγίζειν consistently connoted proximity or approach.[2]

The meaning of proximity in ἐγγίζειν is extended to the limit in five instances in the LXX where this verb translates נָגַע or מְטָא.[3] In Ps 32 6 is found the supplication, "That in the time of distress, in the rush of great waters, they shall not reach him (πρὸς αὐτὸν ἐγγιοῦσι, for יַגִּיעוּ)." Again, in Jonah 3 6 we read, "When the news reached the King (ἤγγισεν ὁ λόγος πρὸς τὸν βασιλέα, for וַיִּגַּע הַדָּבָר אֶל־מֶלֶךְ)." Jeremiah (51 9) laments over Babylon, "for her judgment touches the heavens (ἤγγικεν εἰς οὐρανόν, for נָגַע אֶל־הַשָּׁמַיִם)." The other two instances represent translations of the Aramaic מְטָא and are found in Daniel (LXX) 4 9 and 19, the two conveying exactly the same meaning. Daniel in vision sees a tree "whose height reached to the heavens (ἤγγιζεν ἕως τοῦ οὐρανοῦ . . . ἐγγίσαι τῷ οὐρανῷ)." In these five cases proximity is extended to the point of initial contact as a result of reaching after. It may be granted that the announcement of the Kingdom involves this very point, that it is immediately imminent. Repeatedly the warning is given that the present era has expired and the kingdom is "at hand." But that the Kingdom is due immediately to ensue is quite different from the declaration that it has already been in operation. The concept that the Kingdom, like rushing water pursuing a man or an imaginary tree striving toward heaven, has at last attained its point of revelation is exactly the message of Jesus.[4]

[2] For additional instances consult Hatch and Redpath, *Concordance to the Septuagint*, Oxford, 1897.

[3] It is to be observed that none of these more debatable instances involves the perfect, ἤγγικεν.

[4] For a fuller discussion of the LXX witness, see J. Y. Campbell in *Expository Times*, XLVIII (1936), 91–94. His conclusion: "It is clear that the LXX affords no good evidence that ἤγγικεν ever means 'has come'."

Standing chronologically between these occurrences of ἐγγί-ζειν, the usage in the Apostolic Fathers also is equally clear. Early in the second century Barnabas wrote (6 1), "Let him draw near to the Lord's servant (ἐγγισάτω τῷ παιδὶ κυρίου);" and again (4 3), "The final stumbling block is at hand (ἤγγικεν)." The contemporary author of Hermas also thus used the term in Mandates 11 13. "On no account does he come near (οὐκ ἐγγίζει) to an assembly of righteous men, but shuns them."[5] Among the Apologists ἐγγίζειν is used only in quotations from the LXX, by Tatian once and by Justin eleven times. In every case Otto has translated these occurrences by "appropinquare."[6]

A little earlier than these occurrences of ἐγγίζειν, the usage of NT writers is decisively clear. Note, for example, the story of Paul's conversion in Acts 9 3–8. "But on his journey, as he was approaching Damascus (αὐτὸν ἐγγίζειν τῇ Δαμασκῷ), ... 'But get up and go into the city' ... They had to take him by the hand and lead him into Damascus." Again, in Acts 10 9 we read of the messengers of Cornelius: "The next day, while they were still on their way, and were drawing near to the city (καὶ τῇ πόλει ἐγγιζόντων) ..." In Phil 2 30, Paul refers to the grave illness of Epaphroditus in the words, μέχρι θανάτου ἤγγισεν. Epaphroditus obviously did not 'come' to death; rather, he 'came near' to death. The writer of Hebrews would not have dreamed of writing that δι' ἧς (ἐλπίδος) ἔρχομεν τῷ Θεῷ. He did write: ἐγγίζομεν τῷ Θεῷ (7 19). So also the author of James wrote: ἐγγίσατε τῷ Θεῷ καὶ ἐγγιεῖ ὑμῖν (4 8). Due reverence for the transcendent and holy God dictated the use of ἐγγίζειν in these last two passages. Again, in Jas 5 8 we read, "So be patient brothers until the coming of the Lord. The farmer has to wait for the precious crop from the ground, and be patient with it, until it gets the early and the late rains. You must have patience too; you must keep up your courage, for the parousia of the Lord has drawn near (ὅτι ἡ παρουσία τοῦ κυρίου ἤγγικεν)." In all these contexts we are at present concerned solely with the obvious linguistic conclusion that ἐγγίζειν means "to draw near."

5 Lake, *Apostolic Fathers*, London, 1924–25, *Loeb Classical Library*.
6 J. C. T. Otto, *S. Justini Philosophi et Martyris Opera*, Jena, 1847–49.

The verb occurs forty-one times in the NT.[7] Twenty-eight of these occurrences are of the normal sort, without debate from any quarter, wherein the meaning is "to draw near" to a certain place or person or to a certain time. Seven other occurrences involve the approach of some eschatological fulfillment: "the hour," "the time," "her desolation," "your redemption," "the day," "the parousia," "the end."[8] Examination finds all these terms used with the perfect ἤγγικεν (except Lk 21 28); and the context in every case requires the usual meaning, "has drawn near." In the single exception Lk (21 28), after describing certain messianic preliminaries, concludes, "But when this begins to happen, look up and raise your heads, for your deliverance is drawing near (διότι ἐγγίζει ἡ ἀπολύτρωσις ὑμῶν)." Here the present tense is used, and the context is less decisive but yet is best suited by the usual translation.

Thus far we have noted that in the non-literary and literary papyri of the second and third centuries, in the LXX, the Apostolic Fathers, and the NT, ἐγγίζειν has been employed consistently to mean "to draw near." For this reason it appears quite unjustifiable to interpret the verb in any other way, in the remaining six NT occurrences. Six times the synoptists have written, "The Kingdom of God (of Heaven) ἤγγικεν" — denoting a state of proximity in present time. Mt offers three of these six instances, and uses the verb normally twice besides; Lk offers two, using the verb normally sixteen times besides in his Gospel and six times in Acts. Usage by the three synoptists unanimously agrees with all the above evidence, and no linguistic evidence appears to support the contention that ἤγγικεν can mean "has come."[9]

---

[7] See Moulton and Geden, *Concordance to the Greek Testament*, Edinburgh, 1899[2].

[8] Resp. Mt 26 45; Lk 21 8, 20, 28; Rom 13 12; Jas 5 8; I Pet 4 7.

[9] The six synoptic references have ἐγγίζειν intransitive (cf. Lk 10 9 ἐφ' ὑμᾶς). This intransitive use is general outside the NT also. Besides, ἐγγίζειν is used with the simple gen., dat. or acc. It is used with μέχρι, ἕως, ἐκ and the gen.; with πρὸς and the dat. (Prov 5 8; Lk 19 37; Acts 10 9); with εἰς, πρὸς and ἐπὶ (Ps 26 2; 68 4; Lk 10 9) and the acc. In all these various constructions, the meaning of ἐγγίζειν is the same.

One may further point out that philology in general observes in ἐγγίζειν no contextual problem and reveals no evidence of changing trend in the connotation of the verb, down to A.D. 1100 at the earliest.[10] In this history of the word no variation in meaning has developed, but through all the literature and through the centuries it has constantly been used to mean, "to draw near." In the synoptists the proclamation that the Kingdom of God "has drawn near" is twice attributed to John the Baptist,[11] and five times to Jesus.[12] Insofar as we may determine the Aramaic expression or the thought of Jesus from this Greek literary form, the consistent usage of ἐγγίζειν insists upon the basic translation, "The Kingdom of God has drawn near." Surely we are committed to the necessity of exegesis on the basis of this translation.

This conclusion is further strengthened by other expressions concerning the Kingdom, attributed by the synoptists to Jesus. Luke has Jesus say (21 31), "When you see these things happening, know that the Kingdom of God ἐγγύs ἐστιν. It would be exceedingly difficult, and would demand convincing explanation, to translate this form "has come." In the Lord's Prayer is the well-known petition (Mt 6 10; Lk 12 2), ἐλθάτω ἡ βασιλεία σου, with the aorist imperative expressing the hope for a definite coming of the Kingdom in the near future. Dodd (pp. 36, 42) points out a parallel to this in the Jewish prayer, "May he establish his Kingdom during your life and during your days."[13] Without debate as to the date of origin (Dodd assigns this prayer as early as the first century), one may readily acknowledge the similarity of these petitions. One is attributed to Jesus in the first century, as an instruction to his disciples to continue praying for fulfillment, while the other has been used by Jews even to the present generation. They both anticipate a future coming of the Kingdom.

Another saying of Jesus is that found in Mk 9 1 = Lk 9 27, which

[10] E. A. Sophocles, *Greek Lexicon of the Roman and Byzantine Periods*, Cambridge, Mass., 1914.

[11] Mt 3 2, Mk 1 15.

[12] Mt 4 17, 10 7; Lk 10 9, 11; Mk 1 15.

[13] S. Singer (translator), *Authorized Daily Prayer-book*, 1908, "Kaddish."

Dodd (p. 53) has translated, "There are some of those standing
here who will not taste death until they have seen that the Kingdom of God has come with power." In a note he explains that
there is "no doubt that the correct translation of the Greek is as
given above. The bystanders are not promised that they shall
see the Kingdom of God *coming*, but that they shall come to
see that the Kingdom of God *has already come*, at some point
before they became aware of it." Now this is clearly a mis-
reading of the Greek, which declares that "there are some of
those standing here who will not taste death ἕως ἂν ἴδωσιν . . ."
The aorist subjunctive may refer to a definite event in the past,
present or future, and here with ἕως it is obvious that the event
is expected in the future but before the death of some of Jesus'
listeners. They will not die "until they shall have seen the
Kingdom of God come with power" at that future time. The
perfect participle ἐληλυθυῖαν does indeed indicate, as Dodd
says, "an action already complete from the standpoint of the
subject of the main verb." Its main verb is ἴδωσιν, referring to
the future sight at which time the coming will be fulfilled. If
the "coming" had already transpired as Jesus spoke, and thus
preceded the "sight" still to be experienced, the statement required the aorist participle of antecedant action instead of the
perfect.[14] Futhermore, ἴδωσιν cannot mean, as Dodd proposes,
"to come to see" or "to awake to the fact," for the aorist connotes no such gradual unfolding but rather a definite event to
be observed within that generation.[15]

Such expressions of the Kingdom further support the idea of
its futurity as interpreted in ἐγγίζειν. It appears to us clearly
conclusive that we shall build theological interpretation upon a
false premise in the postulate that "there is no saying of the
unequivocal form, 'The Kingdom of God will come,' to balance
the statement, 'The Kingdom of God has come.'" There is only

[14] Note the synoptic parallels. Lk 9 27 uses the words of Mk, except to omit
ἐληλυθυῖαν ἐν δυνάμει. Mt 16 28 also looks to a future coming: ἕως ἂν ἴδωσιν
τὸν υἱὸν τοῦ ἀνθρώπου ἐρχόμενον ἐν τῇ βασιλείᾳ αὐτοῦ. On the proleptical
perfect see H. J. Cadbury, *JBL*, LVIII (1939), 251–4.

[15] On Mk 9 1 = Lk 9 27 J. Y. Campbell and J. M. Creed join us in refuting
Dodd's translation; see *Expository Times*, XLVIII (1936), 93 and 184 f.

one such statement to interpret, and it is true we cannot have it both ways. The linguistic evidence here reviewed is of one voice on the translation of ἐγγίζειν. We shall therefore build our theological structure more securely upon this premise, that there is no saying of the unequivocal form, "The Kingdom of God has come," to balance the statement, "The Kingdom of God has drawn near."

The other statement of Jesus, upon which Dodd has primarily based his interpretation of "realized eschatology," is the Q passage of Mt 12 28 = Lk 11 20, "If I, by the spirit (finger) of God, cast out demons, then the Kingdom of God has come upon you." "Something has happened," says Dodd (p. 44), "which has not happened before, and which means that the sovereign power of God has come into effective operation." Men are "confronted with the power of God at work in the world. In other words, the 'eschatological' Kingdom of God is proclaimed as a present fact." One is tempted to inquire why the reported activity of exorcism by Jesus at this time can be construed so uniquely to mean that the Kingdom of God is already and for the first time in "effective operation," while the reports of similar activity by other exorcists at other times are found to yield no such conclusion. However, we shall confine our attention rather to a linguistic inquiry of the key verb, φθάνειν.

First, it may be observed that, unlike ἐγγίζειν, φθάνειν is found frequently in the papyri. The older and apparently the original meaning, "to come first, to do first, to anticipate," remains in use into the fourth century at least, and even later in the passive voice. For example, all are agreed that when Paul wrote (I Thess 4 15), ἡμεῖς οἱ ζῶντες . . . οὐ μὴ φθάσωμεν τοὺς κοιμηθέντας, he meant, "we the living . . . shall not precede those who will have fallen asleep."

Yet philologists have given the impression that the original connotation of anticipation has been almost lost from the simple form φθάνειν in NT times. The statement of Blass forty years ago is typical, "The simple verb has almost lost the meaning of 'before'," and this statement is repeated in the Blass-Debrunner Grammatik of 1931 (par. 414, 4). Dodd, seeking to refute Camp-

bell, quotes Schmid (*Atticismus*, iv, 427) to the effect that
φθάνειν is "known to late Greek (NT, LXX, Philo, Pap. Mag.
Leydens.) only in the sense 'come' "; then adds his own remark,
"I do not recall anything in papyri or other hellenistic documents which contravenes this maxim (except so far as the older
Attic usage occasionally crops up)."[16] But this "maxim" is a
false one, nor is it contravened only by Atticisms; for the popular
papyri and other hellenistic documents offer *plentiful* examples
to the contrary.

In the first place, the meaning of "before" can be cited in a
score of typical informal papyri as well as literary documents
through at least the first four Christian centuries.[17] To illustrate,
note the Michigan Papyrus 212, 17, a letter from Dorion to his
son Serenus, in the second or third century. "In regard to the
old farm-building belonging to the house, Julius anticipated
[me] in writing to you that Eutyches is causing us trouble (φθάνει
σοι γράψ[ας] ᾿Ιούλιος)."[18] It is clear beyond question that
φθάνειν here means "to anticipate," and that its use is not
Atticistic.

Of the seven NT occurrences of φθάνειν, that in I Thess 4 15
has usually been acknowledged to mean "to precede, to anticipate." Moulton and Milligan declare that "apart from I Thess
4 15 the verb in the NT has lost its sense of priority." But it
may be necessary also to except the instance in II Cor 10 14,
ἄχρι γὰρ καὶ ὑμῶν ἐφθάσαμεν ἐν τῷ εὐαγγελίῳ τοῦ χριστοῦ.
To be sure, when the meaning is "to anticipate," φθάνειν is often
associated with another verb, one element participial and the
other finite — yet not always so. There are a few instances,
besides I Thess 4 15, where φθάνειν standing alone continues

---

[16] *Expository Times*, XLVIII (1936), 138 f.

[17] *BGU* II, 522,6; *Inscr. Gr. Insularum Maris Aegaei*, XII (Fasc. V), 302,2
and 590,2; *Ryl. P.*, II,119,16; *Mich. P.*, 212,17; *Oxy. P.*, II, 237, vi, 30; III,
472,48; VI,907,14 and 935,20; VII,1070,14; VIII, 1103,6; X, 1252 recto 32;
XII, 1469,11; XIV, 1666,3; *Sulloge I G*, II, 783,35; *Zenon P.*, 57,12; *Wis.*,
6:13 and 16:28; Philo, *Moses* I, 315[II,130,46]; Plutarch *Sulla*, 9:1[i.456F];
Pompey 33:3 [i.637A]; Justin, *Apology*, 12:10, 23:3, 46:1, *Dialogue*, 28:2, 67:2.

[18] J. G. Winter, *Papyri in the University of Michigan Collection*, Ann Arbor,
1936 (*University of Michigan Studies, Humanistic Series*, XL).

to carry this meaning.* In Wis 16 28 we read, δεῖ φθάνειν τὸν ἥλιον ἐπ᾽ εὐχαριστίαν σου ("We must rise before the sun to give you thanks"). Again, in a papyrus later than 27 B.C. we have the phrase, φθάνοντες δ᾽ ἀλλήλους ταῖς εἰς εὐ[ποιΐας] ἐπινοίαις ("anticipating each other in conceiving benefactions").[19] Goodspeed, Moffatt, Weymouth, Twentieth Century and Plummer (*ICC*) conclude in favor of such an interpretation in II Cor 10 14, "I was the very first to reach you with the Gospel of Christ." Yet it must be admitted that neither the construction nor the context is here decisive.[20] But that φθάνειν continues to be used for several Christian centuries to mean "to anticipate" has an important bearing upon the interpretation of the crucial "kingdom passage" in Mt 12 28 = Lk 11 20.

In the next place, it may be observed that the idea of anticipation in φθάνειν extends to the meaning, "to hasten, to be quick," even as early as Plato (*Symp*. 185 E) and Herodotus (VII, 162). In the LXX (III Kg 12 18) צמח was so translated in the clause, ἔφθασεν ἀναβῆναι τοῦ φυγεῖν ("he hastily leaped [into his chariot] to flee"); cf. ἔσπευσεν in II Chron 10 18. This meaning is found in non-literary papyri at least as late as the third century.[21] In a letter of that century (*Teb. P*., II, 417, 10), the writer informs the recipient, "But we will begin the work, for as soon as we make haste to set ourselves to it (ἐπὶ γὰρ ἐ[ὰν] φθάσωμεν ἐπιλαβέσθαι τοῦ ἔργου) we can finish it (completely?)." But the construction in which the meaning "to hasten" is found is in all instances observed different from that of Mt 12 28 = Lk 11 20, in that it is always associated with another verb (participle or infinitive).

At this point, we proceed to examine φθάνειν in its meaning, "to come, to arrive," upon the basis of which Dodd interprets that "the Kingdom of God is a fact of present experience," "the sovereign power of God has come into effective operation," and the ministry of Jesus must be viewed "as 'realized eschatology,'

---

[19] *Sulloge I G*, II,783,35.

[20] Cf. Philo, *Life of Moses*, I, 2; Plutarch, *Sayings of Spartans*, Agesilaus the Great, 28, both quoted below. See also Note 31.

[21] *Amh. P*., II, 72,9; *Oxy. P*., X,1293,25; XI, 1381,63; *Teb. P*., II, 417,10; *Inscr. Gr. Insularum Maris Aegaei*, XII (Fasc. IX), 906,26.

* It is not surprising to find the sense of anticipation in the compound form προέφθασεν, as in Mt 17 25 and the LXX, etc.

that is to say, as the impact upon this world of the 'powers of the world to come' in a series of events, unprecedented and unrepeatable, now in actual process."[22] Whether or not such an interpretation of φθάνειν is possible soon becomes clear through a review of other occurrences of the word. The earliest instance in this review lies in the LXX translation of דָּבַק in Jud 20 42, "So they retreated before the Israelites in the direction of the desert; but the battle pressed them close (ἡ παράταξις ἔφθασεν ἐπ᾽ αὐτούς)." This is precisely the form and syntax of Mt 12 28 = Lk 11 20, and the context makes plain beyond all doubt the sense of pursuit and imminent contact, rather than the idea of an actual conflict.

The LXX contains twenty-six occurrences of φθάνειν, and for twenty-one of these we have an underlying Semitic. Eighteen times φθάνειν stands for the Aramaic מְטָא (eight times in Daniel Th) or the Hebrew נָגַע, and *without exception* the verb has been used to describe either the action of approaching or the precise point of contact, but *not* the participation in some ensuing experience. "I saw him come close to the ram (ἴδον αὐτὸν φθάνοντα ἕως τοῦ κριοῦ)."[23] "He advanced toward the Ancient of Days, and was brought near him (ἕως τοῦ παλαιοῦ τῶν ἡμέρων ἔφθασεν· καὶ προσήχθη αὐτῷ)."[24] "You have slain them with a fury that has reached up to the heavens (ἕως τῶν οὐρανῶν ἔφθακεν)."[25] Most instructive of this group of illustrations is the passage in Dan 4 9–19, Daniel's vision of the tree that grew to touch heaven. The Aramaic מְטָא (ἐγγίζειν in the LXX) is translated by φθάνειν in the Theodosion version (ἔφθασεν ἕως τοῦ οὐρανοῦ . . . τὸ ὕψος ἔφθανεν εἰς τὸν οὐρανὸν . . . ἔφθασεν εἰς τὸν οὐρανόν), and it is evident in this context that φθάνειν means at most "to touch," but not "to break into" heaven.[26]

The non-literary papyri do not offer many illustrations of φθάνειν in the meaning, "to arrive," but those available exhibit

[22] Dodd, *Parables of the Kingdom*, 43, 44, 51.
[23] Dan 8 7 Th.
[24] Dan 7 13 Th.
[25] II Chron 28 9.
[26] J. Y. Campbell has reviewed φθάνειν in the LXX in *Expository Times*, XLVIII (1936), 92.

without exception the use of the term to convey the idea of *just reaching*. This meaning has grown naturally from the older meanings, "to anticipate" and "to hasten." This is an important distinction, for it brings φθάνειν and ἐγγίζειν into synonymity. A second-century(?) letter assures a friend, "We arrived safe and sound in the Oxyrhynchite nome after ten days (ἐφθάκαμεν ἐρρωμένοι εἰς 'Οξυρινχείτην διὰ ἡμέρων δέκα)."[27] In a petition to the Prefect of Egypt about A.D. 145, Ptolemaios pleads, "Since your inbred kindness, my lord prefect, extends to all (εἰς πάντας φθανούσης), I too ask to receive it."[28] Another document of A.D. 255 (*Flor. P.*, I, 9, 9) runs, "When I had arrived at the tombs (φθάσαντός μου πρὸς τοῖς μναιμίοις) . . ." Again, as late as A.D. 709, the connotation of φθάνειν is still limited to the point of attainment in the phrase (*Lond. P.*, IV, 1343,24), φθάσαι τὰ ἔσχατα ("attaining their highest expectations"). Furthermore, in modern Greek it has never come to mean anything different (despite the citation of the colloquial ἔφθασα).[29]

But to return to contemporaries of the evangelists, one may observe the usage of Philo and Plutarch. Philo (*On the Creation*, 8) remarks that Moses "attained the very summit of philosophy (φιλοσοφίας ἐπ' αὐτὴν φθάσας ἀκρότητα)"; and in the same book (5) he uses the phrase, "Within reach of the human mind (τὴν ἀνθρωπίνην διάνοιαν φθάνειν)." In his *Life of Moses* (I, 2), he declares that the fame of the laws has "reached the ends of the earth (ἄχρι καὶ τῶν τῆς γῆς τερμάτων ἔφθακεν)." In *The Confusion of Tongues* (153), Philo allegorizes the words of Gen 11 6, "And they have begun to do this." When evil men attack the invulnerable things of God, he says, "they attain but to the beginning and never arrive at the end (πρὸς δὲ τὸ τέλος φθάνουσιν οὐδέποτε). Therefore, we have these words, 'They

---

[27] J. E. Powell, *Rendel Harris Papyri*, Cambridge, 1936, 103,5.

[28] J. G. Winter, *Papyri in the University of Michigan Collection*, Ann Arbor, 1936, 174,3.

[29] Kuriakides, Λεξικον 'Ελληνοάγγλικον, Athens, 1909², gives for ἔφθασα "I am coming! immediately! here, Sir!" For modern φθάνειν he gives "to arrive, to reach, to get, to come (to), to overtake, to attain, to extend, to equal." Ill., "her hair reaches down to her heels," "as far as the eye can reach."

have *begun* to do'." Still again, in *Allegorical Interpretation* (III, 215) he writes, "Very beautiful is it that the entreaty reached as far as God (φθάσαι μέχρι Θεοῦ): but it would not have reached so far (οὐκ ἂν δὲ ἔφθασεν), but for the kindness of him that called." In none of these cases does Philo use φθάνειν to go beyond its usual meaning "to reach, to attain;" in none of them does it connote engagement in the experience ensuing upon the initial contact.

Plutarch also conforms to this usage. In the *Sayings of Spartans*, Agesilaus the Great (28), this character replied to the question as to how far the bounds of Sparta extended, as he flourished his spear, "As far as this can reach (ἄχρις οὗ τοῦτο φθάνοι)." Plutarch tells of Lysimachus (*On the Fortune of Alexander*, 338A), who "reached such a pitch of arrogance and boldness (εἰς τοσοῦτον ὑπεροψίας ἔφθασε καὶ θρασύτητος) as to say, 'The Byzantines now come to me when I am touching heaven with my spear'."

In summary of this point, we note in the various sources and types of Greek from the LXX down to modern Greek, when φθάνειν is used to mean "to come, to arrive," it is so used in a sense that is limited by the earlier meanings of the verb, "to be first, to do first" and "to hasten." Φθάνειν means "to reach, to arrive," in the sense of straining after and attaining. It refers explicitly to the point of attaining. It describes arrival upon the threshold of fulfillment and accessible experience, *not* the entrance into that experience. It is in this light that NT occurrences also must be construed, particularly where φθάνειν and ἐγγίζειν are mutually involved.

Of the six instances of φθάνειν in the NT, I Thess 4 15 requires the older meaning "to precede." The other five occurrences all involve the newer meaning, "to reach." Paul always uses the aorist tense of φθάνειν in this meaning, but this is followed by ἄχρι with the gen., εἰς with the acc., or ἐπὶ with the acc., as it is also in the sole Gospel occurrence of Mt 12 28 = Lk 11 20. All these prepositional phrases also reflect the idea of reaching to a point of contact.[30]

[30] Φθάνειν, "to reach," is found in a wide variety of constructions, similar to those of ἐγγίζειν: simple gen., dat., or acc.; ἕως, μέχρι, ἄχρι with gen.; ἐν with dat.; ἐπί, πρὸς, εἰς, περί with acc.; and intransitive.

Paul wrote to the Romans (9 31) that "Israel, straining after a law that should bring uprightness, did not come up to it (εἰς νόμον οὐκ ἔφθασεν)." When he wrote to the Corinthians (II, 10 14), he spoke of his coming even to them (ἄχρι γὰρ καὶ ὑμῶν ἐφθάσαμεν),[31] an objective that may be geographical or racial, but which served as the threshold before the door opening upon his subsequent ministry to them. But ἐφθάσαμεν neither refers to nor describes the activity subsequent to the point of his arrival. When Paul wrote to his Philippian friends (3 16), he expressed his "hope of attaining resurrection from the dead . . . I am pressing on to see if I can capture it, . . . straining toward what lies ahead, I am pressing toward the goal, for the prize to which God through Christ Jesus calls us upward . . . Only, we must live up to what we have already attained (εἰς ὃ ἐφθάσαμεν τῷ αὐτῷ στοιχεῖν)." Here again the context clearly implies a definite limitation to a tentative point of achievement. It does not describe future eventualities as a "fact of present experience," nor as "a series of events . . . now in actual process." Once more, Paul wrote to the Thessalonians (I,2 16) about his enemies, "God's wrath has overtaken them at last! (ἔφθασεν δὲ ἐπ' αὐτοὺς ἡ ὀργὴ εἰς τέλος)."* Some have held that this statement is an interpolation referring to the later destruction of Jerusalem. Such an emendation is unnecessary since φθάνειν does not envisage particular events already being experienced, but only the immediate anticipation of such a sequel. The divine wrath which has at last reached the Jews threatens the imminent condemnation which God is expected to pronounce upon the unbelieving, now that his Kingdom is ready to be revealed.

Outside of the Pauline letters, there is only a single occurrence of φθάνειν in the NT, the Gospel passage crucial for the concept of "realized eschatology." In Mt 12 28 = Lk 11 20 we read, "If I am exorcising demons by the spirit (finger) of God, ἄρα ἔφθασεν ἐφ' ὑμᾶς ἡ βασιλεία τοῦ Θεοῦ." This context requires for an adequate interpretation of ἔφθασεν no peculiar translation.

---

[31] Those who find in ἐφθάσαμεν here both meanings of the verb ("We anticipated others in reaching you") make of this a unique case. Alone, φθάνειν means "to anticipate" or "to reach," but not both. Both meanings would require ἐφθάσαμεν ἐλθεῖν (or ἐλθόντες).

* Cf. Test. of Levi 6¹¹ ἔφθασε δὲ αὐτοὺς ἡ ὀργὴ τοῦ θεοῦ εἰς τέλος.

We have found no instance anywhere in the Greek language which requires translating this, as does Dodd, "The Kingdom of God has come upon you" as "realized experience" (p. 50), as "a series of events . . . now in actual process." On the contrary, general usage insists that we translate here, "The Kingdom of God has just reached you." Among all the instances reviewed herein, we may list all those illustrating precisely the same construction and meaning as in this Gospel passage:

> Jud 20 34: φθάνει ἐπ' αὐτοὺς ἡ κακία
>   "Disaster overtakes them"
> Jud 20 42: ἡ παράταξις ἔφθασεν ἐπ' αὐτούς
>   "The battle pressed them close"
> Dan 4 25: ταῦτα πάντα ἔφθασεν ἐπὶ Ναβουχαδονοσόρ
>   "Now all these things befell Nebuchadnezzar"
> Eccles 8 14: φθάνει ἐπ' αὐτοὺς ὡς ποίημα τῶν ἀσεβῶν
>   "The experience which belongs to the wicked
>   overtakes them"
> Philo, Creation, 8: φιλοσοφίας ἐπ' αὐτὴν φθάσας ἀκρότητα
>   "He attained the very summit of philos-
>   ophy"
> I Thess 2 16: ἔφθασεν δὲ ἐπ' αὐτοὺς ἡ ὀργὴ εἰς τέλος
>   "But God's wrath has overtaken them at
>   last."

In all these passages the sense of reaching after to make contact or to overtake persists as the connotation of φθάνειν. Disaster is about to eventuate, the battle pursued the refugees, prophesied events overtook Nebuchadnezzar, punishment confronts the wicked, Moses attained an objective, God's wrath is about to be vented. In each instance fulfillment of events is future, and φθάνειν connotes their imminence. - These contexts afford no precedents by which to find in Mt 12 28 = Lk 11 20 "realized eschatology."

Thus ἐγγίζειν and φθάνειν are synonymous in the meaning "to draw near, even to the very point of contact," but the experience which draws near is still sequential. There is no need for the debate which Dodd seeks to draw with Campbell, "Mr Campbell takes ἤγγικεν at its face value, and tries to make ἔφθασεν conform, while I take ἔφθασεν at its face value, and try to make ἤγγικεν conform."[32] It is quite possible to take both verbs "at face value," obviating any further effort to force either into conformity to the other. That ἤγγικεν cannot mean "has transpired, or is transpiring" must be admitted. That ἔφθασεν is ever used to mean more than "reached, overtook, came into contact" is denied by its consistent connotation. That the two verbs should be translated synonymously with reference to the Kingdom of God, we agree with Dodd. But the only meaning in which the two verbs are naturally synonymous, without straining either, is "to draw near, even to the very point of contact."

The nearness of the culmination of the Kingdom of God is an elastic conception in early Christian thought; ἤγγικεν is the more indefinite term but in at least one instance seems synonymous with the sole usage of the more definite ἔφθασεν (Lk 10 9, 11 20). Both Lukan statements should be translated alike, "The Kingdom of God has reached you." This does not deny the futurity of the Kingdom. Its immediate revelation is expected to ensue, but has not yet transpired. Contrary to Dodd's charge[33] that such a view is the result of a compromise between two sets of sayings regarding the Kingdom as present and future, this view seems clearly and explicitly to be stated in Lk 10 9 and 11 20. It cannot be sustained that these verbs describe a "realized eschatology."

Dodd's argument has apparently influenced his worthy compatriot, R. H. Lightfoot. In *Theology* (May, 1927), Dodd had expressed a similar view, as again in his chapter of Deissmann's *Mysterium Christi*, 1930, 67, n. 1. Lightfoot, in the Bampton Lectures of 1934,[34] translates Mk 1 15 " 'The time is fulfilled, and the kingdom (or reign) of God is upon [you],' for so we are now often bidden by good guides to understand and emphasize the words." In a later note on the same verse he declares, "The words are probably stronger than is often thought, implying 'The time of fulfillment has come, the kingdom of God has

[32] Dodd, *Expository Times*, XLVIII (1936), 138. See also Dodd's note in Bell and Deissmann, *Mysterium Christi*, 1930, 66.

[33] Dodd, *Parables of the Kingdom*, 49.

[34] *History and Interpretation in the Gospels*, London, 1935, 65, 106–7.

appeared'; cf. Mt 12 28, Lk 11 20." It has been suggested that Dodd may have retracted on his stand in this matter, since he has more recently translated Mk 1 15 in the usual sense.[35] But in connection with Mt 12 28=Lk 11 20, he still maintains that reference is to "those who *have experienced* [italics ours] the end of this world and the coming of the Kingdom of God."[36]

Whatever theological necessity or merit may rest in Dodd's belief that "in some way the Kingdom of God has come with Jesus himself,"[37] it appears quite unjustifiable to build that belief upon the contention that ἐγγίζειν and φθάνειν must, or even may, be translated "has come," as "a fact of present experience," "in a series of events . . . now in actual process."

[35] Dodd, *History and the Gospel*, New York, 1938, 123.
[36] *Ibid.*, 125.
[37] Dodd, *Parables of the Kingdom*, 45.

THE EFFECT OF
RECENT TEXTUAL CRITICISM UPON
NEW TESTAMENT STUDIES

As one looked upon the state of New Testament textual studies in the early 'thirties it must have appeared that an unusual number of important events were transpiring. One read in 1930 about the sensational recovery from Egyptian sands of textual witnesses from the third century, earlier by a century than the oldest and best witness previously available. Here were three papyrus manuscripts attesting the Greek text in substantial portions of the Gospels, Acts, Pauline Epistles and the Apocalypse, as that text was employed by Christians in middle Egypt about A.D. 250.[1] Such discoveries come but rarely even in the amazing modern era, and this discovery, 'the greatest since the Sinaiticus' (Kenyon), offered to scholarship an important new basis for its researches on the primitive text.

There soon followed other papyrus acquisitions, each fragmentary but presenting its own element of importance. There was discovered in Dura (Syria) in 1933 the first known Greek witness of Tatian's Diatessaron.[2] The John Rylands Library reported in 1935 the identification of the earliest extant witness to any part of the Greek New Testament, a small fragment of the Gospel of John written before A.D. 150.[3] Other early papyrus fragments were acquired about the same time, notably by Princeton, Yale, and the University of

[1] Frederic G. Kenyon, *The Chester Beatty Biblical Papyri*, Fasc. I–III (London, 1933–7); Henry A. Sanders, *A Third-Century Papyrus Codex of the Epistles of Paul* (Ann Arbor, 1935).

[2] Carl H. Kraeling, 'A Greek Fragment of Tatian's Diatessaron from Dura', *Studies and Documents*, vol. III (London, 1935).

[3] C. H. Roberts, *An Unpublished Fragment of the Fourth Gospel* (Manchester, 1935).

Michigan.[1] Kenyon reflected the expectant mood of that day when he wrote that 'these recent discoveries of exceptionally early MSS.... justify the hope of other discoveries which may clear up the many obscurities that still beset the early history of the Bible text'.[2]

In the last quarter-century scores of medieval copies of the Greek New Testament have been found and, for the first time, have offered their testimony. Although such manuscripts rarely contribute early readings, they are essential to the investigation of later stages in textual transmission. Notable among them was the Rockefeller-McCormick New Testament (Gregory 2400) which was found in Paris and acquired by the University of Chicago in 1928.[3] With a wealth of miniatures to illustrate the text, this manuscript represents two related areas of research especially prominent in recent years: Christian art, and the Byzantine text. Its appearance in America gave an impetus to manuscript discovery and textual research unprecedented in scope and vigour. About the same time, Streeter and Lake were reporting their studies on a newly discovered early recension, the 'Caesarean text', which must henceforth be considered along with the 'Neutral' and 'Western' forms.[4]

Not least in these matters was the transfer to the British Museum, in December 1933, of the famous Codex Sinaiticus from Leningrad, where it had lain since 1862.[5] Although this Greek Bible from fourth-century Egypt had long been available in photographic facsimile and had been thoroughly examined by Tischendorf and by Westcott and Hort, it was an important step of progress to establish

---

[1] See Kenneth W. Clark, *A Descriptive Catalogue of Greek New Testament Manuscripts in America* (Chicago, 1937). Also H. I. Bell, *Recent Discoveries of Biblical Papyri* (Oxford, 1937).

[2] Frederic G. Kenyon, *The Text of the Greek Bible* (London, 1937), p. 195.

[3] Goodspeed, Riddle and Willoughby, *The Rockefeller-McCormick New Testament*, 3 vols. (Chicago, 1932).

[4] B. H. Streeter, *The Four Gospels, a Study of Origins*, 4th ed. revised (London, 1930); Lake, Blake and New, 'The Caesarean Text of the Gospel of Mark', *Harvard Theological Review*, vol. XXI, 4 (October, 1928). Hereafter, the terms Neutral, Western, and Caesarean, will be used without quotation marks although the reader will understand that these terms are always thought of as 'so-called'.

[5] See the pamphlets issued by the British Museum, *The Mount Sinai Manuscript of the Bible* (1934) and *The Codex Sinaiticus and the Codex Alexandrinus* (1938).

the manuscript in London where definitive studies might be freely made.[1] Such were the stirring discoveries and researches that marked the early 'thirties. Scholar and layman alike felt an exciting spirit of progress and many anticipated an imminent *dénouement*.

I. THE CRITICAL TEXT

The ultimate task in textual criticism is to reconstruct the lost original documents of the New Testament. A climax was attained in 1881, 350 years after the work of Erasmus and Stephanus. Three successive stages of progress are discernible in review. The first continued until the days of John Mill and Richard Bentley (early eighteenth century) and was marked by the collecting and collating of many new manuscripts. Their contemporary, J. J. Wettstein, collator and cataloguer, listed about 300 manuscripts which had become known in the West by that time. The second period began with Bengel who first classified manuscript witnesses according to a textual history, and sought to establish textual criteria. The Textus Receptus remained dominant throughout that period. It was Lachmann who, in 1830, opened a new era when he created a critical text *de novo*, planting the seed that flowered with Westcott and Hort.

It has been necessary to recall even so briefly the successive periods in textual history in order that we may understand the work of our own age. The course that began with Erasmus reached its full fruition with Westcott and Hort. It is not given to us today merely to perfect the Neutral New Testament by a process of itemized repairs. In textual criticism we have reached the end of an era and entered upon a new cycle of investigation. For some time it has been evident that textual research since Westcott and Hort is similar to that of the sixteenth and seventeenth centuries, for our time again is marked as an age of collecting and collating. As the early critics sought to perfect the Textus Receptus so critics since Westcott and Hort have sought to perfect their 1881 text. The eclectics, of that day and of this, 'improved' the text here and there though without a fundamental principle to guide them. Years ago, F. C. Grant observed

[1] This was early demonstrated by the study published by Milne and Skeat, *Scribes and Correctors of the Codex Sinaiticus* (London, 1938).

that we must return 'to the point where older scholars such as Griesbach and Lachmann left off'.[1] Really, our day is comparable to that of Bentley in that materials have been gathered in great quantity, while we still await the first proposal for a more adequate history of the primitive text.

But the age of Bentley was succeeded by that of Bengel, finally to produce fruit in the age of Lachmann. So our age, we believe, must lead us to a new era of reclassification according to a new historical insight which is as yet obscure to us. To that new insight the researches of our day will contribute, and in future a better text will be found based upon a superior historical understanding.[2] In the meantime, the text of Westcott and Hort (or another quite similar) continues to serve well the needs of this generation and the next. For today, therefore, our work must be undertaken and understood with the objective of laying a new foundation. There is in it this larger meaning, to transcend the laborious researches of the moment. The responsibility of the present generation reflects its opportunity to lay the new foundation. The discoveries that mark our time may be expected to reveal ultimately a new meaning; and each new product of research to assume its place in a new pattern. It is in this faith that we inquire particularly concerning the effectiveness of textual criticism in the present generation.

With reference to the recovery of the original New Testament text, we may expect to find the informed critic more sober and patient than others. Although many thoughtful Christians have come to believe that this objective has been virtually won, awaiting only a finishing touch, the critic is sobered by the realization that the best critical text so far achieved now holds little assurance of being the original text and that to work back from the one to the other has become increasingly difficult. He is the more patient because of his knowledge that textual research has proceeded in a long cycle—discovery, analysis, reconstruction. The former cycle required 350

---

[1] F. C. Grant, 'Studies in the Text of St Mark', *Anglican Theological Review*, vol. xx (1938), p. 106.

[2] See the discussion of Norman Huffman, 'Suggestions from the Gospel of Mark for a New Textual Theory', *Journal of Biblical Literature*, vol. LVI (1937), pp. 347–59.

years and concluded but recently, with the critical text of Westcott
and Hort. The present generation stands at the *beginning* of a new
cycle, in the search for the original Greek New Testament. The recent
discovery of earlier papyrus manuscripts and the recognition of the
Caesarean recension have not settled problems but created new ones.
They have not completed the pattern but rather have complicated
the solution.

The appearance of numerous critical texts has tended to give the
impression that much progress has been made beyond Westcott-Hort,
and that great discoveries have largely displaced its twin authorities,
Sinaiticus and Vaticanus. A mere roll call of the critical texts produced
since Westcott-Hort is impressive: Weymouth (1886), Brandscheid
(1893), Hetzenauer (1893), B. Weiss (1894–1900), Blass (1895–1902),
Nestle (1898), Saliveros (1902), Antoniades (1904), Souter (1910),
Bodin (1911), von Soden (1913), Vogels (1920), Colombo (1932),
Merk (1933), Bover (1943); besides numerous revisions of some of
these.[1] Translators have made their choices from among these,
reflecting a judgment which they may announce but not explain.
For example, Weymouth (1903) translated from his own 'resultant'
Greek text; Bell (1922), Ballantine (1923) and the R.S.V. (1946)
rest upon the Nestle text; Ballentine (1922), Montgomery (1924),
C. K. Williams (1952), to say nothing of the popular E.R.V. and
A.S.V., reflect the text printed by Souter; Moffatt (1913) used
von Soden; Kleist (1932) translated Vogels; while the Twentieth
Century (1904) and Goodspeed (1923) rested upon Westcott-Hort.
In the midst of such variety it is well to assess the progress made
toward recovering the original Greek base, bearing in mind that we
are here concerned not with the growing edge of knowledge but
with the effects already operative in New Testament studies.

For New Testament studies in the past twenty years, the most used
critical editions of the Greek New Testament number six. Protestant
editions include Westcott-Hort, Souter, and Nestle; while Roman
Catholic editions include Vogels, Merk, and Bover. They fall into
two groups: Souter and Vogels on the side of the Textus Receptus;

---

[1] The Nestle text has appeared in eight editions between 1930 (14th) and
1952 (21st); the text of Merk, in seven editions between 1933 (1st) and 1951 (7th).
Other recent editions are those of Brandscheid, 1932 (3rd); Bover, 1950 (2nd) and
1952 (3rd); Souter, 1947 (2nd); and Vogels, 1949–50 (3rd).

and Nestle, Merk, and Bover on the side of Westcott-Hort.[1] The oldest of these texts is Souter[2] for although a posthumous edition was published in 1947 his canonical text remained unchanged, still reproducing the 1881 text of Palmer.[3] Palmer's text was essentially the Textus Receptus eclectically altered to include many 'readings adopted by the revisers of the authorized version'.[4] The Palmer-Souter text was an improvement seventy-five years ago but today we must recognize that it actually antedates the Westcott-Hort text and disregards much substantial progress achieved since its origin. Souter's text differs from the Textus Receptus far less than any of the other texts named above. A collation with Westcott-Hort through an extensive section (Mark i–v) reveals 191 differences, of which 168 are T.R. readings. This reveals the extent to which the posthumous Souter edition even now fails to avail itself of critical improvement. It is a concession of doubtful wisdom that is still found in the guide prepared for both the American Bible Society and the British and Foreign Bible Society, stating that 'translators and revisers...are at liberty to follow that [text] underlying the English Authorized Version (edited by Dr F. H. A. Scrivener, for the Cambridge University Press), or that underlying the English Revised Version (edited by Archdeacon Edwin Palmer, for the Oxford University Press)'.[5] Nestle recently described the Souter text as 'very similar to that of Westcott and Hort',[6] but our detailed examination of its text clearly reveals that its kinship with the Textus Receptus sharply contrasts it with Westcott-Hort. Today the use of the Souter text places unnecessary obstacles in the path of the interpreter or translator, whether or not he be a textual specialist.

---

[1] In comparing these printed texts we refer to the editor's first choice of each reading, without regard to a possible alternative indicated in the margin or apparatus. Nor are we concerned with proposing or judging possible improvements to be made, but rather with reporting and comparing what the current editions have set before us.

[2] Alexander Souter, *Novum Testamentum Graece, editio altera* (Oxford, 1947). Only the apparatus differs from the first edition of 1910.

[3] E. Palmer, Ἡ Καινὴ Διαθήκη (Oxford, 1881).

[4] Scrivener counted 5788 changes in the entire New Testament (see Philip Schaff, *Companion*, p. 419 n.).

[5] Eugene A. Nida, *Bible Translating* (New York, 1947), pp. 50–1.

[6] Erwin Nestle, 'How to Use a Greek New Testament', *The Bible Translator*, vol. II (1951), p. 55.

The Vogels text, last revised in 1949–50 after a long interval,[1] is only somewhat less influenced by the antiquated Textus Receptus. A similar collation of Mark i–v shows 103 differences from Westcott-Hort, of which seventy-five are T.R. readings. Nestle has remarked of the Vogels text that it 'does not differ much from Souter or Nestle'.[2] But it cannot resemble them both because they differ widely from one another (187 times in Mark i–v, of which only seven of Souter's readings depart from the T.R.). The text of Vogels falls between Nestle and Souter. Actually, Vogels and Souter differ from one another 189 times in these five chapters, with Souter adhering to the T.R. reading 146 times and Vogels following the T.R. forty-three times. But Vogels also differs considerably from Nestle (eighty-seven times, of which seventy-eight are T.R. readings). Indeed a detailed examination of the text of Mark i–v shows Vogels akin to Souter and the Textus Receptus.

In contrast, Westcott-Hort, Nestle, Bover, and Merk form a tight critical group with comparatively little difference among them. Up until 1933 the printed texts of Westcott-Hort and Nestle[3] supplied in the West the basic critical Greek New Testament. Within the next decade there were published the critical texts of two Catholic scholars—the first edition of Merk,[4] followed ten years later by that of Bover.[5] These four critical texts today exert the greatest influence upon the interpretation of the New Testament in Western scholarship. Writing in 1949 (*J.T.S.*), G. D. Kilpatrick referred to Nestle, Souter, and Merk, as 'the three most useful'. But the present trend is away from the 1881 text reflected in Souter, which therefore might well be replaced by Bover. We propose, therefore, a comparison between Westcott-Hort and each of the other three, to set in relief the changes which the years have produced.[6]

[1] Henry Joseph Vogels, *Novum Testamentum Graece et Latine, editio tertia* (Freiburg, 1949–50). The earlier editions appeared in 1920 and 1922.

[2] *Loc. cit.*

[3] Eberhard Nestle, *Novum Testamentum Graece* (Stuttgart, 1898); recent announcement has come of the 21st edition (1952).

[4] Augustinus Merk, S.J., *Novum Testamentum Graece et Latine* (Rome, 1933); the sixth edition appeared posthumously in 1948, edited by S. Lyonnet, S.J.

[5] Joseph M. Bover, S.J., *Novi Testamenti, Biblia Graeca et Latina* (Madrid, 1943), revised in 1950 and 1952.

[6] For this comparison, we employ Nestle 1952[21], Bover 1950[2], and Merk 1948[6], which are the latest editions in hand. Bover published a new edition in 1952, and

Probably the most influential critical New Testament text in use today is that of Nestle. The American Bible Society and the British and Foreign Bible Society especially recommend its use for translation.[1] The fourth edition of 1903 was adopted by the B.F.B.S., which now has in preparation a new edition based upon Nestle's latest printing. Among current critical texts Nestle stands the closest to Westcott-Hort. In the entire Gospel of Mark (one-twelfth of the New Testament), the 1952 Nestle edition shows only eighty-nine changes from Westcott-Hort. A large majority of these are insignificant elements of orthography. Not more than thirty-two instances may be considered substantial; only twelve involve a difference in meaning. All twelve were introduced early into the Nestle text, between 1898 and 1903, and thus do not illustrate improvement in recent years but they still stand in the 1952 edition:

Mark i. 34   χριστον ειναι. Nestle (with Merk and Bover) omits this phrase which Westcott-Hort included in brackets. This was originally omitted by Nestle in 1898.

 ii. 23   παραπορευεσθαι (for διαπ.). Adopted by Nestle since 1898 (with Merk and Bover); Westcott-Hort chose διαπ., in half-brackets.

 iii. 14   ους και αποστολους ωνομασεν. Nestle since 1898 (with Merk and Bover) has omitted this clause which Westcott-Hort accepted.

 iii. 32   και αι αδελφαι σου. Nestle since 1898 (with Bover but not Merk) has added this phrase which Westcott-Hort rejected.

 vii. 24   και Σιδωνος. Nestle omitted as early as 1903; Westcott-Hort included in brackets.

 vii. 35   ευθυς before ελυθη. Nestle since 1898 has added; Westcott-Hort omitted.

 ix. 38   ος ουκ ακολουθει ημιν. Nestle since 1898 has added; Westcott-Hort omitted.

 x. 26   εαυτους. Nestle since 1898 (for αυτον in Westcott-Hort).

 xii. 23   οταν αναστωσιν. Added by Nestle as early as 1903; Westcott-Hort rejected.

 xv. 1   ετοιμασαντες. Nestle, as early as 1903 (for ποιησαντες in half-brackets in Westcott-Hort).

Lyonnet reissued Merk in 1951. The text of Mark in Nestle's 1952 edition shows no change from the 1950 edition.
[1] Nida, *Bible Translating*, pp. 50–1.

xv. 44 παλαι. Nestle, since 1898 (for ηδη in half-brackets in
Westcott-Hort).

xvi. 17 καιναις. Nestle, since 1898 (for και εν ταις χερσιν in
brackets in Westcott-Hort).

The Nestle text of Mark shows only seventy-five changes through
the twenty-one editions between 1898 and 1952 and thirty-five of
these are restorations of Westcott-Hort readings. Only thirty-one
have entered the Nestle text since 1903 (fourth edition), of which
twenty-four are merely orthographic. The other seven involve no
difference in meaning, and six of these represent a return to Westcott-
Hort:

Mark i. 25 ιησους] +λεγων   (so Westcott-Hort).
ii. 17 αυτοις] +οτι   (so Westcott-Hort).
ix. 8 αλλα] ει μη   (so Westcott-Hort).
x. 35 +δυο [υιοι   (so Westcott-Hort).
xiv. 20 +εν [τρυβλιον   (so Westcott-Hort).
xv. 22 μεθερμηνευομενον.
xvi. 1 +η [μαρια   (1) (so Westcott-Hort).

The result of our examination is again to confirm that Nestle's
critical text, described by Erwin Nestle himself as 'based on the
investigation of the nineteenth century',[1] as late as 1952 still rests
heavily upon Westcott-Hort; that few changes have been made from
Westcott-Hort; and that the trend of most recent revision has been
a return toward Westcott-Hort.

The texts of Merk and Bover are somewhat less conservative
though they present few additional substantial changes, of which
only the following (in Mark i–v) involve a difference in meaning:

i. 1 υιου του Θεου. Added by both Merk and Bover, rejected by
Westcott-Hort.

ii. 16 και πινει. Added by Merk, rejected by Westcott-Hort.

A full composite list for Mark i–v of all variants from Westcott-
Hort as found in Nestle, Merk, or Bover totals only seventy-seven
(Nestle 31, Bover 52, Merk 56). Twenty-one times all three agree
against Westcott-Hort; in thirteen readings Bover and Merk stand
together against Nestle and Westcott-Hort. Among these four

[1] Erwin Nestle, 'How to Use a Greek New Testament', *The Bible Translator*,
vol. II (1951), p. 54.

critical texts, Bover stands alone fifteen times; and Merk eighteen times. The conclusion is inescapable that these most used critical texts at mid-century show little change from Westcott-Hort and only rarely present a significant variant.

It remains to ask whether the changes made represent progress toward the original text. It is obvious that this limited revision is not the result of the new manuscript discoveries. The Beatty text of Mark is fragmentary and exhibits few of the Marcan variants under discussion, and in these few instances the editors have more often rejected the $\mathfrak{P}^{45}$ reading. Nor does it appear that the Freer Gospels[1] have played any direct part in recent revision, for all the variants in Nestle were previously known and debated and all have been tried in some good critical text within the last century. Indeed, one notices that many variants slip in and out of the critical texts subject only, it seems, to a shift in judgment. Especially frequent are readings adopted for the first Nestle edition which have in later editions been rejected. This phenomenon of vacillation can be illustrated with a few citations from the early chapters of Mark:

   i. 1   υιου Θεου not in N[1], in N[4], but not in N[20].

   i. 4   ιωαννης in N[1], not in N[4], but in N[20].

          ερημω] + και in N[1], but not N[4], in N[17] but not N[20].

   i. 8   + εν [πνευματι in N[1], but not N[4] nor N[20].

  iii. 4   αγαθοποιησαι in N[1], but not N[4] nor N[20].

  iii. 8   εποιει in N[1], but not N[4] nor N[20].

  iii. 17 ονοματα in N[1], but not N[4] nor N[20].

  iii. 22 βεελζεβουλ in N[1], but not N[4] nor N[20].

  iv. 5   αυξανομενον in N[1], but not N[4] nor N[20].

  iv. 32 κατασκηνουν in N[1], not in N[4], but in N[20].

It is also apparent that such critics as Nestle, Merk, and Bover often differ in judgment. Bover often stands alone and there is some evidence that he—more than Merk—is influenced especially by the Vulgate, as in the following examples:

Mark i. 41 Add αυτου after ηψατο. Supported by D vg.

   iii. 26 μεμερισται και for και εμερισθη. Supported only by vg (*dispertitus est et*).

    iv. 8 εν...εν...εν. Supported only by vg (*unum...unum...unum*).

[1] Henry A. Sanders, *The New Testament Manuscripts in the Freer Collection*, Part I: *The Washington Manuscript of the Four Gospels* (New York, 1912).

There are, however, many Vulgate readings not favoured by Bover and Merk; but Bover especially is influenced by his theory that it is the Western text that attests a pre-recensional form of the second century (*Proleg.* p. xxxi). None of the editors has made his changes because of his own reconstruction of the history of the text; none attempts any such reconstruction. The chief influence that has altered the Westcott-Hort readings is simply a lower status for its 1881 text. The most influential factor in recent criticism is the general view that the Neutral text is itself a derived text which has passed through a process of revision. Along with a demotion of B and ℵ there goes a somewhat enhanced status for D and Θ and their groups.[1] For an editor, this often is enough to swing the scales to the opposite side. The few readings changed in the texts all show an evenly balanced attestation and many were originally placed in brackets in Westcott-Hort. One concludes that a subjective element plays a considerable part in the eclectic procedure of recent textual revision.

The eclectic method is openly embraced in our day.[2] Indeed, it is the only procedure available to us at this stage, but it is very important to recognize that it is a secondary and tentative method. It is not a new method nor a permanent one; it does not supplant the more thorough procedure of Westcott and Hort but only supplements it temporarily. The eclectic method cannot by itself create a text to displace Westcott-Hort and its offspring. It is suitable only for exploration and experimentation. From it may one day come the insight about which a multitude of itemized researches may gather and find unity and meaning. The eclectic method, by its very nature, belongs to a day like ours in which we know only that the traditional

[1] For recent major studies on the Western text consult especially A. C. Clark, *The Acts of the Apostles* (Oxford, 1933); W. H. P. Hatch, *The Western Text of the Gospels* (Evanston, 1937); Frederic G. Kenyon, *The Western Text in the Gospels and Acts* (London, 1938); G. D. Kilpatrick, 'Western Text and Original Text in the Gospels and Acts...in the Epistles', *Journal of Theological Studies*, vol. xLIV (1943) and vol. xLV (1944); and A. F. J. Klijn, *Survey of the Researches on the Western Text of the Gospels and Acts* (Utrecht, 1949). On the Caesarean text consult especially Lake, Blake and New, 'The Caesarean Text of the Gospel of Mark', *Harvard Theological Review*, vol. xxI (1928), pp. 207-404; B. H. Streeter, *The Four Gospels*, revised (London, 1930), pp. 77-107; and the thorough critique by Bruce M. Metzger, 'The Caesarean Text of the Gospels', *Journal of Biblical Literature*, vol. LXIV (1945), pp. 457-89.

[2] An excellent procedure in eclectic criticism is observed in the 1946 Schweich Lectures by G. N. Zuntz, *The Text of the Epistles* (London, 1953).

theory of the text is faulty but cannot yet see clearly to correct the fault. While, therefore, we are indebted to 'the eclectics' for their scholarly judgments, we should not expect thus to be provided with an improved critical text. Paradoxically, the eclectic method as applied today presupposes the *general* correctness of our traditional textual theory. Yet the eclectic method treats each variant independently, with rare exception. By it even the same editor may lead us in several directions, and certainly different editors will do so even though their basic text is the same. For, let us remember, the basic text of such able editors as Nestle, Merk, and Bover is still the structure established by Westcott-Hort. It is clearly not true that for New Testament studies the 'reign of the "Neutral" text has come to an end', as F. C. Grant declared fifteen years ago.[1] Grant actually referred to 'the long undisputed reign'. Certainly there has arisen dispute about the status of the Neutral text; indeed, it is generally agreed that the Neutral text must be replaced by a better. But we do not have that better text and do not yet know how to reconstruct it; meanwhile the Neutral text continues to reign and, I think, must for some generations to come. It has been demonstrated above how little change from Westcott-Hort appears in any of the current critical texts now in general use for Biblical studies.

Furthermore, such tentative changes as have appeared do not represent an integrated theory of the text and therefore can have no such basic theory to validate them as improvements. Objective textual scholarship must still depend upon manuscript testimony, and it is still true that the most ancient manuscripts are the most valuable. We are often reminded today that there is no infallible manuscript or recension. This is not new information, but what was once a concession has now become an insistence. Yet despite the acknowledged fallibility of all manuscripts, there is still a trustworthy quality of good character in certain manuscripts and even in the Neutral text. For the eclectic critic to declare these false at any point calls for persuasive evidence. A judgment is not validated merely because we like the resultant theology or even because it preserves consistency for the author, for these are elusive and subjective factors. Where variants appear, ultimate judgment must rest upon a basic

[1] F. C. Grant, 'Studies in the Text of St Mark', *Anglican Theological Review*, vol. xx (1938), p. 103.

theory of the primitive text. It is true that the critic has many aids besides manuscript witnesses; a choice between variant readings may be influenced by synoptic research, language, style, vocabulary, orthography, harmonization, theology, or history. But these aids represent knowledge to be gained *from* the true text and their influence must be kept under proper restraint if they would guide us *to* the true text. Furthermore, our purpose has been to learn what was originally written—even if the author or editor should be found inconsistent, or illogical, or faulty in theology or history. Yet we do face a difficult problem in those closely balanced variants which have long been the despair of editors. At least, we are still prone to describe them as *balanced*, in terms of the traditional categories and the traditional theory that one of the ancient texts must be more primitive than the others (if only we might know which!). But the principle of competing witnesses has been giving way to a principle of co-operating witnesses. The Neutral, Western, and Caesarean texts have all been found in use in all sections of early Christianity, and though all of our earliest manuscripts (up to A.D. 400) have come from Egypt alone they attest the use even there of all major textual types. The problematic readings in Mark, such as those referred to above, show in each case the combined support of Neutral, Western, and Caesarean witnesses for each alternate reading. The textual critic has not yet developed an objective criterion to decide these cases. Despite the latest discoveries and the newest researches, New Testament studies today reflect the continued dominance of the Neutral text.

Although technical New Testament studies must ultimately be based upon the critical Greek text, it is relevant here to note the effect of recent textual criticism upon the English version. Since 1930 there have appeared at least forty-five independent translations of the New Testament, or its parts (most frequently, the Gospel of Mark). Clearly the most influential of them is the Revised Standard Version, produced by an American committee in 1946. However much change may be noted in this official translation, little of it may be traced to specific readings in manuscripts or in critical editions, and here again it is proper to ask whether this little represents further recovery of the original documents. Of course, most of the eighty-nine changes from Westcott-Hort in Nestle's text of Mark have no reflection in the English idiom. One of the translators, Frederick C. Grant, has written that 'the readings we have adopted will, as a rule, be found either in the text or the margin of the new (17th) edition of Nestle' (1941).[1] Therefore it will be expeditious to review first the R.S.V. treatment of Nestle's changes from Westcott-Hort. In Mark there are twenty-six such changes which are reflected in the English idiom, and of these the R.S.V. has rejected fifteen (nine of which would alter the meaning):

    *ii. 23 διαπ.] παραπορευεσθαι.
    *iii. 32 add και αι αδελφαι σου (omission noted in margin).
    iv. 40 ουπω] ουτως; πως ουκ.
    vi. 9 ενδυσασθαι] ενδυσησθαι.
    vi. 51 λιαν] + εκπερισσου.
    *vii. 24 omit και Σιδωνος (addition noted in margin).
    *vii. 35 add ευθυς before ελυθη.
    viii. 20 λεγουσιν] omit αυτω.
    *ix. 38 add ος και ακολουθει ημιν (omission noted in margin).
    *x. 26 αυτον] εαυτους.
    xii. 32 add και before ειπεν.
    xiii. 2 omit ωδε.
    xiii. 22 δωσουσιν] ποιησουσιν.
    *xv. 1 ποιησαντες] ετοιμασαντες.
    *xv. 44 ηδη] παλαι.

The other eleven changes, of which only three involve a difference in meaning, have been adopted in the R.S.V.:

    *i. 34 omit χριστον ειναι.
    *iii. 14 omit ους και αποστολους ωνομασεν
          (addition noted in margin).
    iv. 5 και (2) omit
    vi. 22 αυτου] αυτης της.
    viii. 12 λεγω] + υμιν.
    xi. 17 ελεγεν] + αυτοις.
    xii. 17 ειπεν] + αυτοις.
    *xii. 23 add οταν αναστωσιν.
    xiv. 7 omit παντοτε (2).
    xvi. 14 omit εκ νεκρων.
    xvi. 17 ακολ.] παρακολουθησει.
    *xvi. 17–18 και εν ταις χερσιν] καιναις.

[1] Luther A. Weigle (ed.), *An Introduction to the Revised Standard Version of the New Testament* (New York, 1946), p. 41.

In addition, there are a few readings adopted by the R.S.V., departing from both Westcott-Hort and Nestle, e.g.:

i. 1   add υιου του Θεου, with Bover and Merk and Westcott-Hort^{mg}.
i. 29   εξελθοντες ηλθαν] εξελθων ηλθεν, with Merk and Westcott-Hort^{mg}.
ii. 22   omit αλλα οινον νεον εις ασκους καινους, differing with all these editors and supported only by D and Old Latin.
x. 7   add και προσκολληθησεται προς την γυναικα αυτου, with Merk and many manuscripts (vs. ℵ B Ψ *et al.*).

In all, there appear to be very few cases in which the R.S.V. departs from Westcott-Hort;[1] these are traditionally doubtful cases and, in a few instances, even highly questionable as to authenticity. Sometimes 𝔓^{45} is deliberately rejected (vii. 4 βαπτισωνται and viii. 15 ηρωδιανων) in favour of Westcott-Hort. Indeed, Grant exclaims that 'it is really extraordinary how often, with fuller apparatus of variant readings at our disposal, and with the eclectic principle now more widely accepted, we have concurred in following Westcott and Hort...still the great classical tradition of modern times'.[2] This is a tribute eminently deserved but often obscured in these days of notable discoveries and theories. Once again, our review of the R.S.V. in Mark has demonstrated how little, and how tentatively, textual criticism since 1930—and much earlier—has altered the New Testament text we study.[3] The effect of textual criticism upon New Testament studies is always a delayed force, and the chief impact upon present studies is the result of the earlier reconstruction of the

---

[1] Apparently the same observation will hold true for the new British translation now in preparation. Professor C. H. Dodd, who is general director of the British group, has reported that the New Testament panel finds 'no existing published text which could be implicitly followed: we should in effect have to construct our own text, which would necessarily be eclectic. We adopt as a starting-point the Oxford text (Souter), but diverge from it where it seems desirable—[our text] will in the end approximate more closely to the forthcoming edition of Nestle, which is being prepared for the British and Foreign Bible Society, than to any other.' If so, then the changes from Westcott-Hort are not likely to be numerous.

[2] Weigle (ed.), *Introduction to the Revised Standard Version of the New Testament*, p. 41.

[3] E. A. Nida, in *The Bible Translator* (III, 2, 81–94) in 1951 discusses 'Spiritual Values in Better Manuscript Readings of the New Testament'. All seven passages there noted are based on Westcott-Hort readings and illustrate improvements of seventy years ago.

Neutral text. The limited and tentative alterations in this text thus far are peripheral and unstable. Any substantial effort to improve the basic critical text must 'mark time' until the whole complex of textual studies reveals a new integrating pattern.

2. THE BYZANTINE TEXT

It is not to be thought that recent textual criticism has been fruitless simply because the Westcott-Hort text has not yet been superseded. Even in the quest for the original text fundamental studies have indicated the need to reconsider the history of the text. The Western and Caesarean forms have grown in stature to stand beside the Neutral, and the Neutral no longer holds a monopoly on the true text. There is less confidence than ever that we have a true understanding of the origins and relations of the early recensions. The newly recognized Caesarean form has created intricate problems. Third-century papyrus texts have not yet been successfully placed in the historical scheme. But although studies in textual history are in a tentative state they have produced important results in making us aware that a new reconstruction is demanded by the evidence, and to perceive the need is to secure initial insight into the answer. Furthermore, while the history of the early text is essential to the reconstruction of that text, it is true also that that history as derived *from* the manuscripts throws light upon the development of the early Church in the different sections of the Roman Empire.

Neither can it be said that textual research has recently been inactive; on the contrary, no time in history has seen such varied and far-flung textual studies as has this generation.[1] The greatest attention has been directed to the Byzantine manuscripts, in a wide range of studies: the Byzantine text and its various types, textual families, the lectionary text, and related studies in Byzantine theology, palaeography, iconography, and church music. Such studies relate, not directly to the beginnings of the New Testament text but to its transmission, interpretation and use in worship. These are the aspects

---

[1] This is impressively demonstrated in the forthcoming *Annotated Bibliography of the Textual Criticism of the New Testament* (126 pages) covering the period 1914–39, prepared by Bruce M. Metzger, to be published by Christophers in London as vol. XVI in *Studies and Documents*.

of New Testament studies which today are immediately affected by textual researches, for these researches seek to learn how the New Testament fared in the expanding Christian community. They may ultimately throw light upon the origin of the text, but for the time being they concentrate upon later developments.

The Byzantine text has recently attained importance in its own right. Even in the days of Tischendorf and Westcott and Hort it was defended by Scrivener, Miller, and Burgon for its excellence and validity. Burgon even contended for its superiority over the Alexandrian text, and pronounced ℵ and B 'the most corrupt' and D 'the most depraved text'. But this was the final effort to retain a primary position for the Textus Receptus, 'now universally admitted to be a secondary form of the text'.[1] So complete was its downfall that the mass of Byzantine manuscripts were virtually disregarded until our own generation, but recent criticism is particularly noted for its fresh attention to them. They have again become of high importance, not because Westcott and Hort were wrong about their secondary status but because it is recognized today that they may bear additional witness to the early text and also to later forms employed in the Church. Their usefulness does not lie in the exclusive preservation of an original reading here and there (which would in itself be difficult to judge) but rather in the retracing of main paths back to the major texts, early or late, from which they once departed.

It is well known that distinctive groups of Byzantine manuscripts have long been recognized, such as Family 1, Family 13, the 'purple manuscripts', and Group 1424. These were at first seen as isolated groups whose broader relationships were unknown, distinctively local texts which reflected the peculiar interpretation of the New Testament at some centre. But this was a beginning in textual classification of the increasing mass of later manuscript witnesses. The most extensive effort at classification was made by Hermann von Soden, in whose *Die Schriften des Neuen Testaments* (1902–13) the late manuscripts (excepting the lowly lectionaries) received the fullest attention. His scheme constitutes the background for much textual criticism in the last quarter-century. Great numbers of these

---

[1] Ernest C. Colwell, 'The Complex Character of the Late Byzantine Text of the Gospels', *Journal of Biblical Literature*, vol. LIV (1935), pp. 211–21.

late manuscripts have in our time been collated and classified. Each investigation may appear unrelated to others and it is not often that a manuscript attaches itself to one of the notable groups. But this extensive and continuing search is accumulating a great reserve of information, until larger patterns appear in which each part will find its place. For example, it is within this generation that the Family Groups 1 and 13 have at last fallen into the larger pattern of the Caesarean form, and since the first small groups were discovered additional members have been recognized so that the families are now much enlarged with sisters and cousins and in-laws. It is perceived that even these late copies of the text, revised though they may be, may like Ariadne's thread assist us in retracing our steps to the source. This is the meaning of such patient labours in textual criticism today.

But there is also an immediate effect upon New Testament studies, for the Byzantine manuscripts have been found useful in teaching us how the Church interpreted the New Testament in the Byzantine era. Textual variation is a living thing. The forms of text have resulted from the shape of thought. Next to knowing how the New Testament originally read, it is important to learn how later generations of believers made it read. The libraries of the world contain thousands of manuscript copies of the New Testament which give full evidence that interpreters differed and sometimes wrote their theological differences into the text. These interpreters have greatly complicated the task of recovering the original text, but their textual variations fill the canvas of the Church's later life and thought. It should be clear that textual criticism is not merely a preliminary exercise in establishing a useful text but is rather a constant associate of church history and historical theology. The textual critic is called upon today to establish not *the* critical text but many critical texts. We now seek to recover, in addition to the original New Testament text, the text used by each of the writing Fathers—the critical text of Clement, of Origen, of Eusebius, of Irenaeus, of Tertullian, of Cyprian, as well as of many a later commentator. Current studies particularly would recover the critical original of local texts and family texts (such as Family 13), and each should be studied in relation to local history and interpretation. Such an association has been pointed out by Kirsopp Lake, who observed that 'the mental attitude of an age is apt to be reflected in its texts.... The t'ird and fourth centuries used the Neutral and Caesarean texts; both are marked by clearness of choice and decision between alternatives. It is not an accident that these centuries were those which formulated the great doctrines of Catholic Christianity, and that the fifth century, which used the Antiochian and Ecclesiastical texts, was in the East chiefly characterized by compromise in doctrine and conflation in text.'[1] Nor did theological motivation cease so early to have its effect upon the text. Specifically, an instance in the Byzantine era is set forth by E. W. Saunders, drawn from his study of an early thirteenth-century manuscript influenced by the eleventh-century commentator, Theophylact.[2] Certain variants in the manuscript find *exclusive* support from Theophylact's commentary on the Gospels in the terms in which he explains the true meaning of each passage. That variants in the New Testament text are often laden with theological significance, and may well have theological motivation, is further emphasized by the present writer in an article exhibiting choices of variant readings in the Pauline text.[3] The task, in such cases, is not merely to determine which was the original reading, but to learn as well how each reading played its part in the life of the Church. This interest, in which the textual critic turns historian and theologian, has been increasing in recent criticism and may fruitfully be extended in future textual studies. It presents a direct challenge especially to the historical theologian to collaborate with the textual specialist to produce the most trustworthy conclusions.

The study of manuscript lectionaries is a special department of textual criticism. It has, however, been greatly neglected and although much knowledge about continuous-text witnesses has been garnered through three centuries we still have very little understanding of lectionary witnesses. Until recently a lectionary has mistakenly been used, if at all, in the same manner as a continuous-text manuscript. For example, Tischendorf cited readings from a few lectionaries in eclectic fashion and merely recorded the lectionary side by side with

[1] Kirsopp Lake, 'Excursus on "The Ecclesiastical Text"', *Harvard Theological Review*, vol. xxi (1928), p. 345 n.

[2] Ernest W. Saunders, 'Studies in Doctrinal Influences on the Byzantine Text of the Gospels', *Journal of Biblical Literature*, vol. LXXI (1952), pp. 85-92.

[3] Kenneth W. Clark, 'Textual Criticism and Doctrine', in *Studia Paulina*, honouring Johannis de Zwaan (Haarlem, 1953). See pp. 90ff. of this volume.

the continuous-text witness, as just another witness to the reading. But the study of the lectionary text has now become a distinctive feature of recent textual criticism, and serious and methodical study of the lectionaries has at last been well established.[1]

Lectionary research has special importance for New Testament studies. In the first place, the reading of the Scripture in corporate worship assumed the lectionary pattern early in the life of the Church. It is generally held, furthermore, that public reading of the lectionary text tended to stereotype it and remove it from the centrifugal forces that shattered the unity of other witnesses.[2] Therefore the lectionary text would be a conservative text and, once understood, should bear valuable witness to the text in the early period of the Church. But textual criticism of the lectionaries can contribute other important knowledge about the early Church. Besides helping to clarify the problem of textual transmission, lectionary studies may throw light upon the early practice of Christian worship. Yet for all the importance of the lectionaries, they have come into their own only in this present generation.

The lectionaries (Gospels and Epistles) do not contain all of the New Testament text (especially notable is the complete absence of the Apocalypse), although some selections appear more than once and often show variant readings. It is because of the lectionary structure that its study is more intricate and difficult and requires a special technique to secure scientific results. For example, it is fairly clear that the lectionary text is composite with a separate development of the week-day system from that of Saturday–Sunday, the latter probably representing the earlier system. If this be so, it is obvious that the two systems must be separately studied and reported. Or again, when the same lectionary in duplicate readings (perhaps within the same system) shows a difference in the text we have a puzzling phenomenon that does not occur in continuous-text witness. Nevertheless, for all its difficulty the lectionary has become a special subject of textual research in this generation. The results of such a study are immediately applicable to certain historical problems

---

[1] See especially Riddle and Colwell, *Prolegomena to the Study of the Lectionary Text of the Gospels* (Chicago, 1933).

[2] Ernest C. Colwell, 'Is There a Lectionary Text of the Gospels?', *Harvard Theological Review*, vol. xxv (1932), pp. 73–84.

of the early Church, and will ultimately provide essential information on the early history of the text.[1]

There are several subsidiary fields of manuscript research especially active in recent years, which contribute to textual criticism: archaeology, bibliology, palaeography, Byzantine liturgy and music, and iconography. An expedition in 1949–50 to the great but neglected libraries of Jerusalem and Sinai has now made available a great mass of new textual material, especially valuable for patristic and Byzantine studies.[2] Again, the recently discovered Beatty papyri are valuable not only for their witness to an early text but as illustrations of the papyrus codices used by Christians in the second and third centuries. They have better informed us about the primitive format of Scriptural writings, a factor which influences conclusions about the text as well as the canon. To know how Christians made their books contributes to a clearer analysis of the fortunes of a text in transmission.[3] Palaeographical studies were greatly advanced in this generation when Kirsopp and Silva Lake published their massive corpus of dated Greek manuscripts.[4] A new technique for dating Byzantine Greek manuscripts has recently been proposed by Colwell, based upon the proportions of uncial and cursive letter-forms.[5] Especially in the field of Christian iconography, studies relating to the New Testament have demonstrated their value for Biblical criticism. 'Pictures and text in manuscripts often travel together over long stretches of time, so that obviously the process of copying

[1] Allen P. Wikgren observes that 'many lections preserve a text which is that of the best and most ancient codices, a fact which should make lectionaries of great value not only in the history of the transmission of the text, but also in any attempt to reconstruct its most ancient form' (*Journal of Biblical Literature*, vol. LIII (1934), p. 198).

[2] Kenneth W. Clark, *Checklist of Manuscripts in St Catherine's Monastery, Mt. Sinai* (1952); *Checklist of Manuscripts in the Libraries of the Greek and Armenian Patriarchates in Jerusalem* (1953), Washington.

[3] See especially C. C. McCown, 'Codex and Roll in the New Testament', *Harvard Theological Review*, vol. XXXIV (1941), pp. 219–50.

[4] Kirsopp and Silva Lake, *Dated Greek Minuscule Manuscripts to the Year 1200*, 10 vols. and index (Boston, 1934–9 and 1945).

[5] Ernest C. Colwell, *The Four Gospels of Karahissar*, vol. 1 (Chicago, 1936), pp. 225–41: 'Some Criteria for Dating Byzantine New Testament Manuscripts.' His proposal has been more fully developed in a doctoral dissertation at Yale University, by Howard C. Kee, 'The Paleography of Dated Greek New Testament Manuscripts before 1300' (n.p. 1951).

of the one must have a bearing on that of the other.'[1] Art and text together reveal the mind of the scribal community. All of this paragraph refers to disciplines that support textual studies and, indeed, most of the works cited are by New Testament specialists, several of them being textual critics. The effect of these researches has not yet been fully felt in New Testament studies but they stand upon the threshold of attention.

3. THE INTERNATIONAL GREEK NEW TESTAMENT

The largest single research project in textual criticism of the present, or of any time in history, is the preparation of a basic critical apparatus. Although the effects of this will be fully felt in the future, it is relevant to describe it here because its substantial effect upon New Testament studies is immediate even while it is in progress. It is a broad international effort, turning chiefly upon an axis of British and American collaboration with the main centres at Oxford and Chicago, and including at present a few representative scholars in European countries. Because so many New Testament scholars are active in it—about 300—it is inevitable that current labours exercise an effect upon testamental studies at once.

The international character of the project is the result of independent initiative in England and the United States, yet the movement in England was the earlier. Some years before the Second World War erupted a group of scholars organized such a project under the leadership of the late Bishop Headlam. It was first reported that their objective was to publish a new critical text along with an improved citation of textual variation. But the effort to replace the Westcott-Hort text was abandoned, a development which further demonstrates the thesis that it is untimely to expect a new critical text in our generation. Under the editorship of S. C. E. Legg, two volumes of the projected series were published in 1935 (Mark) and 1940 (Matthew),[2] and a third volume prepared on Luke but not

[1] Kurt Weitzmann, 'Narrative and Liturgical Gospel Illustrations', in Parvis and Wikgren (edd.), New Testament Manuscript Studies (Chicago, 1950), p. 152. Cf. Harold R. Willoughby, The Rockefeller-McCormick New Testament, vol. III (Chicago, 1932); The Four Gospels of Karahissar, vol. I (Chicago, 1936); The Elizabeth Day McCormick Apocalypse, vol. I (Chicago, 1940).

[2] S. C. E. Legg (ed.), Novum Testamentum Graece (Oxford, 1935-40).

published. The text of Westcott-Hort was printed as a base and the critical apparatus cited manuscripts in support of this text as well as those supporting variant readings. In the apparatus of Mark, about forty uncial manuscripts are cited besides about thirty uncial fragments. The Beatty manuscript ($\mathfrak{P}^{45}$) is the only papyrus cited. From the mass of minuscules, only twenty of special significance are regularly cited (representing Family 1, Family 13, and the Alexandrian and Caesarean types). In Mark, about 200 additional continuous-text minuscules are occasionally reported. In the succeeding volume on Matthew, about half of all these minuscules is omitted while about fifty additional witnesses appear occasionally. In the unpublished Lucan apparatus about fifty minuscules in the printed volumes are dropped and well over a hundred additional minuscules appear for the first time. In all three Gospels, about 350 minuscules appear at least once in the apparatus but only a small, choice group is reported consistently. This procedure is traditional, for no previous editor has attempted to cite all of his witnesses throughout, but the Legg volumes do report from a much larger number of manuscripts than heretofore.

The above description of the first stage in the project provides a background necessary for the understanding of the succeeding stage. The American initiative arose in 1942 and resulted in a definite plan drawn up in 1948.[1] Happily, the American and British groups joined hands, and at this point a new set of principles was agreed upon in international conference. The original plan, therefore, was substantially revised and the objective differently defined.[2] Therefore the volume on the Gospel of Luke, next to be published, will be reworked to conform to the new principles. In it the Textus Receptus will be printed as the base with (as before) evidence cited both for and against this text.[3] The new agreement calls for the citation of all known uncial witnesses and indeed all manuscripts up to A.D. 900.

[1] M. M. Parvis and A. P. Wikgren, editors, New Testament Manuscript Studies (Chicago, 1950).

[2] Merrill M. Parvis, 'The International Project to Establish a New Critical Apparatus of the Greek New Testament', Crozer Quarterly, vol. XXVII (1950), pp. 301–8.

[3] Parvis (ibid. p. 307) states: 'As far as we know, this is the first time that there has been an attempt to compile an extensive apparatus based upon the textus receptus.'

It will include *all* of the extant papyri.[1] An important revision of plan is the basic insistence that every Greek manuscript cited in the apparatus must be *completely* reported so that the apparatus will give full information on each manuscript. The number of minuscule witnesses to be included will be determined by the capacity of the apparatus but sporadic citation has been ruled out. Furthermore, if it were found possible to report the variants of some 300 minuscule manuscripts, they would represent a selection from possibly 900 Byzantine manuscripts to be studied, the criterion of selection being textual distinction.

Another important principle decided is that citation will not be arranged by textual types or groups. Whatever textual relationships may have been recognized in past studies, for the purpose of this reference work all will be levelled and every witness will stand by its own merit. Uncial and minuscule manuscripts will be cited simply in alphabetical and numerical sequence, according to the official designation of each. Nevertheless, in selecting from the great number of Byzantine manuscripts it is purposed to include adequate representation of the various textual types with which present-day critics are accustomed to deal. But the apparatus will reflect the effort to be neutral in all such previous findings and seek to avoid the obstruction of new insights or novel paths of textual investigation. Inasmuch as textual theory appears to have reached an impasse in our time, the fullest scope should be allowed for the discovery of gateways to new progress.

The revised plan further provides that the lectionary witness will be emphasized. A considerable block of lectionaries, whose importance is newly recognized in these days, will be carefully selected for *complete* citation (a recognition never before accorded this type of textual witness). Further, it is proposed to cite all versions into which the Greek text was translated before the year A.D. 1000. To set these translations more clearly against the Greek original, versional variants cited will appear in Greek. Patristic quotations are to be cited with special emphasis upon those Fathers whose text relates to the text-types emerging as dominant in the early cen-

[1] Georg Maldfeld and Bruce M. Metzger, 'Detailed List of the Greek Papyri of the New Testament', *Journal of Biblical Literature*, vol. LXVIII (1949), pp. 359–70. The editors here describe sixty-two extant papyri.

turies.[1] The results of this extensive research to be fulfilled through international co-operation will take the form of eight volumes for the complete New Testament. This type of basic reference work has not been successfully produced since the work of Tischendorf eighty years ago, and never has one utilized the technical principles now to be applied. The present project is necessary for two reasons: first, numerous discoveries of important manuscripts and theories have been made in the interval and, secondly, an improved technique for the *apparatus criticus* of the New Testament text is required in order to support that most difficult and complex problem of all textual criticism—the analysis of the New Testament text in its origins and transmission. If it be granted, in the providence of God, that this pretentious project should find completion, it will mark the end of the first stage of a renewed cycle of textual investigation. The modern period of collecting and collating sources, similar to the period 1516–1734, will have drawn to a close. A new phase may well open then when an adequate *apparatus criticus*, summarizing and ordering the vast data compiled, may provide the source from which new perception and inspiration may arise.

Ultimately, there is only one motivation for textual criticism, and that is the need for a trustworthy text to interpret. Biblical studies may go astray if based upon a corrupted text and, in turn, textual fidelity falls short of virtue if it represents only a mechanical restoration. While the search for the 'true text' does not in itself imply a theory of verbal inspiration, the living word contains a message of life and the importance of that message is one with the importance of the literal word. The textual critic has always been a theologian, but it is equally essential that the theologian shall be a textual critic. Certainly the two functions are indivisible and whether carried on in one mind or in two they must find close partnership. Therefore, the effect of textual criticism upon Biblical studies must be continuous, and the textual critic is called upon at all times to persist in the preparation of a better textual foundation upon which the structure of Christian faith may stand firm.

[1] M. M. Parvis observes that 'this will be the first time that the lectionary text or texts have been adequately cited in any apparatus' (*Crozer Quarterly*, vol. xxvii (1950), p. 307).

TEXTUAL CRITICISM AND DOCTRINE

It has frequently been declared that textual criticism has no relation to Christian doctrine. Research on the text of the New Testament is considered to be a technical discipline whose objective is to recover from ancient manuscripts the proper words of the text. It is said to have no theological significance and to be without effect upon the doctrines of the church. Textual critics have examined hundreds of differing texts and handled myriads of variant readings, and some have concluded that doctrine is unaffected thereby. This view is not antiquated and it is easy to cite recent repetitions of it by preeminent authorities. Vaganay in 1937, estimating that research has so far revealed 150,000—250,000 textual variants, emphatically insists that "there is not one affecting the substance of Christian dogma" [1]. Kenyon in 1940 restated his position, that "no fundamental doctrine of Christian faith rests on a disputed reading" [2]. F. C. Grant in 1946 once more affirmed that "no doctrine of the Christian faith has been affected by the [RSV] revision, for the simple reason that, out of the thousands of variant readings in the manuscripts, none has turned up thus far that requires a revision of Christian doctrine" [3]. The most recent citation is drawn from John Knox's latest publication,

[1] Leo Vaganay, *An Introduction to the Textual Criticism of the New Testament* (Trans. by B. V. Miller; St. Louis, 1937), p. 12.

[2] Sir Frederic Kenyon, *Our Bible and the Ancient Manuscripts* (New York, 1940), p. 23.

[3] Luther A. Weigle, ed., *An Introduction to the Revised Standard Version of the New Testament* (New York, 1946), p. 42.

a most provocative discourse on historical criticism in relation to faith. "We are mistaken," he believes, "if we suppose that any vital concern of faith is involved" in the conclusions reached through our critical researches [1]). It would appear that all of these scholars are insisting that textual criticism is at best a rational procedure belonging to a category apart from that of faith and doctrine.

It is also clear, however, that the concern of most of these scholars — to whom, no doubt, many others should be added — is that no weakening or distortion of doctrine should result from textual studies. They further seek to reassure others, who may fear the effect of textual research upon their traditional faith. But it is also quite clear that every one of these scholars would defend the right and value of textual and historical scholarship, for they have devoted their own lives to it. It remains to be learned, except in the case of Knox, how each would explain this paradox. If textual criticism, whatever its results, cannot touch doctrine — neither to criticize, nor to revise, nor even to support — then fears are groundless and, it may be concluded, our critical labors are futile. Hort long ago insisted that textual criticism is "always secondary and always negative [and] its final aim is virtually nothing more than the detection and rejection of error."

Having cited such an array of authorities, we shall be bold indeed to differ, even though assured of comparable support. Yet a different conception of the textual critic's task may well be urged as a matter of profound importance to our life and labor. In the first instance, it may be suggested that textual criticism be considered as positive rather than negative. It is not merely, in the terms of Hort, to detect and reject error, but is to discover and embrace truth. To exscind a false interpolation or to restore an omitted phrase is to purify the true text. The discovery of an important manuscript will throw fresh doubt on many a passage but offers new hope in the

---

[1]) John Knox, *Criticism and Faith* (New York, 1952), p. 56.

task of recovering the true text. It is reasonable to ask expectantly if textual criticism may contribute to our spiritual well-being, may add assurance in the quest for our creed.

Christian doctrines are imbedded in the New Testament text. They were not created by the authors, but they were interpreted by them. Personal experience and oral tradition have had much to do with formulating and conserving the doctrines of the church, but the written word is an essential interpretation of these doctrines. In its earliest history the text suffered the greater effects of formative conditions in the church, but in its recent history in the West textual criticism has imposed controls that help to repair and establish the text, as well as its influence on doctrine. Streeter has declared that "all the really important various readings" appeared within the first two centuries [1]). Certainly the doctrines of the church have not always been the same. They are not the same in different branches of the church today. But in all cases these doctrines inhere in the Scriptures, and the text is used by all to defend them. The language of the inspired Word is important to the interpretation of doctrine, and the two show interaction with one another. Many variants are of textual-doctrinal character.

Perhaps those scholars who hold that dogma is unaffected by the state of the New Testament text are thinking of great over-arching affirmations, rather than the smaller elements of belief. Belief in God, in the divine Christ, in salvation — these are neither proved nor refuted by any changes in the text. But the great dogmas are ultimately composed, in human experience, of all the many beliefs we hold. These beliefs are directly affected by the condition of our text, and a purer text can increasingly inspire and establish our faith.

The New Testament was originally composed as an interpretive document. Throughout its history it has continued its role as interpreter of doctrine. The freedom men assumed in

---

[1]) B. F. Streeter, *The Four Gospels* (London, 1924), p. 36.

altering its text was inspired by their understanding of Christian doctrine, and by their purpose to make it plain to others. Even Vaganay recognizes that there are "variants having a dogmatic origin . . . . motived by the wish to strengthen a proof or answer an adversary's objection" [1]). Theological history is replete with doctrinal debates on the text of the New Testament. Tertullian charged that Marcion corrupted the text of Paul. Ambrose (*De spir. sanct.* 2 : 6) and Didymus (*De trin.* 2 : 11) accused the Arians and Nestorians of introducing heretical readings. The Emperor Anastasius is said to have deposed a bishop because he tampered with the text. Erasmus and Stunica debated over "dogmatic corrections." Tyndale was accused of wilfully perverting the meaning of the Scriptures. Such a list could be extended almost without limit to demonstrate the interaction of text and doctrine. It is not sufficient merely to claim that offensive readings are false, or that an impure text does not corrupt doctrine. Every interpreter may make the same claim in the interests of his own position, but the arbiter is the textual critic. The textual form of inspired Scripture is inextricably related to doctrinal truth. Textual criticism plays its part at the very center of the church's doctrine.

Another task of textual criticism, beyond establishing the true original text, is to recover and explore the many recensions of later centuries. It is well known that research has indentified many distinctive recensions. Each one is a text in its own right, developed through the theological interests and beliefs of a particular era or locality. Such a text is in itself evidence of the doctrinal characteristics of those who used it. Textual criticism therefore undertakes to recover the true form of every such text, in the belief that this will help to write the history of doctrine. Doctrine does have a history and its changing expression has been reflected in textual variations. Consequently textual criticism deals not merely with words, not with mechanical externals, not with superficial forms, but with

---

[1]) *Op. cit.*, p. 63.

matters vital to theology. Textual research finds no motive in
establishing a critical text which has no relevance to doctrine.
The dynamic for textual research springs from the living
doctrines of the church and for them alone is it inspired to
fulfill its task.

But some will be concerned that we have here implied that
doctrine is a variable thing, modified by the whims of men.
On the contrary, it is because Christian doctrine is believed
to have been expressed in the Biblical text that so much
importance is laid upon textual criticism. The record of our
Lord and the faith of the first believers are mediated through
the words of the New Testament writers. Here lies the genius
of the Christian doctrine. If we are to have the fullest understanding of this doctrine, textual criticism must first recover
the pure text of such witnesses.

II

To illustrate the truth of the foregoing thesis, numerous New
Testament passages might be culled from contemporary
scholars. Instead we shall illustrate it here with a series of
fresh instances of textual-doctrinal variants drawn from the
Pauline Epistles in the earliest witness we possess, the third-
century Chester Beatty papyrus (P[46]) [1]). We shall not refer in
this study to modern versions in the European languages, but
only in the English. As a secondary interest we shall point
out the effect of P[46] upon the critical text, especially where
the evidence to date offers evenly balanced testimony to variant
readings. But our main purpose will be to show the doctrinal
issue involved in each textual problem cited.

---

[1]) This papyrus was acquired in 1930—33; fifty-six leaves by Mr. Beatty, and
thirty leaves by the University of Michigan. It contains the Greek text of the
Pauline letters, lacking Philemon, the Pastorals, and part of II Thess. It was fully
published by Sir Frederic Kenyon, *The Chester Beatty Biblical Papyri: Pauline
Epistles*, Fasc. III Suppl., Texts and Plates (London, 1936—37), Its contribution
to the textual criticism of the New Testament has not been fully exploited.

Romans 8 : 28

This statement by Paul has long been cherished for its assurance that "all things work together for good to them that love God." But an important difference of meaning rests upon a variant in the text, for which the evidence is closely balanced. This variant is the appearance of ὁ θεός as the subject, a reading first adopted by Lachmann in 1831 with the support of A B sah boh aeth and sometimes Origen [1]) though all other witnesses omit it. When later Tischendorf consulted א the term was absent and he omitted it from his text. Westcott-Hort and Nestle have placed ὁ θεός in indecisive brackets. But the new Beatty papyrus includes ὁ θεός. This would seem to tip the scales in favor of Pauline authorship.

To adopt this reading, as Goodspeed and the RSV have in the English version, is to present the very different and important theological view that "God works with those who love him . . . . to bring about what is good." This is a more inspiring as well as a more realistic belief than that "all things work together for good." It is also in better harmony with its context: "the Spirit helps us in our weakness." It was so that Origen understood the passage (even without ὁ θεός being written) in his Commentary on John (xx. 23). "It is necessary for him who wills to fulfill the desires of God also to perform the works of God. For not only the willing but also the divine working, as Paul says, is of God who unites completely with the good man to will, and joins with him to make that will effective, for 'in everything he works for good with those who love God.' "

I Corinthians 2 : 1

Another significant theological idea depends upon one word in this verse. Former texts in Greek and English (with the

---

[1]) Origen, *On Prayer* xxix. 19 (= 1.264) A later witness, Serapion of Thmuis: *Against the Manichees* 29, also writes ὁ θεός συνεργεῖ . . . .

support of $\aleph^c$ B *et al. mu.*) record Paul "declaring unto you the testimony of God" (as in I Cor. 1 : 6). But some recent texts (excepting Nestle and the RSV) follow the choice of Griesbach: "the mystery of God" (with $\aleph^*$ A C). The textual evidence is evenly balanced, at least until P[46] also transmitted the reading [μυστ]ήριον according to Kenyon. There seems very slight possibility that the scribe wrote [σωτ]ήριον (as in 489), and we may agree with Kenyon that this new witness supports here the typical Pauline conception of God's "mystery", rather than "testimony" or "salvation".

Each one of these variant terms conveys a distinctive theological sense. But the latter two appear to be derivitives belonging to later theological development. The idea of the divine "mystery" is a familiar one with Paul, but not one likely to develop from the simple conception of God's "testimony".

I Corinthians 6 : 20

Here is a text about which there is no serious question as to the original form written by Paul. The strongest textual evidence supports the reading: "Glorify God in your body." But numerous Byzantine scribes show a discontent with this "sharp practical injunction" (Robertson-Plummer, p. 129), probably not because of an ascetic suggestion but rather because of a sense of narrow materialism. This is revealed by the theological addition which became popular (cf. ς and KJV): "Glorify God in your body and in your spirit, both of which are God's." At this point Chrysostom explains Paul in the full text: "Now these things he says, that we may not only flee fornication in the body, but also in the spirit of our mind abstain from every wicked thought." Here is a theological extension which brings the statement of Paul into accord with the teaching of Jesus. Lightfoot called the addition "a liturgical insertion", but certainly Chrysostom attributed it to Paul and considered that it completed the theological sense.

I Corinthians 7 : 5

A significant variant here shows the religious habit of early Christians of associating prayer with fasting. Manuscript evidence clearly shows that Paul wrote: "that you may devote yourselves to prayer." But very early the text was altered to read "prayer and fasting." The same association is expressed in textual changes made at Mk 9 : 29 and Acts 10 : 30. Indeed, the original text of Mk 9 : 29, which refers only to "prayer", compares with Mt 17: 21 which reads "prayer and fasting." Similarly Hermas fasted and prayed before receiving his visions (Vis. II. 2.1 and III. 1.1). The Didache (8) gives instructions in the one context on both fasting and praying. In Acts 14 : 23 it is stated that prayer and fasting preceded the selection of elders in the new Asia Minor churches, and in 13 : 3 prayer and fasting preceded the ceremony that launched the mission of Barnabas and Paul.

There can be no doubt that prayer and fasting were closely related elements in the religiously disciplined life. The combination was generally considered as a means to spiritual enlightenment. It would be important to early Christians to believe that Paul referred to this combination in I Corinthians 7 : 5, but textual evidence denies this. Warfield considered this instance to be one of the most likely cases of "doctrinal corrections." Chrysostom's text read: "fasting and prayer", and even Griesbach and Scholtz favored this reading with the support of the uncials K L.

I Corinthians 10 : 19

A most important theological issue placed before Paul was the nature of idols. In the more recent critical texts Paul writes: "What do I imply then? That food offered to idols is anything, or that an idol is anything?" (so $\aleph^a$ B C² *et al.*). However, the textual evidence for this reading is quite evenly balanced, for the latter half of the question ("or that an idol is anything?") is omitted in Alexandrinus and by the original scribes of **א** and C. To these must now be added the witness of P[46] completing a formidable array which may well be enough to weight the scales in its favor. Griesbach was the first modern critic to omit the clause.

From a theological viewpoint, it is much easier to believe that the clause was added than that it was deliberately omitted. Furthermore, the witnesses favoring omission are too early, too many, and too respectable for the omission to be dismissed as homoioteleuton. If the omission is genuine, Paul refrains here from dismissing the idol itself as a nonentity, notwithstanding his declaration in 8 : 4. This more cautious, and more confusing, explanation of Paul about meat offerings, idols, demons, and the many gods, gave way later to a sweeping and inclusive renunciation of all. In the light of this, the rhetorical question would then be more acceptable in the amended form: "Do I imply that food offered to idols is anything? Or, for that matter, that the idol itself is anything?"

I Corinthians 11 : 29

A similar case is that found in the warning of Paul: "Anyone who eats and drinks without discerning the body . . . ." This is the form generally accepted today in Greek and English critical texts. It is supported by only a few witnesses, but they are the best; and P[46] now concurs. But an early "doctrinal correction" appears in **א**[c] C[c] and a host of other witnesses — the insertion of "unworthily" (under the influence of 11 : 27). But in 11 : 29, logic also would reject this term, for already the warning has its condition: "without discerning the body." To add "unworthily" is to impose another condition which only with difficulty may be related to the first. But the theological addition has grown so popular as to completely obscure the original condition in 11 : 29. While many Christians participating in the Eucharist are concerned about their worthiness, they pay no attention to the original condition that they must "discern the body." Here then is an influential theological variant which has affected doctrine as related to the Eucharist.

I Corinthians 13 : 3

"If I give my body to be burned . . . ." How familiar is this passage! It is supported by Clement (*Strom.* IV. 18) and Codex C and a great multitude of later manuscripts. It persists even in Tischendorf and Nestle and in most of the recent English translations, including the RSV. But almost a century ago it was known that the oldest and best witnesses (א A B 33 *et al.*) agreed in a different reading: "If I give my body in order to boast . . . ." and Westcott and Hort decided in their favor. The Twentieth Century translation (1904) was the first English version to adopt this reading, and it stands also in the Goodspeed New Testament of 1923. Robertson and Plummer (*ICC*, p. 291) observed in 1911 that "it is by no means certain that καυθήσομαι . . . . is the right reading." Now the additional witness of P[46] strengthens the case for καυχήσομαι so that the textual evidence would seem conclusive.

Yet for all this, this cherished passage remains uncorrected in most Greek and English texts. An important theological difference depends upon the original form written by Paul. The traditional form, which speaks of burning, does not suit well the primitive Christian era when burning was neither a form of execution nor of torture nor of personal purification. Robertson and Plummer suggest that the figure is merely one to depict the most painful death imaginable, an idea reminiscent of Origen ("the most terrible of all deaths, the being burnt alive"). But this illogically implies that the more painful the death the greater its benefit. If the better attested reading, καυχήσομαι, is attributed to Paul, he was saying something quite different. "If boastfully I dole out all I possess and, further, give my very body, without love there is nothing gained." This picture of sacrifice is further clarified by the comment of Clement of Rome (I. 55): "Many gave themselves up to slavery, and receiving the price paid for themselves fed others." With either of the alternative readings there are interpretive difficulties, but textually the priority should be given to καυχήσομαι with its particular theological implications.

I Corinthians 14 : 38

"If any man is ignorant, let him be ignorant." So the KJV and ASV translate, accepting the ἀγνοείτω of Stephanus (with P⁴⁶ א° A² B Dᵇ *et al.*). But Westcott and Hort, and Nestle, and the English Twentieth Century, Moffatt, Goodspeed, and the RSV all turn to ἀγνοεῖται (with א* A* D* *et al.*). Origen uses both forms of this text and therefore does not help us to determine the original. Perhaps ἀγνοείτω has, more recently, been considered secondary because in three manuscripts of the fourth and fifth centuries we see correctors changing to this. But it is a scribal reading in B and in the third-century P⁴⁶. Since ἀγνοείτω is known as a reading as early as the third century, it is quite possible that the three correctors referred to above are really correcting a tendency to ἀγνοεῖται as a secondary reading.

There is certainly found here an important theological difference. Origen, where he uses ἀγνοεῖται (ignoratur), insists that the statement is not blasphemous (*Hom. on Gen.* IV. 6), and defends this attitude toward a fellow Christian on the ground that God must himself assume this same attitude toward the "ignorant" one. Nevertheless, Origen seems troubled by the idea that such a person is to be discarded. A different interpretation is expressed by more recent exegetes who accept the same reading, namely, that to guard against theological error Paul urges the Corinthians not to listen to one who does not understand and accept Paul's own insights. But if ἀγνοείτω is accepted, then Paul's thought must be understood in the context somewhat as follows: "If any of you considers himself a prophet or a pneumatic, then let him demonstrate his claim by attesting that what I now write to you is an instruction of the Lord. If any one among you fails to recognize this, he simply remains ignorant and such a claim to prophecy is dissipated." Depending upon the Greek word accepted, the interpretations involve different theological implications.

I Corinthians 15 : 51

This is one of the most confused texts, though (and perhaps because) it deals with a most important doctrine. Almost all texts follow B and the mass of Greek manuscripts in reading: "We shall not all sleep, but we shall all be changed." The reference is clearly to Christian believers and the interpretation is not difficult. The *parousia* was expected soon, and for believers (on earth or in Sheol) a mystery of transformation would be enacted. But, though not generally acknowledged, the strongest textual attestation (א A C 33 *et al.*) supports a different reading: "We shall all sleep, but we shall not all be changed." The reference here is clearly to all people, believers and non-believers. Some interpreters suggest that the first clause corrects history, when Paul and his contemporaries had departed this life. A more plausible view is that the statement merely declares that all people are subject to death but some, the believers, will survive death and be transformed. This meaning fits the larger context extremely well. Thus: "Flesh and blood, being mortal, cannot inherit an immortal condition. Rather all of us, being mortal, die. But there will be enacted a mystery, a transformation for believers who die. For believers will be raised up from Sheol as immortal beings and experience a transformation." This better attested text is equally suitable to the primitive Christian theological environment. It also accords with the basic thought of Paul. Indeed, it may imply the same doctrine of resurrection although there is variation in the process described.

Western witnesses present still another reading: "We shall all rise but we shall not all be changed." In this case the reference is to all people. All who have died, good and bad, believer and non-believer, will be raised from Sheol when the trumpet sounds, but only those who survive the jugdment will be transformed. However, Tertullian — who follows this form in *Res. of Flesh* 42 — takes it to mean that only those remaining and in the living flesh can be, or need to be transformed. Since the departed have already passed through a great change, and their bodies have deteriorated, they have no substantial body to be changed. So he understands Paul to mean that, though others will be saved, only those with earthly bodies will be transformed. Yet later he expresses the view that the deteriorated body of the departed will be repaired so that they too will regain a substantial being, subject to a similar transformation.

An entirely new reading for this passage recently came to light, out of the third century. The earliest record of this passage, in P46, attests the form: "We shall not all sleep, nor shall we all be changed." Perhaps this implies no different belief, requiring only to understand the pronouns. Paul might say, in these terms: "Not all of this generation will die before the *parousia*, nor shall all its people experience the transformation mystery." A. T. Robertson (*Intro. to Textual Crit.*, p. 159) comments that these variations may be "due to rival theories of the resurrection or to failure to understand Paul's language." However, it might well be true that such variations represent independent approaches to the same doctrine and adjustments to the changing Christian life.

CONCLUSION

These few selections are typical of numerous passages throughout the New Testament. In every case, doctrinal conceptions are involved and the reading accepted as original makes a difference in doctrinal sense. Major conceptions of God, of man, of sacraments, of inspiration and epistemology, of the supernatural, of resurrection and future life, all are touched in these few examples of textual variation. The Christian's reach to apprehend and apply the great doctrines to life is affected by the Scriptural text he reads. When all such points of textual variation are considered together it is clear that they comprise a substantial body of critical issues which only textual criticism can resolve.

Therefore, it is the great responsibility of textual criticism to refine the New Testament text toward an ever increasing purity. It must lay the foundation on which alone doctrinal interpretation of the New Testament may be soundly based.

THE THEOLOGICAL RELEVANCE OF TEXTUAL VARIATION IN CURRENT CRITICISM OF THE GREEK NEW TESTAMENT*

I

IN these days of "Vatican II" an English version of the NT has been produced which is officially acceptable to both Protestant and Roman Catholic Christians. Originally translated by American Protestant scholars as the Revised Standard Version, it was subsequently revised by Catholic scholars as the Catholic edition and designated as the RSV CE. For three and a half centuries the King James and the Douai-Challoner versions have stood side by side, representative of the major divisions of Western Christendom and conveying the implication that the two English texts express distinctive and important theological characteristics for Protestant and Catholic interpretation.

On numerous occasions when new translations into English have been made, someone has risen to allege that a translation is of too conservative a theological interpretation, or reflects a liberal bias, or even that it reveals a communist flair, and indeed all three qualities may be alleged of the very same translation. Recently, the announcement of a "Bible for Evangelicals" credited the RSV with clarity but criticized it for its Christology, and intimated that the newly announced translation would express the true theology. When the RSV appeared various readers alleged that its text was atheistic, or modernistic, or socialistic, or even blasphemous. We are not here concerned with the justice or injustice of such allegations, for effective refutation has long since been offered. We are concerned rather to recognize that in such instances as these there is attested the belief that variation in a text, whether in the Greek original or in translation, involves a difference in interpretation which is important to the church and to the believer. In the light of such a principle, textual criticism would be allied with exegesis and theology and even with the practical tasks in pastoral care.

Quite apart from the integrity and the skill of the editor of a Greek text or the translator of a version, a difference in the form of expression will often create a difference in the sense and may reflect a difference in the thought of the editor or the translator. Furthermore, when textual variation occurs in the Greek NT, we often do find an alteration of

---

* The Presidential Address delivered at the annual meeting of the Society of Biblical Literature on December 30, 1965, at Vanderbilt University, Nashville, Tennessee.

meaning. It is important to know what the *original* text and the *original* meaning were, but it is also important to recognize the *subsequent* revision of text and thought in the course of the church's history. In the current edition of the Nestle NT, for example, we have more than a single text, for in the *apparatus criticus* we are confronted with thousands of textual variants that involve a difference of form and interpretation. Today, three special factors may increase our concern with, and the importance of, textual difference and its theological import. I refer to the publication of the RSV CE, the recent discovery of third-century papyrus texts in the Beatty and Bodmer libraries, and the unprecedented scope of the International Greek New Testament Project in the preparation of a new *apparatus criticus*. These three developments cast special light upon the relationship of text to interpretation. It is not our primary concern at this time to determine what is original and what is secondary, but rather to demonstrate the variety of reading and of consequent meaning. It has been remarked that "there are no 'spurious readings' in New Testament manuscripts."[1] The intent of such a statement is only to insist that every variation is genuine in its time and place. Although a variant which is a departure from the original text may be described as spurious, yet every intentional and sensible variant has a claim to authenticity in the history of Christian thought. It will be valuable to form a judgment, in the light of all modern textual discoveries and researches, of the extent to which the Greek text of our NT has been subjected to revision and made to carry differences of thought.

About 250 years ago, John Mill, of Oxford, published an edition of the Greek NT.[2] The text itself was a repetition of the traditional Byzantine "Received Text," but it was further reported that his manuscript sources revealed 30,000 variants.[3] This disclosure was shocking to some, and a long and bitter debate ensued. It is most significant, however, that this eighteenth-century debate was not a theological discussion about the variant readings and their meaning; but rather it dealt with a prior issue, whether or not sacred Scripture is a proper subject for critical textual emendation as employed in secular classics.

A hundred years ago Scrivener estimated that the text of the Greek NT showed variance "at least fourfold that quantity," i. e., 120,000.[4] It was in 1886 that Benjamin Warfield estimated between 180,000 and

---

[1] Donald W. Riddle, "Textual Criticism as a Historical Discipline," *ATR*, 18 (1936), pp. 220–24. Cf. also M. M. Parvis, "The Nature and Task of New Testament Textual Criticism," *JR*, 32 (1952), p. 172.

[2] John Mill, *Novum Testamentum . . .* (Oxford, 1707).

[3] Gerard Maestricht, "Dissertation on the Collections and Collectors of Variant Readings," in the Prolegomena of his Greek NT (1711). Cf. also Richard Bentley ("Phileleutherus Lipsiensis"), *Remarks upon a late Discourse of Free-Thinking* (London, 1713).

[4] F. H. A. Scrivener, *A Plain Introduction to the Criticism of the New Testament*, I, p. 3.

200,000 "variant readings."⁵ And in 1937 Vaganay acknowledged a range of 150,000 to 250,000 ("The exact figure matters little").⁶ Now in our time, the International Greek New Testament Project can report on 300 manuscript collations of Luke, and estimate for the entire NT perhaps 300,000 variants. The simple fact of massive textual variations (small and large) is beyond denial or refutation.

The effect of the variable text upon theological interpretation, however, is still subject to difference of judgment. Richard Bentley, who counseled his generation to welcome the great variety of readings, advised nevertheless that there is not "one article of faith or moral precept either perverted or lost."⁷ His contemporary and opponent, Daniel Whitby, insisted that "Mill's variants are of no importance" because "there are scarcely any variant readings which concern the rule of conduct or even a single article of faith."⁸ Nearly 200 years later, Warfield in America brought Bentley's view up to date by quoting him with approval;⁹ as did also his contemporary in England, F. H. A. Scrivener.¹⁰ Another of their contemporaries was Hort, whose estimate of textual variation has been often repeated, that "substantial variation . . . can hardly form more than a thousandth part of the entire text."¹¹ This classic statement, however, must have been rhetorical rather than mathematical, for a tenth of one per cent would amount to merely twenty lines in Nestle. The estimate is absurd and worthless. Another contemporary authority in America was Ezra Abbot, who judged that only one-twentieth of all variants had sufficient manuscript witness, and of this fraction only one-twentieth carried "appreciable difference in the sense": a fourth of one per cent or about fifty lines in Nestle.¹²

Lest it would seem that we are here merely rattling old bones, let us quickly excerpt typical remarks in contemporary publications: Leo Vaganay of France in 1937: ". . . there is not one [variant] affecting the substance of Christian dogma."¹³ Sir Frederic Kenyon of England in 1940: "No fundamental doctrine of the Christian faith rests on a disputed reading."¹⁴ F. C. Grant in America in 1946, commenting on the RSV: ". . . no doctrine of the Christian faith has been affected by the revision,

---

⁵ Benjamin B. Warfield, *An Introduction to the Textual Criticism of the New Testament*, p. 13. Still another estimate was expressed in 1907 by Ira Maurice Price, *The Ancestry of Our English Bible*, p. 201: "almost 150,000." This estimate is retained in later revisions by Allen P. Wikgren (1949 and 1956, p. 222).

⁶ Leo Vaganay, *An Introduction to the Textual Criticism of the New Testament*, p. 11.

⁷ Richard Bentley, *Remarks* . . . , part 1, § 32.

⁸ Daniel Whitby, "Examen of Mill's Variant Readings," appended to Whitby's *Paraphrase and Commentary on the New Testament* (1710).

⁹ Warfield, *Introduction* . . . , p. 14.

¹⁰ Scrivener, *Plain Introduction* . . . , p. 7.

¹¹ Hort, *The New Testament in the Original Greek*, II, p. 2.

¹² Reported by Warfield, *Introduction* . . . , p. 14.

¹³ Vaganay, *An Introduction* . . . , p. 12.

¹⁴ Frederic G. Kenyon, *Our Bible and the Ancient Manuscripts*⁴, p. 23.

for the simple reason that out of the thousands of variant readings in the manuscripts, none has turned up thus far that requires a revision of Christian doctrine."[15] Harold Greenlee in 1964: "No Christian doctrine . . . hangs upon a debatable text."[16] The Kee-Young-Froelich NT introduction in a 1965 edition: ". . . there is no essential historical or theological point that is determined one way or another by textual variants."[17] In the light of this persistent repetition, we may recognize a concern if not fear for the security of the Christian faith and its basis in a variable text.

There has been, of course, a contrary opinion. Hort himself admitted that "it is true that dogmatic preferences to a great extent determined theologians, and probably scribes, in their choice between rival readings . . . ."[18] Kenyon too implies a similar judgment when he writes that through textual researches we "are brought so much nearer to the true Word of God."[19] But such a view seems to be kept in a separate compartment of the mind; and has been expressed cautiously and infrequently, and not at all by the modern writers we have mentioned above who exhibit no constructive viewpoint on the criticism of the text. Rendel Harris insisted that "Dr. Hort cannot be right in divesting the various readings of New Testament manuscripts of dogmatic significance, or in assuring us of the *bona fides* of the transcribers."[20] More recently, C. S. C. Williams has expressed the judgment that textual alteration derives "no less frequently from dogmatic than from other motivation."[21]

In reality the amount of textual variation is a considerable portion. Of course it is true that the great bulk of text shows little or no record of variation. The latest Nestle is predominantly the text of the *Textus Receptus*. But it is the minimal variation for which we search and which we seek to refine, a principle that applies to all other scientific research. The research on a single chemical need not upset the basic table of formulae or the chemist's "creed" but it is essential to learn more of any single chemical. So in the NT text it is the doubtful portion that stands in need of refinement. Its importance far exceeds its fractional size.

Counting words is a meaningless measure of textual variation, and all such estimates fail to convey the theological significance of variable readings. Rather it is required to evaluate the thought rather than to compute the verbiage. How shall we measure the theological clarification derived from textual emendation where a single word altered

[15] Frederick C. Grant, *Introduction to the Revised Standard Version of the New Testament* (L. A. Weigle, ed.), p. 42.

[16] J. Harold Greenlee, *Introduction to New Testament Textual Criticism*, p. 68.

[17] Howard C. Kee, Franklin W. Young, and Karlfried Froelich, *Understanding the New Testament*[2], Introd.

[18] Hort, *op. cit.*, II, p. 283.   [19] *Op. cit.*, p. 104.

[20] J. Rendel Harris, *Sidelights on New Testament Research* (1908), p. 34.

[21] C. S. C. Williams, *Alterations to the Text of the Synoptic Gospels and Acts* (1951), p. 7.

affects the major concept in a passage? Did Paul write θεός in Rom 8 28? This emendation modifies the conception of God who "works for good with those who love him." Should αὐτόν be accepted or rejected in I John 4 19? If accepted, then love characterizes the Christian because of God's initial love for man. By calculating words it is impossible to appreciate the spiritual insights that depend upon the words. We would not contend that even the most theological of variants create a doctrine or cancel out a doctrine, but it is defensible to maintain that variants do "affect" or "alter" or "modify" doctrine. These are the terms used by those who would minimize the importance and the number of variants. Indeed, the only objective and justification of textual criticism is that its emended text should give access to a clearer insight and a deeper faith. Textual variation does not imperil belief in God but it can and does contribute to elucidation of the character of God and of his relation to man. Doctrine consists of a multitude of insights which give meaning to every affirmation. There is far more in Christian doctrine than a brief creedal summation, and the exegesis of variant texts contributes to the enrichment of doctrine.[22]

Many of the denials that textual variation is harmful to the faith are truly denials of allegations never made. We can agree with Hort that "perceptible fraud" is not evident in textual alteration, that "accusations of wilful tampering . . . prove to be groundless," and that dogma has not motivated "deliberate falsification."[23] But these are heinous faults such as we should never allege, and these are not the terms that we should employ. Willful and deliberate, yes. But not tampering, falsification, and fraud. Alteration, yes; but not corruption. Emendation, yes; but not in bad faith. These denials of evil or unethical intention can well be sustained, but such intention is not a proper allegation by the textual critic. He must analyze the text constructively to understand the theological value of any variation, and its place in historical theology.

It is also a false assurance, offered by many, that textual criticism can have no effect upon Christian doctrine. This insistent comfort implies that the text, in any form, deals only with the periphery of doctrine. It also implies a fear that emendation of the text might have evil, but never good, theological consequences. And yet it is impossible for any scholar to provide assurance to any Christian that textual studies will not affect his beliefs, even for the better. Furthermore, the intelligent believer does not ask or want such assurance. His maturity and self-reliance may well be offended by such a surprising counsel as that of Kenyon: "The Christian student can approach the subject

[22] C. S. C. Williams (op. cit., p. 5) has made the judicious comment that whereas "the essence of the Christian gospel remains unaffected by textual variants . . . every such variant . . . has significance for the scholar."

[23] Hort, op. cit., pp. 282 f.

without misgiving, and may follow whithersoever honest inquiry seems to lead him, without thought of doctrinal consequences."[24]

Let us no longer implant the belief that Christian doctrine is unaffected by textual emendation, whether for better or worse. The earliest intentional changes in the text of the Gospel of Mark are still to be seen recorded in the Gospel of Matthew and Luke, revising the sense: for example, the definition of adultery in Mark 10 11 was revised in Matt 19 9 (cf. also 5 32) by the insertion of μὴ ἐπὶ πορνείᾳ. The conception deals with more than sociology and law, and has to do with the unity of husband and wife as creatures and their relationship to the Creator.

It has been demonstrated that Marcion made revision of the text of Luke at many points, for the sake of reinterpretation.[25] For example, at 10 21 he omitted πάτερ and καὶ τῆς γῆς, so that the Lukan address "Father, Lord of heaven and earth" became simply "Lord of heaven." Again in Luke 18 19 he adds πατήρ to distinguish between the Creator and the Christians' Father in the statement: "No one is good except God the Father." Although Origen also adds this word, Epiphanius makes clear the deliberate motivation on the part of Marcion. It is Jerome who explains Marcion's omission in Gal 1 1 of the phrase "and God the Father," so as to read: ". . . through Jesus Christ who raised himself from the dead." In Rom 1 16 Marcion excinded πρῶτον, thus repealing the priority of the Jews: "the gospel is the power of God for salvation . . . to Jew and Greek" — a reading followed even by Tertullian and later preserved in Vaticanus and in the Sahidic version.

So also Origen revised the primitive text at points, although with greater caution and restraint. In John 2 15 there is the frank statement in the episode of the cleansing of the temple that Jesus made for his use a scourge. In Origen's quotation, a delicate ὡς stands before φραγέλλιον, slightly softening the picture of physical violence to "something like a whip." Soon after Origen this little ὡς appears in the gospel text itself as is now newly attested for us in the third-century Bodmer papyri P[75] and P[66]. In John 11 25, Jesus speaks: "I am the resurrection and the life"; but Origen dropped the latter term, recording rather: "I am the resurrection," and his revision is retained by Cyprian and in P[45] and also in the Sinaitic Syriac codex.

In the late second century, Tatian also made revision in the NT text. An example is seen in Mark 1 41, in the response of Jesus to the leper who challenged: "If only you will, you can cleanse me." The text continues: "Jesus was moved with pity (σπλαγχνισθείς)." Tatian re-

---

[24] F. G. Kenyon, *Handbook to the Textual Criticism of the New Testament*[2], p. 7.

[25] J. Rendel Harris especially has marshaled the evidence of dogmatic alterations by Marcion and his followers. See *Sidelights on New Testament Research* (1908), lect. I and appx., pp. 1–35; also "New Points of View in Textual Criticism," *Expositor* Ser. VIII, (1914), pp. 316–34. Later works are: John Knox, *Marcion . . .*, esp. pp. 44–49; and E. C. Blackman, *Marcion and His Influence*.

ports however that "Jesus was moved with anger (ὀργισθείς)," and the exegetical problem here is reflected in the theologically cautious NEB phrasing: "In warm indignation Jesus stretched out his hand, and touched him . . . ." Once again, Tatian introduced a different interpretation at Matt 17 26. When Jesus asks whether it is sons or strangers who pay tax, Simon affirms that strangers do. "Then," replied Jesus, "sons are free"; and (according to Tatian) he further directs, "you too are to pay the collector, as a stranger." This indicates a theological conception different from the original explanation that a Christian should give no offense to an officer of the state.[26]

In the recently acquired gnostic Christian documents of the second century there are instances of textual alteration which revises the meaning in highly important aspects; for example, in the Gospel of Thomas[27] (logion 55) "Whoever does not hate his father and his mother . . .," etc. In the Lukan report of Jesus' words (14 26) there is the intensive sequel: ". . . and his wife and his children . . . and even his very life . . .," but this is omitted in the quotation in the Gospel of Thomas. Again, logion 109 is a paraphrase of Jesus' parable of the treasure hidden in a field (Matt 13 44), with important changes. In Matthew, a nonowner discovers a cache and covers it over until he is able to raise funds to buy the field. In Thomas, the owner himself is not aware of the treasure nor is the son who inherits the field and sells it. When the new owner was plowing he found the buried money, and with his new capital he became a lender. Here in the Gospel of Thomas the simile of seeking the kingdom above all is entirely lost. This particular passage does not help us to re-edit or to interpret the original parable recorded of Jesus, but it does illustrate the freedom with which the account in Matthew was treated from the beginning. Such freedom has been further illustrated by Gärtner[28] and also by Ernest Saunders in his recent discussion of three of the logia.[29] The latter concludes that such usage in the Gospel of Thomas often "assists the NT scholar to determine . . . the earliest form . . . and the meaning of certain NT texts."

Thus far we have recalled only a few of the many examples of textual revision within a century after the recording of the gospel — revision made by fellow evangelists, in patristic interpretations of second-century fathers, and in a pseudonymous gospel of gnostic color. These revisions clearly were made with deliberate intent and, furthermore, they do alter the sense of the text and affect the interpretation. The earliest stage of transmission was marked by an attitude of freedom in theological interpretation. Dogmatic purposes were in view, and constituted the basic attitude in the use of the gospel text.

[26] Illustrations from Tatian are selected from Williams, op. cit.

[27] Cf. R. McL. Wilson, Studies in the Gospel of Thomas, esp. pp. 133–41.

[28] Bertil Gärtner, The Theology of the Gospel of Thomas.

[29] Ernest W. Saunders, "A Trio of Thomas Logia," Biblical Research, 8 (1963), pp. 3–19.

II

A most significant event of our day is the publication of the NT in English bearing the mutual approval of the Protestant National Council of Churches and the Roman Catholic Church.[30] We know it as the RSV with certain revision to meet the approval of Catholic officials. It was wise that the alterations have been set forth in an appendix which is most helpful in interpreting the change that has been made. In view of the long period in which Catholic and Protestant have been served by different English versions, this revised edition throws light upon our major theme.[31] What theological distinction lies in such a text and, further, what theological differences have been resolved in the new RSV CE?

It is clearly recognized that this English translation as originally produced by Protestant American scholarship is basically acceptable to Catholic scholarship as well. The extent of revision in the CE is minimal, amounting to only forty-five changes in the entire NT: thirty-three occurring in the gospels and twelve in the Pauline epistles. Eighteen instances are accounted for by the single change to "brethren" instead of "brothers," all instances intended in the original RSV to refer to blood brothers of Jesus.[32] The singular ἀδελφός is in itself ambiguous, and both the RSV and the CE translate by "brother." In Matt 5 47, where the plural is used to refer to fellow Jews, the RSV is retained in the CE also: "If you salute only your brethren . . . ." The theological distinction in the use of the plural forms "brothers" and "brethren" is clearly implied in the CE note on Matt 12 46, the initial occurrence of ἀδελφοί: "The Greek word or its Semitic equivalent was used for varying degrees of blood relationship."[33] This is indeed a true statement, and beyond it there is the implication that the alteration of the text to "brethren" carries a major theological interpretation, without the necessity to seek any emendation of the Greek original.

Another alteration which affects only the English text is the translation of ἀπολῦσαι in Matt 1 19. Instead of the anachronistic RSV phrase "divorce her," the CE translates (with Knox) "send her away" — which is at once more literal and sociologically better, although in this context

[30] *The New Testament . . . Catholic Edition* (1965).

[31] The Introduction of the CE (p. ix) observes that "for four hundred years . . . Catholics and Protestants have . . . suspected each other's translations of the Bible of having been in some way manipulated in the interests of doctrinal presuppositions . . . not always without foundation."

[32] In this use of "brethren" the CE follows the lead of the late Ronald Knox. The passages are Matt 13 55, Mark 12 31 ff. *et par.*, John 2 12, 7 3 ff., Acts 1 14, I Cor 9 5.

[33] At Matt 12 46 Knox notes: "Since it is impossible for anyone who holds the Catholic tradition to suppose that our Lord had brothers by blood, the most common opinion is that these "brethren" were his cousins; a relationship for which the Jews had no separate name . . . ." No variant for ἀδελφός is found in any NT ms.

there are theological overtones.[34] Once again, in Luke 1 28 the CE
translates (with Knox) κεχαριτωμένη "full of grace," and it relegates
to a footnoted alternative the RSV text "O favored one." Neither of
these forms clearly expresses the theological conception of a unique,
divine attitude toward Mary inherent in the cognate of χάρις and in
the general context.

Besides the alterations in the English text, the CE introduces nineteen
new footnotes. Eleven of these refer to the value of money. Instead of
the RSV note at Matt 18 28 ("The denarius was worth about twenty
cents") the CE explains, "The denarius was a day's wage for a laborer."
Such equations are more realistic, and the change is a welcome one.
Another footnote is found six times in I Corinthians, to the effect that
παρθένος means "virgin." The CE text itself remains unchanged, re-
taining the various RSV translations: "unmarried" (7 25), "a girl" (7 28,
34), "betrothed" (7 36 ff). The theological implication of this consistent
footnote lies under the surface, but finds support at Matt 1 23, where the
RSV does translate the LXX (Isa 7 14) παρθένος with "virgin."

It is of greater importance, however, to comment on those alterations in the CE which involve change in the critical Greek text itself.
There are only sixteen such places, all of them in the gospels. Eight of
these readings are in Luke, of which six are found in the account of the
resurrection. All sixteen variants represent the same textual attitude;
that is, they are restorations of passages which were present in the King
James and Rheims-Douai versions but have been omitted from the RSV.
They are all present in the *Textus Receptus* but were rejected by Westcott-
Hort and Nestle. All sixteen variants require a fine discrimination in
assessing the balance of testimony, and the CE must summon us to a
fresh review of these readings. The formula used in both the RSV and
the CE is similar, but the textual judgment is reversed. The RSV omits
the passage from the text and in the footnote reports its presence in
"some ancient authorities"; whereas the CE returns each passage to
the text (as does Knox), and a footnote reports that "other ancient
authorities omit." Notably these sixteen restorations include the traditional ending of Mark and the Johannine *pericope adulterae*; and both
these textual phenomena are fully and accurately explained in footnotes.
To restore the *pericope adulterae* to its traditional position within the
Gospel of John would appear to be erroneous, especially against the fresh
testimony for omission by both P66 and P75. The CE note on p. 239
acknowledges that the passage "is not by St. John" but is held to be
inspired and canonical. On the other hand, the restoration of the traditional ending of Mark is a wholesome challenge to our habitual assumption that the original Mark is preserved no further than 16 8. Before the
middle of the second century, Justin in his "first" *Apology* (45) writes

[34] Note that in the CE ἀπολελυμένην is translated "a divorced woman" at Matt
5 32, 19 9, and Luke 16 18.

a short passage notably verbatim with Mark 16 20 (οἱ ἀπόστολοι αὐτοῦ
ἐξελθόντες πανταχοῦ ἐκήρυξαν) which looks like a direct quotation.
Similarly, Irenaeus quotes from Mark 16 19.[35] Tatian's text had the long
ending. The earliest translations — Latin, Syriac, and Coptic — all
possess it. Witnesses both for and against the CE restoration as genuine
are early and impressive, and we should consider the question still open
and perhaps "insoluble at present."[36]

Of the remaining fourteen restored readings in the CE, eleven are
"Western noninterpolations."[37] I would consider that all of these were
actually in the original text and that Hort was misled by his principle
that where B and D differed and the latter omitted the reading the
omission represents the true text.[38] Seven of these readings at the end
of Luke are preserved in B and Aleph and now also in P[75]. Such external
testimony outweighs the "noninterpolation" theory, and therefore the
restoration of all eleven passages in the CE gives a superior critical text.

What theological relevance is to be recognized in the textual alteration
of the CE? First, it may be said that few Catholic-*vs.*-Protestant issues
are apparent. Rather, the difference is one of scholarly judgment. Further, there is no consistent theological tendency in the textual revision.[39]
Passages restored to the text on the basis of Greek manuscript support
are, for example: ". . . and he who marries a divorced woman commits
adultery" (Matt 19 9); "And he who falls on this stone will be broken to
pieces; but when it falls on anyone, it will crush him" (21 44).

Shorter restorations are: the word "righteous" in Pilate's disavowal
of "this righteous man's blood" (Matt 27 24); the words "and fasting"
where Jesus speaks of effective exorcism "by prayer and fasting" (Mark
9 29); the words "and pray" in Jesus' instruction "take heed, watch and
pray" (Mark 13 33). The "second cup" passage in Luke 22 19b–20 is restored, a "Western noninterpolation" now attested also by P[75] about a
century after the composition of the gospel and surely a part of the
original text despite the RSV omission.

There are two other restorations in the CE which, on the other hand,
probably were interpolations into the original text. The first is the
phrase in Mark 10 24: "for those who trust in riches." It is a true interpretation of the context but alters the sense with the result that
Jesus makes a general observation, "How hard it is to enter the kingdom
of God." With the added phrase, there is repetition of the preceding
verse. The other probably ill-advised restoration is at Luke 8 43, of the

[35] Irenaeus, *adv. Haer.* iii, 10,6.

[36] This judgment was expressed also by F. C. Grant in *IntB, in loco.*

[37] Matt 19 9, 21 44, 27 24; Mark 13 33; Luke 22 19b–20, 24 6, 12, 36, 40, 51, 52.

[38] Cf. Hort, *op. cit.*, pp. 175 f.; and B. M. Metzger, *The Text of the New Testament*,
p. 134.

[39] For example, one does not find the translation "penance" and "do penance" as
in the Douai version: Matt 3 2, 8, 11; Mark 1 4, 6 12; Luke 3 8, 13 3, 5, 15 7, 16 30, 24 27,
where the RSV has "repentance" and "repent."

woman who "spent all her living upon physicians." That the original text did not contain this is now attested by P⁷⁵, in addition to B (D) syˢ (sa) arm; as against the testimony of ℵΘ syᶜ.

The most impressive alteration in the CE which involves the Greek critical text is the series of six readings in the account of the resurrection in Luke (24 6, 12, 36, 40, 51, 52). The passages added are:

6   ... he is not here, but has risen ....

12   Peter rose and ran to the tomb; stooping and looking in, he saw the linen cloths by themselves; and he went home wondering at what had happened.

36   ... and said to them, "Peace to you."

40   And when he had said this, he showed them his hands and his feet.

51–52   ... and was carried up into heaven. And they worshiped him, and ....

These are all valid scholarly alterations, in which no theological tendency is to be found. Analysis, therefore, of the textual difference between the Protestant RSV and the CE indicates that theological distinction today does not rest upon these modern versions of the NT. We are aware, however, that just as the Protestant has moved from Erasmus to Nestle so the Roman Catholic has changed from Douai to the RSV CE. In both cases, substantial theological change has come about and yet such change is reflected more in exegesis than in textual criticism itself. Both of these statements are illustrated in the "Explanatory Notes" of the CE (Appx. I, pp. 235–46). On Matt 16 19: "Peter has the key to the gates of the city of God. This power is exercised through the church ...." On Matt 19 11–12: "Jesus means that a life of continence is to be chosen only by those who are called to it for the sake of the Kingdom of God." As for the text of the CE, it has found little to alter in the RSV and that little is chiefly scholarly gain.

III

Another major undertaking currently in progress is the International Greek New Testament Project, whose objective is the publication of a new *apparatus criticus*, more adequate for our time than the Tischendorf work of 1869–72.[40] In the preparation of the initial volume, on the Gospel of Luke, the texts of approximately 300 MSS have been collated completely, and this is the most massive attack ever made upon the problem of textual variation. Consequently, it is possible now to estimate more accurately the scope and character of the textual condition of the

---

[40] A description of the project was given in the *Crozer Quarterly* of 1950 (pp. 301–08), by M. M. Parvis. It is not to be confused with a later proposal of the ABS to publish a Greek text with selected variants, especially for missionary translation. The ABS committee overlaps in personnel with the IGNT· executive committee, although the ABS plan is short-term and limited in scope.

Greek NT. The 300 MSS collated include all extant papyri and most uncial copies, as well as Byzantine texts representing known families and recensions, and in addition numbers of early Byzantine copies whose text remains unclassified.

The master file for the Gospel of Luke contains, it is estimated, about 25,000 variants of all sorts. Combing through such a file to select variants of substantial alteration in the text is like extracting a valuable metal from an ore mass, and the yield is about 2 per cent, much higher than the earlier estimates of Hort, Ezra Abbot, and others. But the effect upon exegesis is hardly to be measured by such statistics, when we consider the theological implication of a single letter as in εὐδοκίας of Luke 2 14; or the addition of θεόν in 2 12, where Gregory Thaumaturgus speaks of the "swaddled God"; or the omission of a full verse at Luke 23 34, thus losing the prayer of Jesus: "Father, forgive them, for they know not what they do." How shall one compute such various alterations? In view of the availability of these comprehensive data on the Gospel of Luke, it will be more representative to consider textual alteration in this gospel. We have culled out about 500 variants of more substantial character, from which again to select representative illustration. Rather than to point out a series of single variants, it would seem to be more meaningful to consider longer passages which contain clusters of textual alterations, albeit from different times and sources.

Take, for example, the annunciation in Luke 1 26–35. "In the sixth month, the angel Gabriel was sent from God to a city of Galilee"; although Sinaiticus *et al.* state that this city was in Judea, and Bezae *et al.* omit to name Nazareth in particular. In some manuscripts the person of the angel is transformed into a voice only, which declares "the Lord is with you" (apparently the original text). Attested in the fifth century (ACD) is, however, an extension of this angelic message: "blessed are you among women." And from the eighth century (L) we learn that the angel further pronounced: "blessed is the fruit of your womb."[41] The incredulity of Mary, since she had no husband, is excluded from some fifth-century copies; whereas other copies of the same date substitute her acquiescent reply: "Lo, the servant of the Lord; so be it as you say." Other changes are to be seen in the angel's words: ". . . the child to be born will be called holy"; or, according to some manuscripts: "the holy one of God"; or, again, simply: ". . . shall be called pure."

Such freedom of treatment is quite incongruous with a traditional conception of Scripture. With many of the variant forms, it is easy to recognize primary and secondary text, and yet all the variant forms become part of the narrative in the history of the church. It is the total narrative with all its tangents that constitutes the theological interpretation of the annunciation.

[41] Both additions to the angel's message in 1 28 were drawn from Elizabeth's exclamation in 1 42.

Let us look now at the birth story in Luke 2 1–7. "In those days a decree went out from Caesar Augustus." An Old Latin MS of the fifth century (e) omits the explanation "that all the world should be enrolled." The Protevangelion reports instead that the residents of Bethlehem must register, whereas Bezae reports the residents of Jerusalem, and Codex Boreel the residents of Judea. Continuing the account, everybody went to enroll, each to his own πόλις; a statement that historians have debated over. Codex Bezae and the Sin. Syr. speak rather of a man's πατρίς; Codex Ephrem Syrus, of his χῶρα; and an Old Latin MS (gat), of his *regionem*. So Joseph went up to Bethlehem, but some Byzantine MSS omit the explanation that "he was of the house and lineage of David," while still others include both Joseph and Mary in this lineage (sy[s] *et al.*). The Old Latin and Old Syriac versions here call Mary his wife rather than his bethrothed. The child was born, and she wrapped him, say some late MSS, "in pieces of the Lord's garments." The "manger" becomes in Epiphanius "a cave." We make no effort here to reconstruct an original form of the event. Least of all does it seem feasible to recover what is valid as historical. The entire story breathes of *traditio theologica* in which numerous theologians have had a hand to produce the composite form.

The account of homage paid to the infant Jesus is found in Luke 2 16–22. The shepherds "went hurrying": cf. the sixth-century reading (Ξ) "went believing." "They found Mary and Joseph and the infant": but some Byzantine MSS drop Joseph out of this picture. "And when the time for their purification arrived . . .": yet here D and the Old Latin and Old Syriac all read "his purification," and one MS refers to "her purification," while Irenaeus and others omit the pronoun completely. And Irenaeus omits also the explanatory phrase "in accordance with the Law of Moses."

In the presentation in the temple (Luke 2 33–35) we read: "His father and his mother marveled at what was said." This reading obviously has the strongest attestation and appears in our critical texts. But Origen protests that Joseph is not properly called father, and accordingly a second-century variant (itAΘ) would remove the earthly father and refers instead to "Joseph and his mother." On the other hand, some Byzantine scribes simply wrote "his parents." In the statement of Simeon that follows, some manuscripts omit the prediction: "this child is set for the fall and rising of many in Israel." Retained in other manuscripts, it is altered to refer to "many nations" (Or *et al.*) and to speak of the rising (ἀνάστασις) or "resurrection of the dead" (Cyr). "The thoughts of many hearts" to be revealed are interpreted in some manuscripts as "the evil thoughts" to be exposed (ℵ* *et al.*).

Let us look at one more passage, the confession at Caesarea Philippi: "It happened that as he was praying alone the disciples were with him" (Luke 9 18–23). Here Codex Bezae says nothing of praying, and Vaticanus reports that the disciples rather came up to join him. Jesus asks them: "Who do the people identify as the Son of man?" at least, that is the record in Justin's *Dialogue*. When the direct question is put to the disciples, Peter's response is variously reported: "the Messiah" (sy Jus Or); "God's Messiah" (majority); "Messiah God" (Cop); "Messiah, Son of God" (D e); "Messiah, Son of man"; "Son of the Living God" (Or); or simply "Son of God" (Or). A patristic omission is the clause: "rejected by elders, chief priests, and scribes." It is D it Mcion that omit "and be raised on the third day," whereas other witnesses read "on the third day" or "after three days." Bezae omits "let him take up his cross daily," and numerous others omit the term "daily"; but in some witnesses Jesus invites, "Follow me daily" (a most attractive variant homiletically).

So our inquiry could be greatly extended, passage by passage, to demonstrate the freedom of alteration and interpretation, the substantial portion of the text involved in variation, and the theological quality of many textual alterations. Instead of spot readings in eclectic choice, we have reviewed the larger unit in more comprehensive variation and so have shown the doctrinal play within an episode. Extended analysis could demonstrate the theological quality of each individual witness and distinguish the threads woven into the larger pattern. It is particularly the variation from the common text which provides the clue to distinctive doctrinal tendency, in a manuscript, in a version, in a father, or in a recension.[42]

If we should now concentrate upon one MS, Papyrus 75, we find further evidence that variation in the text and alteration in the sense appeared early. Since P[75] adds a second copy of the Gospel of John from the third century, it is now possible to make direct comparison with P[66].[43] More than a thousand differences between the two manuscript copies are found, and about a hundred of these are of greater importance. A few readings in P[75] will illustrate. In John 4 14, because of the simple change from ἀλλά to ἄλλο, we get the striking saying of Jesus: "Other water I shall give him . . . ." In 6 5, Jesus asks, not "Where can we buy bread?" to feed the multitude but rather, "Where can they buy bread?" In 6 69 Peter's declaration, "You are God's holy one," omits the identification "Messiah." In 8 57, the Jews do not query, "Have you seen Abraham?" but rather, "Has Abraham seen you?" In 9 17 the Jews ask the formerly blind man, not "What do you say about him?" but, "What do you say about yourself?" In 12 8 Jesus speaks of the ever-present poor but does not say, "You do not always have me." Such alterations are early, and many, and are

---

[42] Such a study has been made of Codex Bezae by Eldon Jay Epp (Harvard Ph.D.): "Theological Tendency in the Textual Variants of Codex Bezae . . ." (1961).

[43] Kenneth W. Clark, "The Text of the Gospel of John in Third-Century Egypt," *NT*, 5 (1962), pp. 17–24. See pp. 157ff. of this volume.

neither errors nor heresy. Many of them are mild changes, but they all form a cumulative exegetical mood.

Now returning to the Gospel of Luke in P⁷⁵: we have selected about 125 substantial variants out of about 1,500 differences from the *TR*. A few of these will illustrate more important alterations of text and some will show a theological interest. In Luke 11 11 there appears a unique reading heretofore unreported: "If a son should ask his father for bodily strength (ἰσχύν instead of ἰχθύν), the father will not give him a serpent in place of a fish." In the story of the Prodigal Son (15 24) another unique reading appears. The usual translation has been "They began to make merry," which suggests a rousing party. But P⁷⁵ has the singular ἤρξατο instead of the plural, and the result seems very different as the father exults: " 'My son was dead and has come alive, he was lost and then was found'; and the father became joyous." Still another unique reading is found in 17 14, after the ten lepers cry, "Have mercy upon us." At this point the scribe of P⁷⁵ borrows from Matt 8 3 the reply of Jesus: "I will. Be cleansed, and immediately they were cleansed."

In the account of the arrest of Jesus, Luke 22 62–23 23, the passage shows several textual choices, in which P⁷⁵ agrees with our present critical text. The papyrus includes the statement: "Judas went out and wept bitterly," and also that his captors "beat Jesus." These statements are omitted in the Old Latin version and in early uncials 0171 and D. The papyrus, however, omits the statements: "They struck him in the face"; "It was required to release one man to them at festival time"; and the attribution to the high priests of the outcry for crucifixion. One more example is also a unique reading (24 26): "Was it not necessary that the Christ should suffer these things and enter into his kingdom?" The last word is the unique term, and it was later altered by a corrector to the term now usual to us: his "glory." In general, P⁷⁵ tends to support our current critical text, and yet the papyrus vividly portrays a fluid state of the text at about A. D. 200. Such scribal freedom suggests that the gospel text was little more stable than an oral tradition, and that we may be pursuing the retreating mirage of the "original text."

IV

We would finally conclude that the selective data reviewed above form a consistent picture of theological relevance within the area of textual variation. The amount of textual change that involves theological alteration is a small proportion but it is a nugget of essential importance for interpretation. It is this smaller portion for which textual criticism must search especially. In the course of transmission thousands of textual alterations have appeared in the legitimate lineage of theological interpretation, and all of these must be taken into account in exegesis and doctrinal exposition.

It is of particular interest to realize that many textual alterations first
appeared in Byzantine copies of the NT. It has been widely held and
often repeated that the important alteration of text occurred before
A. D. 200, but this view is considerably modified by the panoramic research of the IGNT Project. It is true that every additional copy collated
yields new readings of exegetical consequence.[44]

We may well begin to ask if there really was a stable text at the
beginning. We talk of recovering the original text, and of course every
document had such a text. But the earliest witnesses to NT text even
from the first century already show such variety and freedom that we
may well wonder if the text remained stable long enough to hold a
priority. Great progress has been achieved in recovering an early form of
text, but it may be doubted that there is evidence of one original text
to be recovered.

In the past we have been accustomed to treat individual readings in
isolation, balancing the testimony pertaining to any reading by itself
apart. But there is much to be said for a different method as well, of
treating a longer passage in a full episode to observe the consistency and
play of the witnesses. The textual critic must recognize the fluidity and
theological vitality in Scriptural accounts, and move on from isolated
words to the broader context. The scrutiny of manuscript support for a
word here and a word there should be overarched by the consistent performance and interpretation of an entire parable or discourse. Furthermore, our attention to original text must not eclipse the valuable theological insight in textual deviation early and late.

The recognition that a textual critic must be also historian and
theologian has obvious corollaries. There must be co-ordination between
all three: the investigation of textual data, the study of theological
history, and research in ecclesiastical history. This threefold alliance is
advantageous, even essential, to each field of research, as it serves to
extend and to inform each specialization with greater comprehension and
refinement. Collaboration of the three fields would make more comprehensive the scholarship of each.

Many new vistas of research await such joint exploration. The
NT text and the theology of each church father, of each regional text such
as fam. 13, or of each major recension such as the Caesarean text — especially where departures from the common text are notable. In any case,
we should not fear but rather should welcome the light that may be cast
by textual criticism upon the history, upon the theology, and indeed upon
the current faith of scholar and layman alike.

---

[44] E. g., Luke 1 28, 34, 2 1, 4, 7 *bis*, 16, 36 (Duke MS 5 = Greg. 2612), etc.

Today's Problems with the Critical Text
of the New Testament

In the preface of an edition of the Greek New Testament we read the editor's assurance: "You now have the text which is accepted by all." This well-known statement may be recognized at once as belonging not to a recent critical edition but to one printed three centuries ago, the Elzevir of 1633. That Latin phrase yielded the term *textus receptus*, used ever since of the Greek New Testament text employed in Western Europe for several centuries. In the first Elzevir edition (1624) the term used was *textus acceptus*. The awkward term "Received Text" is a poor translation and might better be replaced by the term "Accepted Text."

The Elzevir brothers have repeatedly been charged with making a presumptuous and erroneous claim, but it must be acknowledged that they wrote only the truth. Comparison of the printed editions beginning with Erasmus and for three centuries thereafter reveals that scores of editors continued to produce the same text with but slight alteration. Furthermore, it is often overlooked that even prior to the printed editions thousands of manuscript copies had been reproducing the same basic text throughout the Byzantine centuries. The editors were truly correct in describing their product as a *textus receptus*, since it was then all but universal among publishers and scholars. It is well known among us that the Era of the Received Text lasted until mid-nineteenth century.

The threat to the long established *textus receptus* began to cast a long shadow even as the Elzevirs coined their term, but the text in common use did not easily yield up its accustomed prestige. The contest was long and often bitter before the text accepted by all was supplanted by what we call today the critical text. The Oxford Press ended its long series of printings of the traditional *Textus Receptus* only sixty years ago. We of the twentieth century are the first in 1500 years of Christian history, i.e., since the fifth century, to possess the critical text which is in general use today. Indeed we are inclined to feel highly gratified that we have recovered this text, through discovery and scholarly processes. It is a common opinion that we now possess the true text, trustworthy for interpretation. This opinion is illustrated in a new book by Fred L. Fisher entitled *How to Interpret the New Testament*: ". . . the text that is now accepted is open to question in very few places . . . of minor significance."[1]

This recapitulation from the history of criticism brings us to the first of today's problems to be noted here. It is this: that the Westcott-Hort text has become today our *textus receptus*. We have been freed from the one only to become captivated by the other. The persistence of the Byzantine text has been repeated in our own rigid adherence to Westcott-Hort. The psychological chains so recently broken from our fathers have again been forged upon us, even more strongly. Whereas our textual fathers, such as John Mill and Richard Bentley, actively debated the character of the text in their day, our generation of theologians finds easy contentment with our current *textus receptus*.

Even the textual specialist finds it difficult to break the habit of evaluating every witness by the norm of this current *textus receptus*. His mind may have rejected the Westcott-Hort term "neutral," but his technical procedure still reflects the general acceptance of the text. A basic problem today is the technical and psychological factor that the Westcott-Hort text has become our *textus receptus*.

Perhaps someone will remonstrate that there have been many critical texts produced since 1881, which is true. Some-

---

[1] Cf. J. R. Harris, *Four Lectures on the Western Text* (London: C. J. Clay and Sons, 1894), who warned against the "cult" of Westcott-Hort.

one will adduce the Nestle series of twenty-five editions since the beginning of this century. With each new edition we are prone to hasten to the bookstore to obtain the latest text. Our problem lies here, that few scholars are aware that the latest Nestle is a close copy of the 1881 text, and that edition succeeds edition with little or no textual change. All the critical editions since 1881 are basically the same as Westcott-Hort. All are founded on the same Egyptian recension, and generally reflect the same assumptions of transmission.

In order to test this assertion as a hypothesis, eight Duke students have recently collaborated in the collation of numerous critical texts against Westcott-Hort, in two sample passages (Mark 11 and John 12). These passages were chosen because the chances of alteration would seem the greater in the light of researches on the Caesarean text and on recent papyrus acquisitions.

This group has observed that in John 12 Westcott-Hort shows between twenty and thirty changes from the earlier texts of Lachmann and Buttmann, other than orthographic details. But in the many editions after Westcott-Hort only slight alteration has taken place. For example, the British and Foreign Bible Society edition of 1958 (which is the equivalent of the Nestle 1957[23] edition) shows in John 12 only two slight differences from Westcott-Hort. In 12:30 ἰησοῦς is transposed with καὶ εἶπεν and in 12:32 ἐάν replaces ἄν; and in both instances all or nearly all editions agree in this departure from Westcott-Hort. Again, take the Tasker edition which purports to be the *New English Bible* base. In John 12 it departs from Westcott-Hort four times. In 12:9 and 12:21 this edition spells two second aorist forms with ον rather than αν. The two other changes from Westcott-Hort are the same two cited above in the BFBS text. All four changes have nearly unanimous agreement in other editions. It is apparent that none of these formal changes can be reflected in the NEB translation. A final example may be seen in the 1966 American Bible Society edition, which is avowedly based on Westcott-Hort and expressly altered wherever the committee determined. In John 12 there are five alterations made, including three of the four just mentioned. Another is the addition of the article in ὁ ἰησοῦς (12:12) and the other is the transposed σὺ λέγεις in 12:34. Can there be any doubt that these editions are a near replica of Westcott-Hort? They are typical of the many editions that have appeared. Since 1881 twenty-five editors have issued about seventy-five editions of the Greek New Testament. The collation of these many "critical" texts consistently exposes the fact that each of them is basically a repetition of the Westcott-Hort text of which we may be permitted to declare with truth: "You now have the text which is accepted by all." Indeed, we have continued for eighty-five years to live in the era of Westcott-Hort, our *textus receptus.*

Psychologically it is now difficult to approach the textual problem with free and independent mind. Where textual emendations are at issue we have literally moved in frequent circle, with alternating favor between two choices. Eclectic experimentation and sporadic emendation constitute the order of our day. Critical alteration in the frequent editions has been slight and amounts only to intermittent patches. The main fabric is still that of Westcott-Hort. A recent expression of Colwell's, though relating to a different factor, is truly applicable here also: "Hort has put . . . blinders on our eyes." However great the attainment in the Westcott-Hort text, the further progress we desiderate can be accomplished only when our psychological bonds are broken. Herein lies today's foremost problem with the critical text of the New Testament.

Another of today's problems with the critical text may be brought to attention by quoting the 1633 Elzevir preface further: ". . . in which text we present no alteration or corruption." This claim we have been unwilling to grant, and yet we are faced with it once again today in the Westcott-Hort claim of textual neutrality. They maintained that "the books of the New Testament as preserved in extant documents assuredly speak to us in every important respect in language identical with that in which they spoke to those for whom they were originally written."[2] They exalted the text of Vaticanus because "neither of the early streams [Western and Alexandrian] of innovation has touched it to any appreciable extent."[3] We realize that theirs is a qualified claim to originality for the text that is now our *textus receptus*, and yet we tend to overlook their caution in our own habit of reliance upon the text now accepted by all.

Kilpatrick describes our common assumption, that "the Neutral text alone preserved . . . something like its original purity."[4] At the same time we are all aware that several distinctive recensions circulated in the early church whose relationships were really not as Westcott-Hort described them. Not only is it true that the modern *textus receptus* is not always and everywhere original, but it is further true that we cannot yet explain the origin and the status of any of the earliest recensions. We recognize recensions that existed but we are yet unable to trace a course of transmission among them. The textual history that the Westcott-Hort text represents is no longer tenable in the light of newer discoveries and fuller textual analysis. In the effort to construct a congruent history, our failure suggests that we have lost the way, that we have reached a dead end, and that only a new and different insight will enable us to break through. An acceptable theory of recensional relationships must recognize the true status of each recension. Kilpatrick has argued for the originality of certain "Syrian" readings. Tasker has again cautioned that the "Western" text is "much more valuable than Westcott and Hort supposed." But such contentions are based upon the evidence of a few individual readings only. We have not yet been able to discover the pattern wherein the recognizable recensions were woven in the life of the

[2] B. F. Westcott and F. J. Hort, *The New Testament in the Original Greek: Introduction*, 2nd ed. (London: Macmillan and Co., 1907), p. 284.

[3] Westcott and Hort, *New Testament*, p. 150.

[4] G. D. Kilpatrick, "The Greek New Testament Text of Today and the *Textus Receptus*," in *The New Testament in Historical and Contemporary Perspective: Essays in Memory of G. H. C. Macgregor*, ed. H. Anderson and W. Barclay (Oxford: B. Blackwell, 1965), p. 189.

church. The true critical text must be found to be in conformity with the correct account of transmission. This now appears as one of today's chief problems.

There has seldom if ever been a time when more illuminating manuscript resources have come into the hands of textual critics than in our own day. We do recall that fifth-century Alexandrinus reached London a few years after the King James Bible appeared. A century ago fourth-century Sinaiticus emerged from monastic obscurity. But the critic today has for the first time extensive third-century papyrus texts. The Beatty Library in Dublin thirty-five years ago acquired the notable codex of the Pauline Corpus, and portions of the Four Gospels and the Acts, and one-third of the Apocalypse. The Bodmer Library in Geneva recently acquired two copies of John and one of Luke and a fragment of the General Epistles.

Initial examination of these earliest witnesses has shown primarily text in harmony with Westcott-Hort. But more detailed analysis propounds a most difficult problem. These early Egyptian copies do not agree with one another. There is sometimes agreement with Vaticanus, again a distinctive agreement with Sinaiticus, again they attest the Caesarean recension, and yet again some fragments favor Bezae.

What then shall we say of the testimony of these newest and earliest witnesses? They come to light with joyous announcement and high expectation, only to reveal that they further complicate where we hope for clarification. Recensional variety is now seen to have originated as early as A.D. 200. Although we are now enabled to move earlier, the picture does not clear. We have acquired new evidence that textual bifurcations occurred in the earliest stage of transmission. What is more, it is now clear that variant recensions originated *prior* to Hesychius and Lucian. The textual history postulated for the *textus receptus* which we now trust has been exploded. As if this were not enough, we are forced also to admit that the earliest Egyptian text itself was not homogeneous. What now shall we say about our modern *textus receptus?* What solution can be found to this new problem of our day?

Another problem has been newly created by this recent acquisition of extensive third-century papyrus texts, which are both blessing and bane to the critic's labors. More than two centuries ago, John Albert Bengel first classified the manuscripts accessible then. His was a simple twofold division into Asiatic, Byzantine copies of the later centuries, and the more ancient African witnesses consisting of the Old Latin version and Codex Alexandrinus — the last manuscript so named because of its known derivation (and perhaps its origin) in Alexandria itself. Johann Salomo Semler in 1767 developed a threefold classification by further dividing Bengel's ancient African witness into the Western Latin with Codex Bezae, and the Eastern Greek of codices ABCL and Origen which latter he assigned particularly to Alexandria. Finally, in Westcott-Hort's picture this last classification was again divided into the Neutral and the Alexandrian types. Such is the critical background when P^{66} and P^{75} appear in our day as witnesses from Upper Egypt in the early third century. They now provide evidence that the "Egyptian" text of Vaticanus and Sinaiticus was already in use in the distant provincial South no later than A.D. 200, far from the great city of Alexandria. A tendency to center upon Alexandria when discussing cultural origins in Egypt is thus largely nullified. What is more, the Egyptian origin of the new papyri, whose texts bear resemblance to our earliest uncial codices, influences the long debate as to the provenance of the Codices Sinaiticus and Vaticanus. An Egyptian origin becomes the more probable (as long ago urged by Kenyon and Lake), and this too is an important factor in the effort to reconstruct the account of textual transmission.

A problem commonly unrecognized lies in the fact that even now we have recovered no copy of New Testament text prior to the fifth century, except for Egyptian Christianity. Successive discoveries of superior witnesses have created an impression that overreaches the facts. All the manuscripts so far recovered, including the most sensational of recent discoveries, may enable us now to recover no more than the early text in Egypt, whether in Alexandria or in southern communities. No source exists in modern libraries to supply direct knowledge of regional texts elsewhere prior to the fifth century. Since it is not yet possible to recover primitive texts elsewhere than Egypt, we are unable for the first stage of the New Testament text to make geographical comparison, and therefore we cannot discern transmissional relationships between different regions.

We can recognize recensions in fifth-century manuscripts and later in other Christian centers; but it is still a problem in our day that we lack any copies of regional recensions, although there is reason to believe that such variety of text did exist. That we now possess no textual witnesses outside of Egypt prior to the fifth century is completely true for the Greek text. However, it is necessary to acknowledge a slight exception to the general statement, if we should refer to versional witnesses. Two of our copies of Gospel text in the Old Latin may have been written in the latter part of the fourth century: Codex Bobbiensis produced in North Africa, and Codex Vercellensis in Northern Italy; both attest the existence of the Western text prior to Codex Bezae. And from within Egypt a few copies of Coptic text survive from the fourth century; chiefly the Bodmer bohairic papyrus of John, the Michigan sahidic papyrus of John, and a subachmimic papyrus of John published by Sir Herbert Thompson. All of these versional witnesses further affirm that regional recensions existed early and that within the confines of the Nile Valley Christian communities early introduced variety in the text. Although it is a problem that all our earliest copies of New Testament text were produced solely in Egypt, it is yet a prior problem to clarify for Egypt alone the history of the church and the transmission of the text in use there in the earliest centuries.

Still a further oversight has been common; the failure to realize that for much of the New Testament text it is still true that we rest where Westcott-Hort did eighty-five years ago, on the great Codices Vaticanus and Sinaiticus. Despite the exciting discoveries of ancient papyri, a large portion of the New Testament text has not yet been recovered from earlier generations. In the last hundred years there have come to light about forty New Testament papyri written earlier than fourth-century א, B, and W. In these papyri twenty-one New Testament books are represented. The most extensive and best preserved of these are the Bodmer papyri (P⁶⁶ and P⁷⁵) containing two copies of John and one of Luke, all largely preserved. The Beatty papyri of Gospels, Acts, Paul, and Revelation are fragmentary but yet extensive, especially for Paul. But beyond these five papyri, the rest are mutilated and only fragmentary. Actually, there is very little overlapping of text except for the Gospel of John. Although all these papyri come from Egypt, or close by, they yield an assortment of readings difficult to classify and so complicate our problem of recovering the text of the Egyptian Church. Surely these witnesses to the text must some day give direction to textual research, but for the present they present to our limited view conflicting and complicating testimony. But it is quite true that the early papyri offer little in the text of Matthew and Mark, and of Acts and the Catholic Epistles. Therefore for portions of these books and other areas of the New Testament, we are entirely lacking early witness. We possess no papyrus text of the Pastoral and the Johannine Epistles prior to the fourth century.

Another current problem with the critical text today is that emendation has been eclectic and quite sporadic and unsystematic. Since the appearance of Westcott-Hort nothing but eclectic revision has been introduced into any critical edition. Insofar as the original effort continues for the reconstruction of the original text, the method employed has been eclectic exclusively. In contrast to this modern condition, we may note, the course of past criticism has included certain notable breakthroughs, creative innovations. For example, when manuscript gave way to press in 1516 a new comparative method was employed to improve the text by comparing two or more variant copies and making a deliberate selection of the trusted reading. Successive editors enlarged the scope of comparison, not only between an increasing number of copies but even between regional witnesses, and they came to place a greater reliance upon the latter technique (so Griesbach). The introduction of this comparative method reduced the centrifugal factor that was inherent in scribal labors, and countered it with a centripetal influence of the editor-printer. The logic of this method led naturally to still another notable insight and novel method; namely, to weigh the character of each witness. And the climax of this principle was the breakthrough achieved in Lachmann's novel text. Of course, the next high point was attained when Westcott and Hort applied the historical method to produce an orderly account of recensional relationships. Each breakthrough in textual revision has been the result of a new insight that has given rise to a novel method productive of a major change. There has been no such breakthrough since 1881; and this is true in spite of the most illuminating discoveries such as the Caesarean text and family groups and even substantial third-century papyrus copies.

We live in a generation of eclectic criticism, and necessarily so. We have not found emancipation from this limited treatment of the text because we do not yet possess the key to unlock the meaning of our rich resources. We feel the want of an insight that would dictate a different procedure and produce a different result. Therefore we are constrained at present to move in a narrow range of sporadic and unsystematic retouching of the text. The text now received by all has been but slightly and uncertainly patched. Eclecticism has great value but as a method it must be acknowledged to be a concession to the limitations of our time. We cannot approve eclectic emendation as a permanent technique of criticism because it is by its very nature tentative.

Eclectic repair has been subjective and tendentious. In repeating such an allegation we mean to be descriptive rather than disparaging, but it is necessary to recognize the truth about our method today. Colwell recently observed that we have "appreciated the internal evidence of readings" but have mistakenly assumed that we avoid the subjective whenever our conjectures are supported by manuscript testimony. A disciplined subjectivity is a legitimate critical instrument, especially when we do acknowledge our use of it. Nevertheless, it should be recognized that it can never represent the final judgment. Eclectic emendation is always a tentative proposal, subject to weightier overarching evidence whenever such evidence can be discerned. Because of its subjective character, eclectic emendation cannot escape bias, however inadvertent. When one examines a limited textual unit such as a single word or a short phrase apart from the broad context, the selection between variant choices depends upon short-range reasons and therefore partial judgment must be supplemented by private inclination.

If this is the true condition of our textual criticism today, then it is wise to conclude that the best New Testament text at present is indeed our current *textus receptus* plus the critical apparatus. To the degree that the true text still remains unresolved, to that extent we are persuaded to utilize the *apparatus criticus* as an integral part of the text. To the extent that textual judgment awaits resolution, the individual theologian is required to assume personal responsibility for at least a tentative interpretation.

We have now made our way to a final problem of our day. We require a critical history of transmission. The critics of Westcott-Hort's construction have been many, and let it be said that one cannot separate Westcott from Hort. Both were responsible for the text; the text and textual history are one, and both editors must subscribe to the fundamental theory of transmission on which the text is erected. In the foregoing review of current problems we have here recalled some of the evidence that the Westcott-Hort explanation of transmission is untenable, even while it serves as foundation for our *textus receptus*. The traditional complaint is strongly supported by new and additional sources. It is often remarked that the Westcott-Hort text carries us back only to the fourth century. Now we do possess extensive third-century texts which first encouraged the hope that a fresh critical insight might appear. But this hope diminishes when it is revealed that these papyrus texts merely demonstrate the earlier existence of such texts as Vaticanus and Sinaiticus, and our problem is merely moved a century earlier. We still cannot perceive the origins and the influences and the relationships of the variant texts in use as early as A.D. 200. Possibly the best approach to this problem might be through the text of the Gospel of John, for which we do possess more abundant and more varied early witnesses.

A different basis for renewed hope may here be suggested. It is possible that the key we require is to be found in patristic study, especially of the earliest period. Long ago R. M. Grant decried that the necessary collaboration in textual and patristic studies has failed us, in "disintegrative specialization," but we need not be resigned to this condition. Psychologically, it is necessary first to dismantle the Westcott-Hort structure, to abandon the course wherein we have encountered a barrier. Further, we might gain by removing the traditional textual labels that prejudice and confine exploration.

Since our earliest manuscripts, along with the Alexandrian Fathers, have thrown light especially upon textual forms in Egypt, we need to examine particularly the Fathers *outside Egypt*. And as a final suggestion, attention might be turned to the travels of the Fathers: Clement, from Southern Italy to Alexandria; Origen, from Alexandria to Caesarea; Marcion, from Pontus to Rome; Justin Martyr, from Samaria to Rome; Irenaeus, from Ephesus to Rome and to Lyon, and so on. Certainly it is not suggested here that the barrier before us will yield at once to these devices, for in that case a solution must ensue herewith. It is, however, suggested that some such approach, some new angle, some novel experiment must be tried if we would in our time achieve a breakthrough to cast light upon the history of transmission. This is the fundamental need before we may move on to a thorough and systematic renovation of the critical text.

The remedy we need can come only through a better diagnosis. The true diagnosis will of necessity be a new and different one. Such diagnosis should be promoted through the reference work projected by the International Greek New Testament Project. Upon a successful diagnosis depend all the issues of debate which have been discussed above. Perhaps apology should be offered for our occasional review of familiar knowledge, but where the weaving is left unfinished old threads must be picked up. We have sought directions for the completion of the pattern in this conspectus of today's problems.

THE MAKING OF THE TWENTIETH CENTURY NEW TESTAMENT [1]

It is you who are the Salt of the earth ; but, if the salt should lose its strength, what will you use to restore its saltness ? It is no longer good for anything, but is thrown away, and trampled underfoot.

It is you who are the Light of the world. A town that stands on a hill cannot be hidden. Men do not light a lamp and put it under the corn-measure, but on the lamp-stand, where it gives light to every one in the house. Let your light so shine before the eyes of your fellow-men, that, seeing your good actions, they may praise your Father who is in Heaven.

Do not think that I have come to do away with the Law or the Prophets ; I have not come to do away with them, but to complete them. For I tell you, until the heavens and the earth disappear, not even the smallest letter, nor one stroke of a letter, shall disappear from the Law until all is done.

Matthew v. 13-18. (*The Twentieth Century New Testament.*)

SINCE the publication of the first edition of the King James Bible in 1611, the New Testament has been re-translated, in whole or in part, more than 300 times. During the last fifty years, translation has been especially active and has yielded about 100 different versions, of which 45 include the New Testament or the entire Bible. Each translator has had his special purpose, often reflected in the form of his title. For example :

1895   Ferrar Fenton : *The New Testament in Modern English.*
1897   Robert D. Weekes : *The New Dispensation.*
1899   F. W. Grant : *The Numerical Bible.*
1900   Henry Hayman : *The Epistles of the New Testament . . . in the Popular Idiom.*
1901   James Moffatt : *The Historical New Testament.*
1903   R. F. Weymouth : *The New Testament in Modern Speech, an idiomatic translation into Everyday English.*
1918   E. S. Buchanan : (Lk, Jn, Acts) *An Unjudaized Version* (based on Latin).
1920-34   National Adult School Union : *The Books of the Old Testament in Colloquial English.*

[1] A lecture delivered in the John Rylands Library on Wednesday, the 8th of December, 1954.

1922   Chaplain F. S. Ballentine : *A Plainer Bible for Plain People in Plain American.*

1925-32   Arthur E. Overbury : *The People's New Covenant . . . from the Meta-Physical Standpoint . . . a revision unhampered by so-called ecclesiastical authority.*

The lineage of the official English Bible is clearly traceable from the King James Version, through the English Revised Version of 1881, the American Standard Version of 1901, to the Revised Standard Version in 1952 in America, whose British counterpart is even now in the making. But less well known is the continual production of private translations which have their day—and, indeed, reflect their day. The best of these private translations have had large effect upon the periodic official translations. *The Twentieth Century New Testament*, in particular, was a pioneer of modern speech versions. It had an important effect upon its generation, and a significant influence upon subsequent versions. If, in addition, its story contains something of romance and mystery, its fascination does not in the least diminish the strategic importance of this version which made its appearance with the new century.

The title-page mentioned no translator by name and, whoever had done the work, he or they have remained unknown until a recent day. A short preface, dignified and restrained, gave no hint of the trials and tribulations through fourteen years of difficult labours. Twenty years ago, perhaps the last survivor of the partners carefully deposited the secretary's records in the John Rylands Library, and these were recently made available through the kindness of the Librarian, Professor Edward Robertson.[1]

It is certain that no translation had ever been undertaken by so unusual a procedure, or by so strange a group of translators, and it will be of interest to inquire in due course as to the quality of the finished work. The earliest record is a letter of 29 September 1891, which refers to beginnings in the previous year,

[1] In 1898, Professor Edgar J. Goodspeed (later famed as a New Testament translator) was a youthful member of the staff of the University of Chicago when he visited England and learned of this translation project. In his subsequent teaching, he was wont to refer to this otherwise obscure story and also mentioned the deposit of the records in 1933. They now form Rylands Eng. MS. 750.

reported only by word of mouth.   Mrs. Mary Kingsland Higgs,
who lived in Greenacres, Oldham (near Manchester), was the
wife of a Congregational minister.   She was a leader and teacher
of youth, and had four children of her own, and had become
disturbed because the young people did not understand the
idiom of the traditional Bible.   She wrote of her problem to
W. T. Stead, the editor of the new *Review of Reviews*, and herself
began to prepare an idiomatic translation of the Gospel of Mark.
In another corner of England lived a signal and telegraph
engineer, Ernest de Mérindol Malan of Newland, Hull, who also
had four children.   He was the grandson of a noted Swiss
Reformed preacher (Dr. Caesar Malan) and followed the custom
of reading the Bible to his children.   The family was bi-lingual
and Malan observed that the modern French version by Lasserre
was better understood than was the traditional English Bible.
He too wrote to W. T. Stead, of whose Helpers' Association he
was a member.

Mr. Stead referred the two correspondents to one another,
and they soon began collaboration in translating the Gospel of
Mark.   As they progressed, they expanded the plan to include
the Four Gospels and the Book of Acts.   They also sought to
enlist additional partners, and in 1891 W. T. Stead printed a
notice inviting " co-workers in the task of translating the Gospels
and the Acts of the Apostles into our every-day speech ".[1]   It
explained the purpose, to place an Englishman " on the same
footing as his forefathers of the sixteenth and seventeenth
centuries, for whom the Authorized and other English versions
were printed in the ' vulgar tongue ' "—an objective reminiscent
of Wycliffe and Tyndale and Luther.   Malan optimistically
declared : " If each worker undertook a few chapters and
submitted the same to all the other translators . . . the work
would soon be done and ere long we may hope to present to all
English-speaking working men and women, and children of all
classes, a version which they could read without difficulty."   It
was perhaps well that he could not then know that the task was to
require an arduous fourteen-year period, throughout which many
physical and mental trials would afflict the group of partners.

[1] *Review of Reviews*, iv (1891), 288, 391, 554 ; vi (1892), 250 ; vii (1893), 317.

When the King James Version and the Revised Version were planned, the most prominent Hebrew and Greek scholars in Britain were selected for the work. But in the making of *The Twentieth Century New Testament* the universities had no part and officialdom played no hand. It was a common objective, sought by common men, in the interest of common people.

The first appeal for assistance brought together in 1891 a strange conglomerate of twenty persons. For a long time they collaborated only by correspondence and never met one another. This had one fortunate result, when, in January 1892, Malan requested an autobiographical sketch from each to serve as an introduction to all—fifteen of these sketches are preserved among the papers, thus serving to introduce the translators to us also.[1]

From the first, Malan became the driving force in the project and served as its secretary. He was but 33 at the start, but he carried the heaviest burden in the problems of translating, revising, financing and publishing. Meanwhile, he advanced in his career as an engineer until an appointment in 1895 required him to travel abroad and removed him somewhat from participation. As early as 1892, he fell ill under the double strain, complaining of influenza, brain-fever and over-work, but nevertheless continued in the project with increasing assistance from others. His grandfather was a leader in the Reformed Church in Geneva, but Ernest was educated in England as well as in a Moravian school on Lake Geneva. He was baptized and confirmed in the Church of England. As an adult he was prominent in the Congregational Church in Howden, but later (1890) in Hull joined the Wesleyan Church. He writes of having been influenced by Henry Drummond's *Natural Law in the Spiritual World*, of losing sympathy with creeds and dogmas, and of becoming a teetotaller since 1888. These few facts of his life suggest a distinctive personality, frequently in tension, reaching independent decisions.

Also assuming a vigorous part in the project was Mary Ann Kingsland Higgs, a few years his senior. Her father was a Congregational minister whose last appointment was at Bradford

---

[1] A picture of each also was requested but all were subsequently returned except that of Malan, which alone is preserved in the file.

(1862-76), as minister of the College Chapel. There he died when the daughter was 22 years old. Two years previously she had become the first woman to receive a science degree at Girton College, Cambridge ; then had stayed on as Assistant Lecturer. At 25 (in 1879), she married a Congregational minister, a graduate of the University of London ; and together they promoted the building of churches and schools in various parishes. There were four children, and, in addition, youth groups in the churches whom she sought to train. Her health broke when she was 34 years of age, and two years later her husband lost his church. Yet this was the very time that she was translating the Gospel of Mark, and about to undertake the long and difficult task for the New Testament as a whole. Years later, we find her publishing religious tracts, and one in particular in 1910 shows her to be a perceptive pioneer in the early movement of religious education. She was, indeed, a most remarkable woman, and before her death in 1937 had been honoured with the Order of the British Empire.[1]

Let us briefly meet a few others of the more prominent members. The Reverend Henry Bazett described himself as a Huguenot ex-curate, although he had been ordained in the Church of England. As a graduate of Oxford, he had first become a schoolmaster in Wales. He was secretary of the White Cross Army, and a member of the Social Purity League. Only two of his four children still lived. His own health broke and he sought convalescence in America, where his leisure permitted the reading of socialistic books. Upon returning to England he sent a letter of resignation to Bishop Thorold of Rochester, which he also submitted to the Manchester *Guardian* and other papers. For a while he was active in the Women's Trades Union Association, and the Consumers' League. He had since become a Classics Master and private tutor to his young cousins on a farm in Cape Town, and recently published *The People's Version of James' Letter*. His health required him to move back northward and he settled in Southwick near Brighton during the years of his participation in the project.

[1] Hartley Bateson paid high tribute to her in *A Centenary History of Oldham* (1949).

Thomas Sibley Boulton was only 20 years old. He had been educated in Birmingham, the last four years under the Reverend E. F. M. MacCarthy. At 16 he became an accountant. He read Ruskin and Kingsley, and embraced socialism. At the age of 18 his health broke. Subsequently, he became a Master in Music and Language and then returned to college. He abstained from both alcohol and tobacco. He wrote of his desire for " a re-union of Christianity ".

W. M. Copland was a Headmaster who had been educated in Aberdeen where he distinguished himself at the University. For one year he read for Divinity, but after reading Isaac Taylor renounced creeds and dogmas. For thirty years, so he reported, he had rejected the Trinity, the Immortality of the Soul, and a Personal Devil as pagan superstitions contrary to scripture. He was often in poor health. Calling himself " a Radical in Politics and Religion ", he declared that " the Lord Jesus . . . has promised to come back to put matters right. [I] expect this in connection with the present gigantic preparations for war— Russia's designs on the East, etc."

The Reverend Edward Bruce Cornford, 30 years of age, had taken a Cambridge degree in Theology, shifted to the study of Medicine, and travelled abroad. He had worked in the slums of Walworth, and returned to read Theology with the Very Reverend Dean Vaughan, Master of the Temple, and was ordained at Farnham by Bishop Harold Browne. In 1888 he had published a moralistic story in *Our Boys Magazine*.

W. M. Crook was the eldest son of an Irish Wesleyan minister. He stood high in his studies at Trinity College, Dublin, and later was a Master in Classics. At 21 ill health caused a temporary withdrawal. He later became a lecturer for the National Liberal Club and The " 80 " Club, and was a Radical Home Ruler.

The Reverend Peter William Darnton was the son of a manufacturer of musical instruments. He did not attend a university but entered business at 16. Yet he was " bookish " and spent the evenings at the Mutual Improvement Society learning to speak and to write. At 22, he returned to schooling and became a Congregational minister though he begrudged the time required for sermon-making. A widower with four daughters, his last pastorate was at Bristol where he entertained the Revisers as late as 1903.

The Reverend Edward Deacon Girdlestone was possibly the oldest member, at 63, and a stalwart associate. He and his father were Anglican clergymen. After college and teaching, he was ordained at 23 but two years later decided that this had been a mistake. In a state of indecision he continued intermittently to work and to preach. In his mid-thirties he married a woman of means and soon retired. Later as a widower he re-married at 50, and for a while tutored privately. He claims a number of published articles, mostly socialistic.

The Reverend E. Hampden-Cook was a Congregationalist, a " broad Evangelical ", 32 years old. He once attended Owens College and Lancashire Independent College, but received his degree from Cambridge. His pastorates stretched from New South Wales and New Zealand to London, Wales, and Cheshire. In 1903, he prepared the posthumous Weymouth translation for publication. He reported his belief " in three personal advents of Christ, holding that the second took place in A.D. 70, and that there is a third yet to come, death being meanwhile to the individual the coming of the Lord ".[1]

A. Ingram was a Presbyterian, born in Aberdeen. He listed successive occupations as cowboy, grocer, draper, lawyer's and accountant's clerk, and journalist since 1880. He was a widower with three children.

One of the more prominent associates was the Reverend Henry Charles Leonard, a retired Baptist minister selected by W. T. Stead to serve as treasurer. He was one of the Revisers, and performed the special task of making Synoptic parallels consistent. During the period of his participation, a series of misfortunes included the death of his wife in 1895 after a long illness, the loss of one eye and other " oft infirmities " of long standing.

Finally, let us meet the only other woman among the partners. She was Mrs. Sarah Elizabeth Butterworth Mee, who was related to Sir Joseph Butterworth, an emancipationist. Her father was

---

[1] Schaff-Herzog, *Religious Encyclopedia*, xii. 554.

a woollen manufacturer in Huddersfield, but had lost much of his money. She was educated at the school run by the daughters of the Reverend Daniel Walton. At 29 she married the Wesleyan minister, Josiah Mee, and bore him six children while they worked in numerous circuits. Her health failed at 36, and later she is found to be the President of the Women's Health Association, and occasionally doing Temperance work. She taught a Sunday School class for twenty years. She, and at least one other of the partners, knew no Greek, but they served on the English Committee to review the translation for its proper idiom.

There is not the space here to introduce other members of the group, but these will serve to inform us as to its general composition. After the initial stage of the work, twelve more workers were enlisted but unfortunately their biographies were never requested, perhaps because personal conferences had to some extent replaced correspondence. Altogether, thirty-five persons were associated with the translation, including as advisers three prominent scholars : G. G. Findlay of Headingley College, J. R. Harris of Cambridge, and R. F. Weymouth, retired Headmaster of Mill Hill School.

Certainly this company of translators is no ordinary assemblage, and it is difficult to imagine a more disparate group. The members range in age between 19 and 63. In education they vary widely. They represent all parts of the British Isles. About half of them are clergymen, of which probably none is a typical representative. Others are schoolmasters, business men, and housewives. They belong to the Church of England, Wesleyans, Congregationalists, Presbyterians, and Baptists, and one speaks of himself as a Huguenot. Among them, there are many whose records show a procession through successive religious affiliations. Several of the clergymen have experienced repeated doubts as to their calling, and some have forsaken their orders altogether.

It is a company of liberal and independent thinkers, strong-minded, and even opinionated. Their struggle with life—social, political, and intellectual—is reflected in the tensions and ill-health which they report, for hardly a single biography lacks this element. It was grim realism, in the Articles of Association drafted in 1898, that included a provision : " If any partner shall die, retire, or become lunatic. . . ." As a group, their children are numerous, and domestic problems have created a heavy and constant strain. Among them are many Socialists, some self-styled Radicals, and almost all have engaged in numerous social services toward reform and uplift. They hold in common a sympathy for the mass of workers. A number of them have written articles on social and religious reforms, and some have previously engaged in translating, or at least in re-phrasing, the English New Testament.

Compare such a group with the scholarly and academic group which had produced the English Revised Version only a decade before. It is a non-professional group, whose translating was motivated by social causes and by the desire to mediate the Word of God in a plainer English idiom. A more fascinating company of workers can hardly be imagined, and fascination becomes greater when we see them against the background of their time. They worked during the last decade of the Victorian era which was ablaze with political and social revolution. The Home Rule controversy was at its height, and one member who had been reared in an Irish Wesleyan family openly declared his advocacy of Home Rule. The Socialist movement was everywhere astir, and many of the translators affirmed their sympathy with it. Free education for the poor had but recently been granted, the electorate had been enlarged, and new land regulations were being pressed into law.

In the realm of religion, there were under debate the problems of Church and State, freedom of worship, atheism and the Oath, the observance of the Sabbath, ritualism, and marriage and burial regulations. It was truly an age of social ferment and popular reform. It is not suggested here that *The Twentieth Century New Testament* was designed as a propagandist instrument to apply to such controversies, but in its reverent sincerity it was nevertheless a natural expression of its time. It reflects in its chosen phrases a humanistic and naturalistic approach to re-ligious and social concerns. It has frequently been pointed out that the New Testament documents were originally composed in colloquial language and for the common people. The last decade of the nineteenth century was such an age as to commit the New Testament once again to the ordinary man, and to provoke the purpose of these translators—all of whom shared the life of the common people—" to present to all English-speaking men and women " a version of the New Testament adapted to their common need and understanding. At the beginning of the project the Secretary wrote of his hope " that the whole work will be undertaken in a prayerful spirit, each worker asking for Divine guidance for both himself and his fellow-workers ".

II

Yet it is not enough to recognize the powerful human forces that surged about and within the group of translators, even as they worked. We must consider certain critical questions concerning the product of their labours. How well conceived were the method and the principles by which they proceeded ? How well were they equipped for their task ? What were the quality and the influence of the translation they produced ?

Malan's second Circular, sent out in December 1891, outlines organization and procedure, though these were considerably altered as the project developed. The plan, in general, now represents standard practice in group translating, and therefore stands as an illustration of how translations are made. Here are the steps :

1. The original twenty collaborators were divided into five groups, each consisting of three to five members ; and a Gospel or the Book of Acts was assigned to each group, and a portion thereof allotted to each member. Parenthetically, it may be noted that two years later assignments were similarly made for the Epistles and the Revelation.
2. Each member was to translate his assigned portion, and to circulate instalments to receive the criticism by each member of his group.
3. When all this has been accomplished within the groups, each group is to interchange and criticize the work of the other groups.
4. Then the original translator of a portion shall consider all criticisms, but is free to exercise his own discretion about accepting them.
5. Each group shall choose one of its members as Reviser, who shall be its representative on a Revising Committee to which the resultant draft shall be submitted.

6. Translations are to be circulated among Revisers, and such changes as are approved by two-thirds are to be noted in red ink. (We pause here to note that the Revising Committee was thus composed of five Revisers and therefore no less than four votes would fulfil the two-thirds requirement. A note in 1895, however, refers to six Revisers at that time—which simplified the arithmetic.)

7. Each group Reviser is to criticize the translation prepared by his own group, and to present and defend the same before a meeting of the Revising Committee, where finally a majority would rule. (It is to be noted here that at this stage a three-fifths vote would prevail; whereas in the later stage, a two-thirds vote.)

8. Each translator, having been thus represented, shall abide by the decision of the Revising Committee.

9. An English Committee, selected from the translators, is to review the translation to improve the English idiom.

10. All translations are to be printed on " slip sheets " which will circulate widely for criticism, even outside the company of translators.

11. At a later stage in the project, an effort was made to organize an American Company for collaboration. But it was debated whether American scholars should be invited to criticize the slip-sheet text or a later, tentative publication. Ultimately, nothing came of the proposal and no American participation developed. It should here be recalled that an American Company had been formed to collaborate on the 1881 revision and were even now preparing the American Standard Version which was to make its appearance in 1901.

12. Finally, a full but tentative publication in three parts would allow wider circulation and fuller criticism ; from which would derive the definitive publication in one volume.

Surely no group translation was ever prepared with greater precaution or better safeguards against error or private whims. In general, the plan was adhered to, with a few modifications. For example, some members later refused to criticize the translation of another in the group, and therefore instead of circulating a first draft within the group all members were instructed to submit their work to the separate criticisms of Peirson and White. Since this change was not made until January 1895, it affected only the Epistles and the Revelation. Such modifications of the original plan were simply sensible adjustments to developing circumstances. In February 1892, the Secretary began to circulate a " Word-book " which started off with eighty-eight problematic terms (e.g. εὐαγγέλιον, χριστός, κύριος, δοῦλος, μετανοῖα, etc.), and inviting comment on their proper translation. It contained also questions about the final format. The

" Word-book " was kept in continual circulation among the members, who added answers, comments, and questions as it went round.

Organization and procedure required arrangements for finance. Each translator was to work at his own expense. Subscriptions from the translators would defray the cost of revising, editing, and publishing. The copyright would be held by the entire company, and at one time it was expected that individual subscribers might obtain a profit. It was first estimated that £100-150 would be needed, to put 5,000 copies of the Gospels and Acts on sale at 1s. The amount would be divided into £1 shares to be taken up by the translators as far as possible, and then by private subscription. Each subscriber must pay to the Treasurer immediately 2s. 6d. per share, and each would be liable to the extent of his fully paid-up shares. Because they were strangers to one another, W. T. Stead was to nominate a Treasurer who must bank all funds in the name of the Company and render audited accounts to the subscribers. He selected the Reverend H. C. Leonard, a retired Baptist minister of Isleworth, Middlesex; and Malan and Homer completed the Finance Committee.

It was first stated that any profits would be paid as dividends on the shares. Later it was decided only to reimburse each subscriber, and to use the surplus to finance the translation of the Epistles, to advertise, to distribute some free copies and to make possible a lower selling price. This shift in policy caused the resignation of one member. There were continuing financial difficulties, for after five years of operation it was reported that out of twenty-five members only ten had made any contribution. A year later £100 had been raised but the estimate of need had gone much higher than in 1891. It became necessary to divide the Company into Members and Associates ; the Members being those who had contributed at least £1 a year—and only they held votes. But in 1897, W. T. Stead offered to publish the translation in book form, and to pay any profits to the subscribers (who now held a 42-year copyright in England). An American copyright was arranged through Fleming H. Revell Company, and Mr. Leonard's warning against piracy in America lost its force.   By 1901, the tentative edition of the New Testament was on sale at 2s. 8d., the three parts having been previously put out separately at 1s. 6d.   Already 40,000 copies of Part 1, the Gospels and Acts, had been sold (17,000 of them in America).   By 1901, subscriptions had amounted to £200 but expenses had gone over £300 ;   however, by the end of that year profits totalled well over £300.   The final edition appeared in 1904, showing substantial revision of the tentative form.   In London, it was published by the Sunday School Union at 1s. 6d., and the American publisher was Fleming H. Revell.   The anonymous Preface was prepared by Girdlestone, who commended the translation, " undertaken as a labour of love, to the good-will of all English-speaking people, and to the blessing of Almighty God ".

The choice of the title had been most carefully considered. In January 1893, the Secretary first requested suggestions.   In his Circular (No. 16) of the following September he reported six titles submitted, which he revised into the following choices :

The New Testament in Every-day English.
The New Testament in Modern English.
The New Testament in Current Language.
The New Testament in the English of To-day.

In correspondence, the first two were favoured by equal numbers and the matter was referred to the Revising Committee, with the result that a still different title was adopted :

The New Testament.   People's Version.

But four years later the Company approved Girdlestone's proposal of the title :

The Twentieth Century New Testament.

The tentative edition of 1898-1901 embraced the birth of the century ;   while the final edition celebrates its 50th anniversary this year [i.e. 1954].   Between the two, Weymouth published his *New Testament in Modern Speech* (1903).

When one inquires into the linguistic competence of the translators, he finds little in the record that is helpful.   It may safely be assumed that the fourteen clergymen had formal training in the Greek New Testament.   Others had certainly studied Classical Greek and a few were specialists in Classics. Girdlestone especially shows an astonishing perception when he writes in the Preface : " The Greek used by the New Testament writers was not the Classical Greek of some centuries earlier, but the form of the language spoken in their own day." Today this is a commonplace, but Girdlestone's insight anticipated Adolf Deissmann by many years. Grenfell and Hunt were still young scholars, still digging up papyri in Egypt. It was therefore an " advanced " conception as to the nature of the Greek, which enabled these translators to set a precedent for the treatment of the New Testament text.

Nevertheless, the heterogeneous Company presented a problem, which was reflected in the communication of November 1891 : Our task is " to secure on each group sufficient scholarship to ensure, that, while aiming at a good and clear vernacular, the work will bear criticism as a rendering of the Greek text ". It is " not possible to ensure perfection among a body of voluntary and amateur translators ". Five years later it must have been disheartening to report that the first slip-sheet edition of Mark required so much emendation that a second edition had to be printed, and yet Mark had been translated by Mrs. Higgs and Malan (who had collaborated upon it even before the project began), along with the Reverend Mr. Leonard (the retired Baptist minister and Treasurer)—all of whom were recognized leaders in the venture. When later the Epistles were finished, it was necessary to appoint a special committee " to bring about some uniformity ". " The work has been of all qualities," the Secretary wrote, " excellent, flowing modern English, and merely verbal translation." Yet, for all this, when the Gospel of Mark was finished in 1896, Dr. Culross of Bristol exclaimed : " Your Mark is a triumph." When the first edition of Acts was printed, Weymouth pronounced it "admirably done ".

There had been care to include in each of the five groups at least one member with good linguistic ability, who was likely to serve as Reviser. It was also an important factor that a few reputable scholars were allied as advisors, at least briefly. Professor J. Rendel Harris, of Clare College, Cambridge, was briefly associated in 1901, though it is not known what contribution he made. Professor G. G. Findlay, of Headingley College, Leeds, agreed to revise John during the summer of 1892, having recently begun to publish a literal translation entitled " John's Good News ". But he resigned that fall and it is not known whether or not he fulfilled his promise. R. F. Weymouth had published the *Resultant Greek Text* in 1886, when he retired as Headmaster at the Mill Hill School. Since then he had been engaged in translating the New Testament alone, and from 1895 to 1897 was allied also with the group project. In his Preface it is stated that while " full co-operation . . . has not been found practicable . . . there has been in certain parts free communication and interchange of manuscript " ; and he graciously adds, " Which party is the more indebted it is difficult to say ". When he resigned in 1897, it was attested by the Secretary that " he has rendered us valuable help ". The tentative edition preceded that of Weymouth, which appeared posthumously in 1903 under the editorship of one of the partners, Hampden-Cook. But the final edition of 1904 benefited directly from the Weymouth version.

The greatest advantage to *The Twentieth Century New Testament* was the choice of a Greek text to translate. In 1891, the first instructions were to " use any Greek text, but as a general rule that underlying the English Revised Version ".[1] But in the same year that this version appeared, Westcott and Hort published a new critical Greek text. It was perhaps T. W. Whitall who urged the use of Westcott-Hort, for late in 1891 he had supplied copies to all the translators, and thus in one stroke made a most significant contribution—for Westcott-Hort was the best critical text that had yet appeared. The Secretary further directed that Bishop Westcott was " to be consulted if punctuation or sense is changed by a translator ".

The ultimate translation was true to the stated principle : " to grasp the sense of the original Greek " and to express it in modern English, " not departing from the original more than is absolutely necessary in order to bring it more into harmony with the English idiom ". The values of coins, and measures of space and time were turned into their English equivalents. The

[1] This text had been edited by Palmer, and was printed the same year as the English Revised Version (1881). It was later re-issued by Souter.

translators were urged to use Saxon words, and to be consistent in translating the same Greek word everywhere. The problem of Gospel parallels was committed to the special attention of H. C. Leonard, with the objective of exhibiting the true relationship between the Gospels.

The Company agreed to use the modern " you " instead of the antiquated " thou ", exception being made in prayers, in the speech of God, and in quotations from the Old Testament. A modern format was achieved by arranging the text in a single column, and in paragraphs, while relegating chapter and verse numbers to the margin. Modern English punctuation was adopted, including quotation marks. Paragraph titles were inserted to aid the reader, and Old Testament references were given in the bottom margin. Poetry was printed in its proper form, and Old Testament quotations were clearly set off from the main text " to enable the reader to see how familiar the writers were with the very words and phrases of the Septuagint ". It was originally planned to print short explanatory notes, but Leonard early opposed this and his view prevailed.

Each book has a brief introduction. The order of the books is influenced by chronological considerations. Leonard had proposed in 1892 that the order of Westcott-Hort should be followed : and the final edition uses this order, with some modification.[1] The four Gospels stand first, but Mark is at the head—reflecting the recent theory of Markan priority in time.[2] After Acts, comes the Epistle of James (as in Westcott-Hort) but it is separated from the other General Epistles which because of their late date are placed after the Pauline Letters. The Letters of Paul are arranged according to the current theory of their chronological sequence. After all the genuine letters come the Pastorals in a neutral position, followed by the " anonymous " Letter to the Hebrews, and then the rest of the General Epistles (in the order : Peter, Jude, John). The Revelation of John comes last without regard to its earlier dating.

[1] The order in Westcott-Hort, following early manuscripts, is : Gospels, Acts, Catholic Epistles, Pauline Epistles, Revelation.

[2] The proposal of Carl Lachmann (1835) that Mark was the earliest of the Gospels is virtually universal in acceptance today.

III

Now, if " the proof of the pudding is in the eating " it would be well for us to sample a few passages from the 1904 *Twentieth Century New Testament* (in the order found there). Section A contains " The Historical Books "—the four Gospels and the Book of Acts—with Mark standing first.

Mark i. 4 (KJ and ERV) states that John " preached the baptism of repentance unto the remission of sins ". This literal translation of the Greek does not yield a clear sense, and the 1904 edition strives for greater clarity : " . . . proclaiming a baptism upon repentance, for the forgiveness of sins ". This revision illustrates at once both loss and gain. For in the first clause a theological refinement intrudes, in the interpretation that repentance must be anterior to, or is a prerequisite of, baptism ; whereas the Greek phrase has a simple genitive whose meaning is left undefined. But in the second clause, a valid improvement is recognized in the phrase, " for the forgiveness of sins ". These judgements against and in favour of the 1904 translation are reflected decades later in the American Revised Standard Version (RSV) of 1946 : " preaching a baptism of repentance for the forgiveness of sins." Here the second clause follows exactly the translation of 1904.

In Mark iv. 19 there is the allegory of the seed sown among the thorns (KJ and ERV) " . . . the cares of the world and the deceitfulness of riches . . . choke the word ". The 1904 translation runs : " . . . the cares of life, and the glamour of wealth . . . completely choke the Message." The change from " the cares of the world " to " the cares of life " is the result of emending the Westcott-Hort text at this point, in unwisely accepting βlov (observed then in Bezae and the Old Latin) in place of $\dot{a}\iota\hat{\omega}vos$ which has much better support. But the next phrase, " the glamour of wealth ", was well inspired as it corrected the interpretation of $\dot{a}\pi\dot{a}\tau\eta$. This general sense persists in subsequent translations such as Goodspeed's (1923) " the pleasure of being rich ", and the RSV's (1946) " the delight in riches ". However, when the 1904 edition inserted the word " completely " it was done gratuitously, for nothing in the Greek text suggests it other than the result of fruitlessness. So once again it may be observed that judgement upon this verse is mixed, for and against, and is set off by the 1946 RSV: " the cares of the world and the delight in riches . . . choke the word."

In Mark x. 42 Christian humility is contrasted with the rulers of gentiles who (KJ and ERV) " lord it over them and their great ones exercise authority over them ". Originally these two clauses said the same thing, but today the phrase " to lord it over " has come to imply arrogance and oppression. This implication must have been present in the 1904 translation, because the second clause is made to accord with it : " lord it over them . . . and their great men oppress them ". But this translation is misleading since neither of the clauses in Greek necessarily refers to oppression but only to the gentile conception of the dominant ruler in contrast with the idea of eminence through humble service. The intrusion of the reference to oppression may well be one evidence of the influence upon the translators of the social tension and protest of their day.

Another sample is taken from the story of the woman anointing Jesus' head. In Mark xiv. 6 the ERV retains a stiff and literal translation : " She hath wrought a good work on me." How much better is the style and sense of the 1904 translation : " This is a beautiful deed she has done for me ! " As recently as 1946 the RSV followed this lead, finding it necessary to make one slight revision : " She has done a beautiful thing to me."

Once again, we may sample at Mark xv. 2 where the question is asked, " Are you the King of the Jews ? " And the answer (KJ and ERV) : " Thou sayest." The debate over this obscure answer has been long and varied. For example, Westcott-Hort first suggested that the original Greek sentence may have been either declarative or interrogative. If it be taken as a question, it may remind us of the parrying between Pilate and Jesus in John xviii. 33-4 : " Are you the King of the Jews ? " " Do you raise this question yourself, or have others said this to you about me ? " But if—more plausibly—the Markan phrase is declarative, it may remind us of the similar response in Matt. xxvi. 25 where Jesus has referred to his betrayer and Judas asks, " It is not I, is it ? " and Jesus replies (literally) : " You have said."

There is no question here that Jesus is confirming this identification and the 1904 version translates acceptably, " ' It is ', answered Jesus ". So in Mark xv. 2 the version translates the same Greek idiom in the same way : " It is true."   So translated, it amounts to an important affirmation on the part of Jesus before Pilate that he is the anointed leader of the Jews. But perhaps the evangelist was more subtle than this and intended that his idiom should be ambiguous. In this case, the wiser part is to translate ambiguously as does the RSV : " You have said so ", and the 1904 version may be said to have gone too far with its theological interpretation.

Now turning to the Gospel of Matthew, it is of interest to observe the beatitude in v. 5, " Blessed are the meek ". Here the 1904 version renders it : " Blessed are the gentle." This does not make easier the acceptance of an erroneous interpretation, that the gentle shall inherit the possessions of earth. It does, however, avoid the misunderstanding that arises from the popular caricature of meekness, and may therefore be applauded.

Another important revision is found in Matt. vi. 4, 6, 18, where the KJ translates that God " will reward thee openly " for your religious actions " in secret ". The 1904 edition translates : " Your Father who sees what is in secret, will recompense you." The reward may be no more ostentatious than the secret deed. This difference from the KJ rests upon the Greek text, since Westcott-Hort follows ancient manuscripts which omit the phrase, ἐν τῷ φανερῷ. The ERV in 1881 had already acknowledged this correction in the text, and Weymouth in 1903 also agreed to it as did the RSV in 1946.

Matt. x. 8 offers an interesting sample, in the familiar phrase (KJ and ERV) : " Freely ye received, freely give." The adverbial term here translated does not mean, as the English may, generously or abundantly. The 1904 translators were quite correct in their version : " You have received free of cost, give free of cost ", and we find the recent RSV in agreement : " You have received without pay, give without pay."

Once more in Matthew (xxvi. 27), there is the ritualized direction (KJ and ERV) : " Drink ye all of it." This is ambiguous without punctuation and many have mentally punctuated it as " Drink ye, all of it." But the 1904 edition is clear, and correct, when it renders the equally clear Greek : " Drink from it, all of you."

There is a difficult point in Luke xxii. 38, where the disciples at their Passover meal say to Jesus, " Lord, behold, here are two swords ". Jesus replies (KJ and ERV) : " It is enough." Many find it difficult to believe that the evangelist reported Jesus as commending the sword, and so the 1904 version translates his answer in one word of indignant remonstrance : " Enough ! " But a few lines earlier it was Jesus himself who reportedly advised to sell one's cloak in order to buy a sword. However great the theological or moral difficulty may be, the obvious text means " Two swords are enough ", and the 1904 edition has interpolated an inconsistent sense.

In 1904, it was a bold stroke to correct John i. 5 (KJ) : " And the darkness comprehendeth it not ", obscure though this traditional phrase was. The ERV had not helped at all when it altered this to " apprehended it not ". It was a radical departure when the 1904 translation rendered the sentence : " And the darkness never overpowered it." This sense was both clear and correct and has been followed in many later translations as in the RSV : " And the darkness has not overcome it."

Another passage well clarified was the obscure verse of Acts v. 24. When the imprisoned apostles mysteriously disappeared, the leaders (KJ) " doubted of them whereunto this would grow ". The ERV did no better with this verse, but the 1904 edition made sense of it, as follows : " They were perplexed about the Apostles and as to what all this would lead to." All important translations since have resembled this phrasing.

In Acts xxii. 22, in the course of Paul's defence, an interruption occurs when Paul speaks of his gentile mission. The KJ and ERV explain, " They gave him audience unto this word ". The English here is at best ambiguous but seems to say merely that they gave attention to his remarks. But the 1904 edition renders clearly what is also clear in the Greek : " Up to this point the people had been listening to Paul." This idea is essential to the story and is reflected in later translations, as when the RSV renders : " Up to this word they listened to him."

It is at the end of Paul's defence before Agrippa, in Acts xxvi. 28, that the latter remarks (KJ) : " Almost thou persuadest me to be a Christian." The ERV introduces a variant note : " With little persuasion thou wouldst fain make me a Christian." But both are rejected when the 1904 edition translates : " You are soon trying to make a Christian of me." The American Committee in 1881 had urged that the phrase be translated : " In a short time . . .", and the same sense was properly adopted in 1904. It is again reflected in the approval of the RSV : " In a short time you think to make me a Christian."

IV

Section B of *The Twentieth Century New Testament* is composed of " The Letters " and this includes both Pauline and General Epistles, arranged in a chronological sequence acceptable to the translators.

The first sample here may be noted in 1 Thessalonians ii. 6, where Paul writes (KJ and ERV) : " We might have been burdensome as apostles of Christ." This obscure passage gives way to clarity in the 1904 edition : " We might have burdened you with our support." However, the improvement here is only partial as it points the way toward the complete sense of the passage well expressed in the RSV : " We might have made demands as apostles."

Again, in 1 Corinthians iii. 9 Paul explains his status and relationship by a simile : " We are God's fellow-workers. Ye are God's husbandry." But the KJ and ERV have altered the simile found in the original Greek and this is restored by the 1904 translation : " You are God's harvest field." Goodspeed has followed this closely (" You are God's farm ") and the RSV almost exactly : " You are God's field."

Another statement of Paul in 1 Corinthians x. 24 is indeed perplexing when he exhorts (KJ) : " Let no man seek his own, but every man another's wealth." The ERV saw the need to correct this to " . . . but each his neighbour's good." But the 1904 edition really established the form for this verse : " A man must not study his own interests, but the interests of others."

This pioneer phrasing has since been followed closely by all the best translations.

In the Hymn of Love in 1 Corinthians xiii, the 1904 edition again pioneered when it translated ἀγάπη as " love " rather than the traditional " charity ". Here again it has been followed in all Protestant translations since. In this same chapter there occurs Paul's familiar remark (KJ and ERV) : " If I give my body to be burned. . . ." The 1904 edition was the first English version to translate instead the Westcott-Hort text at this point : " Even though I sacrifice my body, that I may boast. . . ." This reading was later approved by Goodspeed, but the RSV translators stood by the traditional text.

Turning next to the Roman letter, we read that Paul had planned to visit Rome. Then follows in i. 13 the obsolete phrase : " . . . but was let hitherto." The ERV properly changed " let " to " hindered ", but it was the 1904 edition that first gave a fresh and satisfactory phrasing to the sentence : " . . . until now I have been prevented ", and others since have followed this exemplary form.

Also in Romans (viii. 28), the KJ and ERV report Paul's words : " All things work together for good, to them that love God ". An important difference is noted in the 1904 edition : " God causes all things to work together for the good of those who love him." The change is derived from the Westcott-Hort text and has been accepted in subsequent translations.

In Philippians iii. 20 we read (KJ) : " Our conversation is in heaven." This obsolete and inaccurate translation was improved in the ERV : " Our citizenship is in heaven." But again it was the 1904 edition which first presented a fully satisfactory phrasing : " The State of which we are citizens is in heaven." The contemporary Weymouth version (1903) has a similar expression : " We are free citizens of heaven." But a much closer similarity is found in the RSV (which follows Goodspeed) : " Our commonwealth is in heaven."

Many have been confused by Paul's advice in Philippians iv. 6 (KJ) : " Be careful for nothing." This may appear to commend improvidence and indifference toward the future. But a more acceptable sense is derived from the 1904 edition :

" Do not be anxious about anything." The RSV acknowledges the excellence of the phrasing, by revising only slightly : " Have no anxiety about anything."

An illustration of improvement may be noted in Hebrews xi. 40 where the KJ and ERV read : " . . . God having provided some better thing concerning us." The 1904 edition made two important changes in this clause : " Since God had in view some better thing for us." These changes have since been acknowledged as valid corrections and the recent RSV accepts both : " Since God had foreseen something better for us."

Another illustration may be found in xiii. 16 (KJ and ERV) : " To do good and to communicate forget not." The word " communicate " (like the word " provide ", above) is a borrowing from the Latin Vulgate, rather than an adequate translation of the original Greek term. Although it may have conveyed the true sense in the sixteenth century, the twentieth century required the correction which the 1904 edition made : " To do good and to share what you have." Exactly the same phrase is preserved in the recent RSV.

A final sample is taken from 1 John iv. 19 (KJ) : " We love [him] because he first loved us." Although the KJ acknowledged that the pronoun " him " is not found in the Greek text, it supplied it as essential to the proper meaning. However, the revisers in 1881 exscinded this addition and *The Twentieth Century* version concurred, as did all other subsequent translations. Far from requiring the insertion of the pronoun, the declaration contains a nobler sense in the literal form of the 1904 edition : " We love because he first loved us."

These are but a few selections of the innumerable changes which the *Twentieth Century* translators brought to the English version of the New Testament. They were a reverent, but a bold and zealous company who dared to give a fresh phrasing to the English translation. They made many corrections and created many phrases which have been adopted by translators of great learning. One of these translators recognized their pioneer achievement when (in 1937) he wrote : " The 20th Century was the first of the many modern speech translations which have given us back the coherent readability of the New Testament."

When we read *The Twentieth Century New Testament* in its definitive form, it is difficult to remember that it was produced by so strange a company as we have met. Somewhere along the line, some transforming miracle seems to have occurred. We are forced to conclude that the devotion to their task has made of them better scholars than they were at first. It is to their credit that they were always responsive to suggested revision, even to the last. Still, it is amazing to find that the finest scholars of later years paid tribute to their work by adopting many of the same phrases and perceptive insights. Much of what we may say in praise of this version of 1904 may sound commonplace today, but under the conditions of half a century ago it was extraordinary. It shares with Weymouth's New Testament the honour of inaugurating the truly modern-speech versions. Though it no longer remains in print, and is difficult to secure, its virtues have been preserved in the editions of reputable successors. It holds an honoured place in the procession of versions; and the hope of the Company of translators, as expressed in the Preface, has been amply fulfilled : " . . . that, by this modern translation, the New Testament may become a living reality to many, by whom the Authorized Version, with all its acknowledged beauties, is but imperfectly understood or never read."

THE TEXT OF THE GOSPEL OF JOHN IN
THIRD-CENTURY EGYPT

Recent years have seen the startling recovery and the publication of third-century copies of the Greek New Testament text. Some of these early copies are of considerable extent and are surprisingly well preserved. These new acquisitions are highly significant because they provide the textual resources for a fresh approach to the primitive text and the textual history, at a time when research has reached an impasse.

All of these new acquisitions are papyrus manuscripts and they offer direct testimony particularly to the text of Egyptian Christianity. Furthermore, these recent acquisitions include substantial texts from the third century, whereas the basic sources for earlier textual studies have been of the fourth century. The two latest acquisitions, of the Bodmer Library in Geneva, contain third-century texts of the Gospel of John and one of the Gospel of Luke, thus providing for the first time two primitive copies of the Gospel of John with substantial overlapping throughout chapters 1-14. It is this new condition that has suggested the present study on the text of the Gospel of John in third-century Egyptian Christianity [1].

We possess today about twenty-five papyrus copies of Greek New Testament text which were written as early as A.D. 300. Most of these are only small fragments and, prior to the recent publication of the Bodmer manuscripts P 66 and P 75, these fragments have rarely offered dual testimony to any part of the text. For example, there are four papyrus copies (P 1, 37, 45, 53) which contain text in the Gospel of Matthew. Three of these are short fragments and one (Beatty MS P 45) has fragmentary text through six chapters

---

[1] The Bodmer Papyri appeared as follows: *Papyrus Bodmer II, Évangile de Jean* (Geneva, 1956 and Supplement 1958); *Papyrus Bodmer XIV-XV, Évangiles de Luc et Jean* (Geneva, 1961), two volumes with photographic facsimile.

(xx 24-xxvi 39). However, there is no significant textual variation where two witnesses become available. For another example, we may note that there are five papyrus copies (P 29, 38, 45, 48, 53) which contain text in the Acts of the Apostles. Four of these are short fragments and one (Beatty MS P 45) has fragmentary text through thirteen chapters (iv 27-xvii 17). Yet here again it is true that there is no significant textual variation where two witnesses become available. Other parts of the New Testament text (Mark, Luke, Pauline and Catholic Epistles, Apocalypse) also are represented among our third-century Egyptian papyri. Yet there is no substantial text in these parts where two witnesses become available from the third century.

The situation, however, has been significantly altered by the recent discoveries, with respect to the text of the Gospel of John. Since we now have two well preserved witnesses in the Bodmer manuscripts (P 66 and P 75) whose texts largely overlap through the first fourteen chapters of the book, it is now possible to consult two Egyptian Christian scribes for their extensive textual witness in the third century.

It would be premature to estimate the ultimate effect upon our critical text, and yet it is immediately clear that there must be a radical revision of textual method. For almost a century, since the researches of TISCHENDORF and WESTCOTT and HORT, it has been the habit of textual critics to evaluate any newly discovered manuscript in terms of the fourth-century codices Vaticanus and Sinaiticus. When the Beatty manuscripts were discovered thirty years ago this traditional method was applied, despite the fact that the new witnesses were a century earlier than the standard employed. Other third-century fragments have been evaluated in the same customary manner, and consequently have been described as a textual "mixture" of recensions that belong to the fourth century. Surely this traditional method wrongly inverts the chronology of textual development, and leads to meaningless scholastic description, and obstructs the way to clear and constructive conclusion.

Now with the comparative testimony of two third-century texts of the Gospel of John (P 66 and P 75) we are released from this false inversion, and are now required to analyze the third-century testimony for itself. It follows from this that the highly regarded fourth-century codices which we have long known must themselves be subjected to a fresh evaluation in terms of the new third-century witnesses which we now have at hand. Therefore our method and our mental habit must henceforth be radically revised. The reputation of the Codices Vaticanus and Sinaiticus were attained in an earlier century when they were the newest acquisitions and the earliest copies. At that time it was not possible to judge them on the basis of earlier witnesses. Today the third-century papyri of Beatty and Bodmer (P 45, 46, 47, 66, 75) are themselves the newest acquisitions and the earliest copies. It is these papyrus witnesses, so extensive and substantial, which must be studied and evaluated in order to form an independent judgment of their character—not in terms of codices still to be written a century later, but rather in terms of the primitive and explicit witness which they themselves record. This is the first requirement in our method and research. Only when such an analysis shall have been completed shall we be in a position to re-examine the status of the fourth-century codices, Vaticanus and Sinaiticus. To study the manuscripts in correct historical sequence is much more likely to reveal their true textual history and to yield the true autograph of the Greek text.

Therefore, our attention should now be directed to the textual character of the two Bodmer copies of the Gospel of John (P 66 and 75). In order to form an initial impression of this textual character we shall here select a number of readings which are ideologically significant. In order to free the mind from the usual textual standard which is represented in the fourth-century codices Vaticanus and Sinaiticus, we shall consider the testimony on an eclectic and rational basis in terms of literary criticism (i.e. internal evidence). The textual character of each manuscript witness will gradually form in the mind as we observe its behavior, although this brief study can suggest only tentative direction toward conclusions. At least we are in a position for the first time to examine the Greek text of the Gospel of John which circulated in Christian communities of Egypt in the third century.

We shall look first at certain controversial readings on which P 66 and P 75 offer a united testimony [1]). For example, in John i 18 there is a theologically critical choice between ὁ μονογενὴς

---

[1] For the text of P 75 the recently published transcription has been checked at such points with the photographic facsimile, but for P 66 this is not possible until a facsimile becomes available.

Θεὸς and ὁ μονογενὴς υἱός. In the fourth century, Codex W in Egypt recorded ὁ μονογενὴς υἱός and this reading, which is also in the Textus Receptus, has been more widely accepted through the centuries. But Codices ℵ and B, which also belong to the fourth century and to Egypt, both attested the reading μονογενὴς Θεὸς which expresses a more radical theological conception. Our new witnesses are united in their third-century testimony favoring μονογενὴς Θεὸς and as yet we have no manuscript from the third century to oppose this reading [1]). Furthermore, Θεὸς may be considered the reading more difficult of acceptance and therefore, on the basis of the textual rule, it is to be preferred as original, and so the testimony of P 66 and P 75 becomes the more persuasive.

Another controversial choice is to be made in John i 34 [2]). The scribe of Codex ℵ records the declaration of John the Baptist: "I have witnessed and testified that this is ὁ ἐκλεκτὸς τοῦ Θεοῦ, but a corrector changed this Messianic phrase to ὁ υἱὸς τοῦ Θεοῦ. The scribes of Codices B and W also wrote ὁ υἱὸς τοῦ Θεοῦ. Now from the third century comes the combined witness of P 66 and P 75 reporting the phrase ὁ υἱὸς τοῦ Θεοῦ (rather than ἐκλεκτὸς).

Exactly the same division among the early witnesses is found in John iv 24, where again the scribe of Codex ℵ reports the words of Jesus: „Those who worship Him must worship in a spirit of truth" (ἐν πνεύματι ἀληθείας) [3]). The corrector altered this to ἐν πνεύματι καὶ ἀληθεία, which is the form found also in B and W. Now the third-century papyri, P 66 and P 75, both bring prior testimony for the form „in spirit and truth".

Another textual variant of considerable interest and importance occurs in John vi 11, in the story of feeding the five thousand. A ceremonial procedure is reflected by the corrector of Sinaiticus who wrote that Jesus gave the loaves to the disciples and they in turn distributed to the crowd; and this form is later preserved in the Textus Receptus. But the original scribe of Sinaiticus had described more simply that Jesus gave the loaves to the people; and this

---

[1]) P 75 and the corrector of Aleph read ὁ μονογενὴς Θεὸς, whereas the article is not found in P 66, B and Aleph.

[2]) See A. von Harnack, *Studien zur Geschichte des Neuen Testaments unter der alten Kirche*, I (1931), 127-32. Cf. Luke xxiii 35.

[3]) It has been noted that the Gospel of John repeatedly refers to the Holy Spirit as "the Spirit of Truth"; but it must be recognized also that this term always has the articles: τὸ πνεῦμα τῆς ἀληθείας (cf. xiv 17, xv 26, xvi 13).

simple form is found also in Codices B and W. This shorter text is now attested by all three third-century papyri from Egypt, P 66 and P 75 and the little fragment P 28.

Additional instances further tend to set Codex Sinaiticus off from the other earliest witnesses. This is illustrated in John v 25 where Codices B and W read: "the hour is coming καὶ νῦν ἐστιν"; whereas Codex ℵ* omits the last clause. The third-century testimony of P 66 and P 75 includes the words. It is so again in vii 8 that Codex ℵ stands apart, in recording that Jesus said: "I am not going up (οὐκ ἀναβαίνω) to this feast." Codices B and W record rather that he said: "I am not yet (οὔπω) going up . . .", which suits better the completion of the story when he actually does go up to the feast. Indeed, many critics have concluded that the original οὐκ was offensive to the scribal exegetes who altered the text to a more acceptable οὔπω. But our new witnesses from the third century, however, agree in reading οὔπω; and as yet we have no third-century text with οὐκ.

Another textual variant appears in vi 52, where Codices ℵ and W record the Jews as saying: "How can this man give us flesh to eat?" But Codex B here reads: "How can this man give us his flesh to eat?" This latter form seems necessary to the context, and it is now attested by P 66 [1]). Once again, in vii 1 it is Codex W that records that "Jesus walked in Galilee and had no authority (ἐξουσία) to walk in Judea". Here again many a critic has concluded that the Christological difficulty of this statement was softened by scribal correction to ἤθελεν which is found in B and Aleph. But now this view suffers from the united testimony of P 66 and P 75 that in third-century Egypt the text read ἤθελεν. Once more, Codex W in ii 22 records that "Jesus arose (ἠνέστη) from the dead"; whereas Codices ℵ and B and the fragment 0162 attest the more usual passive form ἠγέρθη. The new papyri, P 66 and P 75, provide an exclusive third-century witness for ἠγέρθη.

Certain readings show Codex B standing apart from the early group. In iii 34 the original scribe of this manuscript wrote: "Not by measure does God give", and the passage thus may be construed with the sequel: "The Father loves the son and has given everything into his hand". But the corrector added τὸ πνεῦμα, which is present also in Codices ℵ and W; which alters the statement to

---

[1]) A lacuna in P 75 renders its testimony uncertain.

read: "Not by measure does God give the spirit" and this has been construed with the foregoing passage: "he whom God has sent speaks the words of God". The decision between the two variant forms is now strongly affected by the united testimony of P 66 and P 75, both of which read τὸ πνεῦμα.

Once again, in vii 39 Codex B stands apart in the passage: "The spirit had not yet been given" (ἦν δεδομένον). That the perfect participle is a later gloss is suggested by the testimony of Codices א and W, and now by that of P 66 and P 75 also, all of which omit the participle. Origen and Clement of Alexandria both exhibit the same text, and therefore the Egyptian testimony for the omission of δεδομένον is irrefutable and the textual character of the two new papyri from the third century is rendered the more trustworthy.

Thus far, all the readings cited above show P 66 and P 75 in agreement with one another. But in many other readings these two papyri oppose each other. For example, in iv 37 P 66 reads: "In this situation there is a true saying that though one man sows it is another who reaps". Codices א B W also contain this passage, whose omission could be considered an accidental *homoioteleuton*. However, P 75 omitted the saying in the third century, and its addition could be a gloss of moralizing. Again in vii 13 the reading of P 66 is later preserved in the Codices א B W: "No one spoke openly about him (περὶ αὐτοῦ) because of fear of the Jews". But P 75 alone reads: "No one spoke openly on his behalf (ὑπὲρ αὐτοῦ) . . ." In viii 57 Papyrus 66 (as well as B and W) reads: "You are not yet fifty years old, and you have seen Abraham?" But Papyrus 75 and Codex א* preserve the reading which accords better with the context: ". . . and Abraham has seen you?" The same division of witnesses is seen in ix 17 where the Jews ask the man whose sight was restored (according to P 66 B W): "What do you say about him?" But according to P 75 and א they ask: "What do you say about yourself?"

In an occasional passage the early testimony is already considerably confused, as may be noted in viii 38:

P 75	ἃ ἠκούσατε . . . λαλ[εῖτε]
P 66 א*	ἃ ἑωράκατε . . . ποιεῖτε
א corr B W	ἃ ἠκούσατε . . . ποιεῖτε

The textual affinity among the earliest manuscripts shows no high consistency since the lines of support are crossed again and

again. The individual witnesses of the fourth century follow now
P 66 and now P 75. This fact may be observed by examining the following list of selected instances. [1])

iii 20	P 66	ὅτι πονηρά ἐστιν	P 75 ℵ B W	omit
iii 25	P 66 ℵ*	ιουδαίων	P 75 ℵ corr B W ιουδαίου	
vi 5	P 66 ℵ B W	ἀγοράσω- μεν	P 75	[ἀγορασ]ωσιν
vi 64	P 66 ℵ	ἦν ὁ μέλλων παραδιδόναι	P 75 B W	ἐστιν ὁ παρα- δώσων
vi 69	P 66	ὁ χριστὸς	P 75 ℵ B W	omit
ix 27	P 66	ἠκούσαται [= ε]	P 75 ℵ B W	οὐκ ἠκού- σατε
ix 38-39a	P 66 ℵ corr B	ὁ δὲ ἔφη . . . εἶπεν ὁ ἰη- σοῦς	P 75 ℵ* W	omit
x 7	P 66 ℵ B W	ἡ θύρα	P 75	ὁ ποιμήν
xi 12	P 66 ℵ B W	σωθήσεται	P 75	ἐγερθήσεται
xii 8	P 66 ℵ B W	μεθ ἑαυτῶν . . . ἔχετε	P 75	omit
xii 34	P 66 ℵ B W	τίς ἐστιν οὗ- τος ὁ υἱὸς τοῦ ἀνθρώπου	P 75	omit
xiv 21	P 66 ℵ B W	ἀγαπηθήσε- ται	P 75	τηρηθήσ[ε]- τ[αι]

It is appropriate now to make some summary observations growing out of our examination of the texts of the Papyri 66 and 75, from
third-century Egypt.

1. We are mindful that these papyri cannot claim unquestioned
priority on the ground alone of their greater antiquity.

2. We cannot blindly follow their textual testimony even when
the two are in agreement with one another.

3. The textual character of P 66 and P 75 cannot be discovered
by reference to the fourth-century standard of ℵ B W, but must be
based upon their individual performance in specific readings, in
numerous passages.

4. The testiomony of P 66 and P 75 is adequate evidence that

---

[1]) Note that P 75 exhibits a shorter text, frequently (and sometimes
alone) omitting terms found in other witnesses.

their variant readings were known and used in third-century Egyptian Christianity.

5. We observe that P 66 and P 75 frequently differ in text, despite their kindred origin in time and place; and that the Egyptian text of the third century already shows variety of reading. [1])

6. The fourth-century texts of א B W show no consistent indebtedness to either P 66 or P 75, but rather each agrees now with one and now with the other.

7. Nevertheless, there is a notable affinity between the third-century P 75 and the fourth-century Codex Vaticanus, whose textual relationship is closer than that of any other pair among the earliest witnesses.

Similarly, the text of P 66 has the stronger affinity with Codices א and W throughout the text here examined.

8. Finally, it is our judgment that P 75 appears to have the best textual character in the third century; and that it is this text of P 75 that bears most closely upon the textual character of Codex Vaticanus in the fourth century.

Although this cannot be considered to be the unique orthodox text, it does appear that the textual descent from P 75 to Vaticanus contains the more consistent and significant textual quality. We conclude therefore that the key to the true textual history is P 75, our newest available witness for the text of the Gospel of John in third-century Egypt.

---

[1]) Victor Martin, *Papyrus Bodmer* XIV-XV, Tome I, 25 (footnote): „Il semble donc qu'il n'existait pas, en Egypte, au commencement du IIIe siècle, une recension unique des textes évangéliques faisant autorité."

Observations on the Erasmian Notes in Codex 2

It is a commonplace that Erasmus in editing the Greek New Testament text of 1516 used a late Byzantine manuscript of the Gospels for printer's copy, in which he entered marginal notes by way of editing his text. It is equally common, also, to repeat the criticism that Erasmus used a recent copy from among his sources for the Gospel text and that this was a basic cause of an inferior text.

A recent examination in Basle of the manuscripts used by Erasmus has produced certain observations which seem worthy of emphasis, tending as they may toward clarification and correction of the usual account of how the *textus receptus* arose.

I

In the first place, there are observations arising from the physical state of the Gospel manuscript in question (Gregory's Codex 2: U. of Basle, A. N. IV 1). The original scribe has written in a light-brown ink, and from this all other notes are easily and certainly distinguishable.

There is the bold, black ink of a minor corrector, apparently earlier than Erasmus, who is responsible for a few changes in the text — no one of which was altered by Erasmus. In this sense, Erasmus had an older collaborator whose changes in Codex 2 became a part of the text printed in 1516, with no more than tacit approval by Erasmus[1].

But the most obvious markings in Codex 2 are sweeping lines of red crayon, which are mainly in the margin. Inasmuch as no distinctions between markings in this manuscript have been

---

[1] There is also one red-ink correction, at Luke 1, 20, where μὴ is supplied after scribal omission.

described in the past, one might suppose that he is here looking at the notes of Erasmus. But a different conclusion quickly follows, based on two simple facts. One is that Erasmus used a different writing material. The other is that the red crayon nowhere edits the text. It simply marks off the manuscript text into equal blocks for printing, and indicates in the margin the number of the new page in the printed edition and its position in a quire of twelve. This is the work of the printer; perhaps Froben or a staff member. But the text remains unaffected by these red markings. They are not editorial nor Erasmian, and are extraneous to any analysis of the Erasmian notes.

The notes of Erasmus himself were written in a pale-brown watery ink of thin line, so inconspicuous that to pick them out requires the closest attention. Erasmus did not as a rule write in the margin, although Gregory[1] and a host of others say so. Exceptionally he used the margin for a longer textual note, and in the entire Gospel of Luke (145 manuscript pages) there are twelve such marginal notes. But generally the pale notes of Erasmus are superimposed upon the scribal brown, or occasionally inserted between the lines.

These notes of Erasmus appear with greater frequency at the beginning of Codex 2, but then gradually diminish — as is so often the case with a $\delta\iota o\rho\vartheta\omega\tau\dot{\eta}\varsigma$. Beyond the Gospel text, Erasmus used Codex 2 of the Acts and Epistles (U. of Basle, A. N. IV 4) in which to continue his editing, but the pale-brown ink appears in only a few places in this manuscript[2]. Although this manuscript also served as printer's copy, Erasmus found slight occasion to alter its text, and almost none after fol. 54 v, despite the fact that he had two other witnesses for Acts and three others for the Epistles[3].

II

Other observations center about the date of Codex 2 of the Gospels. Some have held that it was written in the fifteenth

---

[1] C. R. Gregory, Textkritik I (1900), 128: Erasmus "had written his own notes in the margin".

[2] The red crayon instructions of the printer extend through the Book of Acts (fol. 59 of the manuscript, and page 322 for the printed form) and then disappear except for an occasional recurrence.

[3] Gregory, ibidem, 263, correctly states that he "corrected the text here and there" and sent this manuscript to the printer.

century, not long before Erasmus used it. The recent personal examination left no doubt that Gregory's twelfth-century dating is right, and that we must evaluate the work of Erasmus on this basis.

If one should hold the theory that a fifteenth-century exemplar produces an inferior text because it is so late, then it follows that a twelfth-century exemplar must produce a better text because it is so much earlier. Therefore, if one will agree that Codex 2 is of the twelfth century, he must expect the Erasmus text to be the better for it. But from this theoretical entanglement two important truths emerge. One is that Erasmus was not guilty, as often accused, of resting his text upon a manuscript of later date and of greater corruption. The other is that there is no *a priori* assurance that his twelfth-century copy was better than a later one, or that a manuscript of the fifteenth century would have been substantially inferior.

The one other Gospel source Erasmus had was Codex 1 (U. of Basle, A. N. IV 2) which was also of the twelfth century; but Gregory (who dated it as early as the tenth) considered it a notably bad text. Codex 1 had little effect upon Erasmus' work, but even if he had chosen to use it for printer's copy his text would have been substantially the same. Indeed, among manuscripts after about 600 A. D. there is seldom a substantial difference to be observed except for local or family resemblance. In fairness to Erasmus, it is required of the critic to set forth what criteria might have been applied for the selection of his manuscript sources, or which manuscripts might have been chosen to yield the superior text desiderated. It is doubtful if we could do this now from our favored vantage point, much less he from his in 1515.

Erasmus may be defended even against his own oft-quoted admission of haste[1]. Suppose he had taken ten years instead of ten months; could the result have been much different, under the circumstances? A case in point is the Complutensian New Testament, praised by many for the care and time expended as

---

[1] "... *praecipitatum fuit verius quam editum.*" It is not clear that Erasmus meant that he had been careless or negligent in preparing the text. The context suggests rather that he was dissatisfied with the haste and pressure of the printer. In any case, typographical errors are not properly to be charged to Erasmus.

well as for the superior manuscript sources borrowed and bought. Yet we must agree with Bishop Marsh who characterized that text as corresponding to the modern manuscripts in opposition to the ancient[1]. Scrivener quite rightly noted that "the text it exhibits does not widely differ from that of most codices written from the tenth century downwards"[2].

It is true that the Erasmus text is largely a printing of Codex 2, just as the Westcott-Hort text is largely a printing of Codex B; yet the Erasmus text is a typical Byzantine text and is the only sort of text conceivable two centuries before John Fell and John Mill.

III

Next, let us observe what Erasmus actually did to the Gospel text of Codex 2. The first answer is: very little. He gave his attention to the correction of accents and breathings. Beyond this, he made fewer than three notes to the page, and two-thirds of these were mere itacisms. Hardly one note to a page, on the average, can be considered of even minor importance. What Erasmus did to the text of Codex 2 was too slight to merit much concern or praise[3]. The wonder of it is, not that he finished the job so quickly, but rather that he took so long to do so little.

We should not attribute to Erasmus the creation of a "received text", but only the transmission from a manuscript text already commonly received to a printed form in which this text would continue to prevail for three centuries more.

---

[1] Bishop Marsh, Lectures on the Criticism of the Bible, p. 96 — quoted in Tregelles, Printed Text (1854), p. 8: "Wherever modern Greek manuscripts — 13, 14, 15 century — differ from the most ancient Greek manuscripts, and from the quotations of the early Greek fathers, in such characteristic readings the Complutensian Greek Testament almost invariably agrees with the modern, in opposition to the ancient manuscripts. There cannot be a doubt, therefore, that the Complutensian text was formed from modern manuscripts alone."

[2] F. H. A. Scrivener, Plain Introduction to the Criticism of the New Testament (1894⁴), II, 180. It is relevant to recall that Scrivener was a staunch defender of the Byzantine text.

[3] The celebrated case of I John 5, 7 was exceptional, and has left a distorted impression of Erasmus' work. His edition of 1516 was chiefly a mile-stone in printing.

However, there is a residue of changes of some importance, in the Erasmian notes of Codex 2[1]. For example, in Luke 1, 50 Erasmus changed the scribe's γενεὰς γενεῶν to γενεὰν καὶ γενεὰν (a reading later supported by א). Again, in Luke 1, 77 where the scribe had written ἐν ἀφέσει ἁμαρτιῶν ἡμῶν rather than the alternative ἁμαρτιῶν αὐτῶν, Erasmus rejected both pronouns and left the phrase impersonal[2]. In Luke 3, 10ff., in the account of the preaching of John the Baptist, there are three occurrences of ποιήσωμεν written by the scribe as subjunctives. Erasmus changed all these to the future indicative[3], which would seem to suit the context better. But the later critical text agreed instead with the scribe, restoring all to the subjunctive.

In Luke 6, 26, Jesus alludes to those ancestors who spoke well of the ψευδοπροφῆται. This was the term as written by the scribe of Codex 2, and also by the scribe of Codex 1 (the other source). Nevertheless, Erasmus crossed out ψευδο, and so the 1516 edition had only the simple form[4]. But the edition of 1519 was to restore the compound form, since then confirmed as authentic. In Luke 6, 31 ("as you wish men to treat you . . ."), the scribe wrote the indicative θέλετε, which Erasmus changed to the subjunctive θέλητε.

In all these instances so far cited, the Erasmian notes were made in the body of the text, which is the usual practice. One of the more significant changes occurs in the margin at 2, 43. Opposite the scribe's ἰωσὴφ καὶ ἡ μήτηρ, Erasmus has substituted οἱ γονεῖς, now attested by the best manuscript support. The relevant verb ἔγνω Erasmus neglected to change, but nevertheless the 1516 edition did change it to ἤγνωσαν.

Another marginal note is at Luke 3, 3, where the scribe writes only of John's baptism of repentance, to which Erasmus adds εἰς ἄφεσιν ἁμαρτιῶν; and this addition too is now well attested.

---

[1] The remainder of this paper is based upon the text of Luke, chiefly chapters 1—8 (on 53 pages of Codex 2). Passages selected for illustration are the more significant readings dealt with by Erasmus.

[2] So the 1516 edition; but in 1519 it read αὐτῶν.

[3] To be quite accurate, it should be specified that an earlier corrector using black ink had already so changed the word in its third occurrence (3, 14) so that Erasmus needed only to mark the other two. This instance is strong evidence that the black-ink corrections ante-dated Erasmus.

[4] In the British Museum copy of Erasmus 1516, a modern corrector has written the compound form in the margin.

At Luke 5, 16 the scribe wrote simply that Jesus was in desert areas praying, as the specific term ὑποχωρῶν was omitted. Erasmus inserted this in the margin, and this change is now well approved.

One of the marginal notes of Erasmus is not a written word at all, but rather his drawing of a hand with a pointing finger. Opposite 11, 49, it points to the scribe's ἀποστελλῶ (with double *lambda*, one of which Erasmus cancels with noticeable vigor)[1].

Once again we find an unusual marginal note at Luke 12, 21f. — this time instructing to omit rather than to add[2]. The scribe has copied here: ταῦτα λέγων ἐφώνη ὁ ἔχων ὦτα ἀκούειν ἀκουέτω. Underlining this, Erasmus has commented in Latin *"sup"* plus a long tail, which we interpret to mean "superfluous". The passage is omitted in all editions until it appears in the 1550 margin. The same phenomenon recurs at 14, 24f., where Erasmus by the same procedure cancels out the scribe's πολλοὶ γάρ εἰσιν κλητοὶ ὀλίγοι δὲ ἐκλεκτοί. Both omissions are today well attested.

It would be a false assumption that wherever Erasmus has revised the text in Codex 2, the change was derived from Codex 1. Yet there are a few notable instances of such probable influence. At Luke 5, 27 in Codex 2, there appears a pale-ink marginal addition which is present in the text of Codex 1: καὶ μετὰ ταῦτα ἐξῆλθε. So again, at 6, 28: προσεύχεσθε ὑπὲρ τῶν ἐπηρεαζόντων ὑμᾶς[3]. Scrivener has cited a few places in the text where Erasmus "must have followed Codex 1"[4]. But examination of the key manuscript, Codex 2, reveals no pale-ink notes at many such points. The 1516 edition is not indebted to Erasmus nor to Codex 1, but merely conforms to Codex 2 itself. For example, Scrivener cites Luke 1, 16 where Codex 1 reads πρός rather than ἐπί. But so also does Codex 2 in which Erasmus has entered no note. He cites also Luke 2, 43, in which the Codex 1 reading is ἤγνωσαν (agreeing with 1516). But Erasmus had not changed the

---

[1] This occurs in a quotation from the σοφία τοῦ θεοῦ on the lips of Jesus. The scribe placed a circumflex over the *omega*, which indicates that he really intended it for the future form which Erasmus desired and spelled properly.

[2] Erasmus usually excinds merely by crossing out the unwanted words in the text.

[3] Erasmus should have begun this addition with καί, as it appears in Codex 1. However, his error was corrected in the 1516 edition.

[4] F. H. A. Scrivener, Introduction (1894⁴), II, 183, n. 2.

form ἔγνω in Codex 2. He cites 9, 15 (κατέκλιναν rather than ἀνέκλιναν) but here again there is no pale-ink note nor is there any variance between Codices 1 and 2.

In all the editorial notes of Erasmus thus far mentioned above, the printed edition of 1516 agrees with the pale-ink revision. Furthermore, these changes by Erasmus have in most cases come to be supported by later discovery and research, so that as far as Erasmus went in editing Codex 2 he merits chiefly commendation rather than the customary condemnation.

The last observation to be presented here is of greater surprise and importance. It is this, that the printer did not accept everything that Erasmus proposed. The 1516 edition is not a replica of the text of Codex 2 as revised by Erasmus, but rather is it true that there are a number of departures from the text that was submitted by Erasmus for the printer. A revision written in by Erasmus was sometimes disregarded, and where Erasmus made no change the printer himself sometimes revised[1]. If Codex 2 was printer's copy — and this appears to be certain — it is equally clear that someone reserved the right to revise that copy, in both minor and major points[2].

In Luke 2, 23, in the clause πᾶν ἄρσεν διανοῖγον, Erasmus changed the participle from neuter to masculine, but the 1516 edition disregarded this note. In 2, 36, speaking of Anna the prophetess, the scribe wrote the masculine form προφήτης and Erasmus made no correction — but the printer did. In place of the scribe's ὑπέστρεψαν in 2, 39, Erasmus made a marginal revision to ἐπέστρεψαν, which the printer did not follow. In the Lukan genealogy there are numerous differences in spelling between Erasmus and the printer — too many to cite here.

In Luke 4, 9, Satan gives the direction: βάλε σεαυτὸν κάτω. Erasmus changes the aorist to the present form, which is followed by the printer. But in the same clause, the printer himself inserts ἐντεῦθεν. In Luke 8, 27, there is an instructive situation. Where the scribe has first written ἐξελθόντι δὲ αὐτῷ the black-ink corrector has changed the pronoun to τῷ ἰησοῦ, which Erasmus allows to stand. But the printer turns the phrase into

---

[1] See above, in 2, 43 ἔγνω thus revised to ἤγνωσαν; and in 6, 28 (footnote).

[2] Minor revisions by the printer are illustrated in itacisms in Luke 4, 37; 5, 31; 16, 7.

a genitive absolute, though the second edition in 1519 returns to the dative pronoun. Again, in 9, 1 the scribe copied συγκαλε- σάμενος δὲ. Erasmus substituted ὁ 'Ιησοῦς for δὲ, but the printer conflated the two. It is clear that when we seek to identify the manuscript sources of such a text there is no *a priori* assurance that somewhere there is a neat and exact textual fit.

The instances here cited from the Gospel of Luke form adequate illustration of the surprising fact that the Erasmus edition is not a mere reproduction of Codex 2 as Erasmus revised it. Who was responsible for the gap: Froben, or the Lutheran John Oecolampadius of Weinberg, or Nikolaos Gerbel? Or did Erasmus make oral and later revision of his own work? It is even possible that the basic text prepared by Erasmus was subject to collaborative revision, and that the 1516 edition was not solely the work of Erasmus.

The Posture of the Ancient Scribe

It is well known that the complex of buildings at Qumran included a second-storey room now identified as a *scriptorium*. Furniture in this room was reported as including writing tables and benches, as well as two ink wells with dessicated ink in one.[1] This interpretation became a general assumption and it has been often repeated in publications. But four years ago B. M. Metzger raised questions about it, in arguing persuasively that scribes did not write on tables. He suggested that the "table" was really the scribe's bench, that the "bench" was his footrest, and that the scribe wrote on his lap.[2]

The writer was convinced by Metzger's argument that the Qumran scribes did not write on these tables, but the alternative identification of bench and footrest seemed less convincing. Therefore there remained an open question as to a satisfactory understanding of the *scriptorium* furniture. Recently an opportuniy was afforded to examine this problem, first by a study of the assumed table and bench now exhibited in the Palestine Archaeological Museum as well as the similar furniture in the National Museum in Amman,[3] and also by fresh attention to artistic portrayal of the scribe at work as attested in Byzantine manuscripts.

Attention was directed first to the set of furniture in Jerusalem. What is exhibited there is the shell of plaster which once covered these mud-brick structures. This shell was carefully moved to the Museum when first discovered on the site.[4] It is at once obvious that the dimensions of table and bench as exhibited bear no true relation to the original structures. As the table has been reconstructed on a frame, it stands 66 cm. (26 inches) high,

---

1. R. de Vaux, "Fouilles au Khirbet Qumrân," *Revue Biblique* 61 (1954), p. 212.

2. B. M. Metzger, "The Furniture in the Scriptorium at Qumran," *Revue de Qumran* 1 (1958-59), pp. 509-15; "When Did Scribes Begin to Use Writing Desks?" *Akten des XI. Internationalen Byzantinischen-Kongresses* 1958 (1960), pp. 355-62.

3. Originally all of the *scriptorium* furniture was exhibited in the Palestine Archaeological Museum. In the fall of 1959 one long table (Kh.Q. 967) and the companion bench were sent, still on the wooden frame mounting, to the younger museum in Amman. It fell to the writer in 1961, preparatory to a study of these objects, to direct the re-assembly of these exhibits in the same manner and on the same frames as originally in Jerusalem.

4. R. de Vaux, *idem*, "Ces morceaux énigmatiques ont été consolidés avec de la colle de pâte et de la toile et transportés a Jérusalem. Patiemment assemblés . . ."

almost as high as our normal desk. The bench, also mounted on a frame, is 34 cm. (13½ inches) high, which compares with our normal chair of 17½ inches. As one looks at these pieces they appear to serve suitably as writing table and bench. However, it is admitted that the Museum frames were merely mountings for the display of the fragments, and are not intended to represent the original dimensions of the structures.[5] Therefore we must start our inquiry *de novo*.

Fig. 58. Furniture from the Qumran Scriptorium as mounted in the Jerusalem museum.

Careful measurements reveal that the taller object was actually 44 cm. (17½ inches) high, only two-thirds of its mounted height at present.[6] One portion of the plaster on the side is preserved from top to bottom and even shows the curve where it merged into the floor surface. A cross-section appears as an inverted trapezoid, imperfectly isosceles. The top surface is 38.5 cm (15⅛ inches) wide, whereas the base is only 15.5 cm. (6⅛ inches)

5. The able curator, Joseph Saad, offered this explanation. His experienced assistance on all occasions is here gratefully acknowledged.
6. De Vaux gives the height as 50 cm., in *L' Archéologie et les Manuscrits de la Mer Morte,* Schweich Lectures of 1959 (1961), p. 23; as he had in the original report of 1954 (see footnote 1).

wide. The sides recede almost equally. For this taller object, the evidence is
sufficient for a confident reconstruction; for the lower object, this is not
true. The surviving fragments of the latter reveal it originally stood between
19 and 25 cm. (7½ to 10 inches) high, approximately two-thirds the height
as now mounted. Furthermore, this bench was attached to the east wall, and
consisted of a horizontal top surface, noticeably concave, extending 32.5
cm. (12¾ inches) out from the wall and then sloping steeply downward
for 19 cm. (7½ inches). At this point it either merged into the floor level,
as shown by the curve of plaster fragments, or possibly led into another
horizontal plane which formed a footstool of undetermined height and width.
The present mounting assumes a pedestal of 15 cm. (6 inches) height and
width, which is probably too high and too narrow if indeed there was originally a pedestal at all.[7]

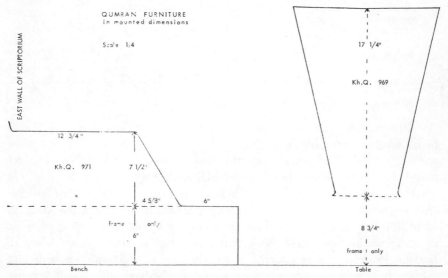

Fig. 59. Cross-section drawing of furniture as mounted.

So far, scholars have merely looked at the furniture or at pictures of it
as now mounted, and imagined its probable utility on this ground. But no
conclusions are safe without an actual test of various postures, observing the
correct dimensions and assuming in turn the different possible interpretations. It devolves upon us therefore to make a simple study of anatomy and
to consider in a practical way how the physical proportions of a scribe may
be disposed in relation to these *scriptorium* structures. We may assume con-
servatively that a typical Qumran scribe would be about five and a half feet

7. The furniture now exhibited in Amman is similar to that in Jerusalem and the dimensions
vary but little. In Jerusalem there may be two shorter tables, and on one of them the outside
apron drops vertically rather than receding.

tall, and such a one will became our model here. This stature, which is the same as the writer's, should well represent the Semite of Palestine at the turn of the era.[8] Inasmuch as it is not feasible to place one's weight on the original plaster shell, the writer has constructed objects of the same dimensions as the original *scriptorium* structures and himself has thus tested different possible positions, taking various measurements in the process.

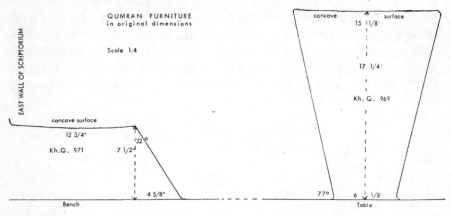

Fig. 60. Cross-section drawing of furniture in original dimensions.

We shall first test the assumption that what we possess are the scribal bench and writing table. If such a scribe sat on the concave bench against the wall, he sat 7½ inches above the floor or the platform where his feet rested. His knees would be 5 inches higher than the 17¼ inch table. He would be most uncomfortably doubled over trying to write on the table, his arms necessarily encircling the obstructing knees. If he spread the knees so as to lean forward between them, this posture would cause an intolerable muscular strain. Some have suggested that a scribe would sit cross-legged, but the footrest as reconstructed is too shallow to accommodate both feet (although it may have been deeper), and furthermore this would require more space for the feet under the table so that our table would have been located farther away, requiring an even deeper leaning and greater stretching. Incidentally, it must be stressed that the table top is not only concave but is also uneven and rough.

If we suppose that the bench had no footrest and that the scribe's feet rested on the floor, his body would be doubled up even more; if he had squatted cross-legged under these circumstances, the table would have been inconveniently far away. It has been pointed out that the sides of the table recede and it has been supposed that this probably allowed the knees to fit

8. So Ludwig Köhler, *Hebrew Man* (1956), p. 23.

underneath[9] so that the table need not have been far away. But the knees come so high that they would strike the table top, except when crossed in squatting. But then the problem is to find sufficient space for the crossed feet rather than the knees. We possess no evidence—other than anatomical considerations — to indicate the original distance of the fixed table from the bench attached to the wall.[10] There is no conceivable posture of the scribal knees and feet that would permit the table to stand sufficiently close for writing. If our scribe was stout, or taller than the model, our problems are all the greater. The anatomical test clearly shows that it is highly improbable, if not quite incredible, that the Qumran scribe copied his texts on this table.

Fig. 61. Scale model: Scribe on low bench using writing table.

Now let us test the assumption that what we possess in the way of furniture is a slightly concave bench and a footrest, as is especially suggested by the sloping surface in the lower structure along the wall. Reversing his direction so as to face eastward, the scribe would be sitting 8 or 10 inches above his footrest, thus forming the lap at a slight angle from the horizontal

9. De Vaux, L' Archéologie . . . p. 23f.
10. If we assume that the table was functionally related to the bench and so stood as close to it as operational requirements permit, the table would have extended about four feet into the 13-foot width of the scriptorium.

plane — which would be satisfactory for writing. But the slope on the footrest is too steep to rest the feet flat on it, particularly if the footrest was only 8 inches high. Therefore the feet, probably bare or thinly covered, must have rested with the arch against the *edge* of the footrest. Such a posture would have been tolerably comfortable, even without a backrest. However, there is no mark on the plaster edge of the footrest, of nick or wear or stain, as would be expected from such constant usage. Furthermore, the footrest structure is unnecessarily wide and complex for such a simple purpose, and its concave top would thus be unaccounted for. The usual footrest of a scribe is a simple horizontal platform and this Qumran form would be

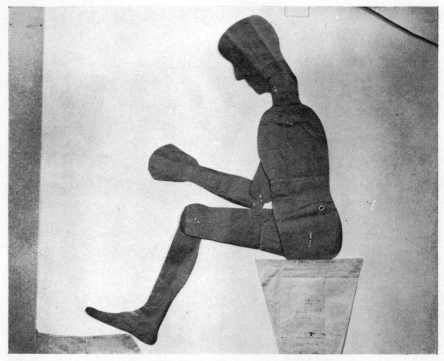

Fig. 62. Scale model: Scribe on high bench with footrest, writing on lap.

unique. Add to these objections that the scribe would sit closely facing a blank wall, or even looking into the light (unless the light should come from above). The furniture stood along the eastern wall, no doubt to take advantage of the morning light — a feature found to be usual in ancient libraries.[11] It is more likely that the Qumran scribe sat facing the west rather than the opposite. Still another objection, based on an anatomical factor, is

11. The eastern wall was 43 feet long and since the width of the room was only 13 feet no scribe would be far from the light. De Vaux (*L' Archéologie . . .*, p. 26) speaks of "large bays open toward the east."

seen in de Vaux' observation that the narrow-based high bench would not stand the weight of several scribes;[12] three or four would weigh 500 to 600 pounds. This bench was made basically of mud-bricks and was fixed into the floor, but it had an over-hang of 4¼ to 4¾ inches on each side. All things considered, it does not appear to be an acceptable interpretation to identify the furniture as bench and footrest.

Fig. 63. Scale model: Scribe on low bench, writing on lap.

We propose here a third interpretation, which is a modification of the first. The bench along the wall is truly a bench on which the scribes sat while writing on the lap. The table is truly a table but the scribes did not use it for writing. This interpretation avoids most of the difficulties inherent in the other two. It also finds confirmation in the fact, which the preponderant evidence supports,[13] that ancient scribes did not use a table for writing.

That the upper-storey room (No. 30 in the Qumran chart) is properly identified as a *scriptorium* appears to be a safe conclusion. In whatever way the furniture was used, and whatever posture the scribes assumed, this conclusion can hardly be challenged, especially in the light of the finding of

12. *Idem*, p. 23.
13. B. M. Metzger (see footnote 2): de Vaux (*L' Archéologie* . . . , p. 24); "Il est bien vrai que l'absence de tables a écrire dans l'antiquité . . . est une opinion recu . . . "

the two ink wells there. Hence we are called upon to understand the scribal operations in this long, narrow room (43 x 13 feet). Our proposal envisages a different function of the table and therefore a different relationship between bench and table. The anatomical problems of scribal posture may thus be cleared away.

We may see the scribe seated on the concave bench along the eastern wall. His bench is low (compared with ours), only 7½ inches in height. His feet rest 7½ inches lower, probably on the floor itself or possibly on a low platform. The relationship of his knees to the table, and the distance to the table, are of little consequence since he does not try to write on the table. The knees rise to form a slope of one in three, which is quite suitable for lap-writing, as the leather sheet lies about 14 inches from the eye (although this is adjustable by the movement of the head). Perhaps there were windows in back of the scribe above the low bench since the *scriptorium* apparently stood alone on the upper level, but we can only conjecture this, since the wall was not preserved.

Our scribe could sit back against the wall for support, which would compensate for the shallow seat of 12¾ inches (compared with our usual chair seat of 15 inches). He was free to move his feet on the floor or a platform (wider than the museum frame shows) and so raise or lower his knees since the table need not be so near him. His knees are not an obstruction to overcome, but are a necessary part of the equipment. His body can thus be relaxed and reasonably comfortable. Such a posture and such an operation are fully in accord with scribal practice as abundantly portrayed through early Christian centuries.

Now as to the table: what was its purpose? It contained the necessary equipment for writing such as the ink wells that have survived. It may be supposed that it held an exemplar also. Someone has suggested that a scroll might have been laid out on the table so that several scribes, copying at different points in the text, might simultaneously produce copies of the same work. This is not impossible but seems dubious since it would call for equal progress among the scribes. Mrs. Katharine Pedley has proposed that the table was used for preparation and repair of the skins and scrolls.[14] For this function alone the table might be located anywhere and so bear no relation whatever to the bench. This, again, is not impossible, and yet such occasional service need not prohibit the regular use as an equipment table convenient to the scribes.

This conception of the table's utility was suggested by study of Byzantine representations of the evangelists at their writing. This evidence has

14. Katharine Greenleaf Pedley, "The Library at Qumran," *Revue de Qumran* 2 (1959-60), pp. 21-41. She suggests that the table might have been in the center of the room.

been pointed out before and we cite it here again because such portraits suggest and support the interpretation here proposed. With variations of detail within the Byzantine tradition, the evangelist sits on bench or chair (of greater height than the Qumran bench) with his feet set on a low platform one foot before the other. He writes on a codex or sometimes on a scroll, occasionally on a loose sheet, but always on the lap or knee. There is a low

Fig. 64. Typical Byzantine scribal posture: the Evangelist Matthew in the tenth century manuscript 74 at the National Library of Athens.

table or chest beside him — rarely in front — which is never used as a writing table. It serves the purpose of holding the writing equipment, on top or even inside a chest. From this table or chest there rises a column supporting a lectern upon which rests the exemplar, a codex or sometimes a scroll. Such portraits are found from the fourth century on, through a thousand years. They show a practice consistent with scribes who obviously never have thought of using a table for writing. It would be contrary to logic to argue that such a convenience, once contrived, might have been forgotten or discarded. It is simpler to understand that in the interpretation of the Qumran furniture we are not permitted the anacronism of inventing a scribal posture like our own.

Père de Vaux has insisted that because it is possible to cite a few illustrations of table-writing from as early as A.D. 400 we may so interpret the Qumran practice. But anatomical difficulties pertaining to scribal posture at Qumran render his interpretation infeasible, and so constitute an independent testimony to the practice of writing on the lap. The artifacts of Qumran are more persuasive than occasional pictorial citations. At the very least, the benches and tables in Jerusalem and Amman should be remounted according to their true dimensions, in order to convey a true impression of their original disposition and utility. The simple test of anatomy yields surprising evidence as to the conceivable posture of a Qumran scribe.

THE MEANING OF ᾽ΕΝΕΡΓΈΩ AND ΚΑΤΑΡΓΈΩ IN THE NEW TESTAMENT

THE problem here discussed was originally raised by such a passage as that found in Gal. 2 8, where active forms of the verb ἐνεργέω twice occur. Former translations appear flat and colorless at this point in Paul's earnest defense of his *divine* authority as an apostle. Paul is saying: ὁ γὰρ ἐνεργήσας Πέτρῳ εἰς ἀποστολὴν τῆς περιτομῆς ἐνέργησεν καὶ ἐμοὶ εἰς τὰ ἔθνη. Recall the King James version: "For he that *wrought effectually* in Peter to the apostleship of the circumsion, the same *was mighty* in me toward the Gentiles." The Revised Versions are characteristically consistent, though not superior, in translating both these occurrences of the verb by "work." Their only other change makes datives of advantage of Πέτρῳ and ἐμοί (thus Lightfoot also). "He that wrought for Peter— wrought for me also." The Twentieth Century translation offers the meaning "to give power." Weymouth returns to the meaning "to be at work." Moffatt translates ἐνεργέω "to equip"; and Goodspeed "to actuate." Our contention is that these are all under-translations, short of the mark, modernizations not only in language but in idea. They do not live in the first century Christian experience. They all apparently refer to an inner human capacity, rather than to that external supernatural divine spirit which had possessed both Peter and Paul. The translations live in the realm of humanism, rather than of supernaturalism. Yet no quality is more characteristic of the first century than its supernatural imagery and belief.

Here stands Paul insisting that his apostolic authority came, not from men nor through any man, but directly through Jesus Christ, and from God who had raised the Christ from among the spirits of the dead where supernatural forces are in control. He proceeds to point out his lack of contacts with the apostles, and that on the few occasions he had for such contacts they "contributed nothing new" to him. Then comes the climax of his claim. "For he who infused the supernatural spirit for Peter in order that he might authoritatively preach among the Jews, infused me too with that same spirit, so that I might as authoritatively preach among the pagans." He had been possessed, and the spirit in him was its own authority. He was in mystical union with Christ, who was master in the realm of spirits, and thereupon rested the authority of Paul the apostle. So we claim, our translators have been too reserved, too quiet in transmitting this vigorous imagery of Paul and his contemporaries.

The difficulty with the word ἐνεργέω is further evidenced by the variety of ways it has been rendered in the same passage by different translators, as well as the variety of expressions used by the same translator in different passages, certain of which have been notoriously difficult because of this very word.

I

The active voice of ἐνεργέω is used in the New Testament eleven times—seven times by Paul, three times in Ephesians, and once in a doublet of Mt=Mk.[1] The King James revisers render it variously as "to work or do, to work (miracles), to work effectually, to be mighty, show forth themselves (mighty works)." The Revised Versions are identical, and consistent with a slavish literalness, in translating always "to work." With the Twentieth Century translators there begins an increasing variety of renderings in the effort to fit the traditional meaning of the word into the several contexts. "To be active, to give power, to endow, to work or be at work, to exert (power), to bring about

[1] Mt 14 2=Mk 6 14, I Cor 12 6, 11, Gal 2 8 (twice), 3 5, Eph 1 11, 20, 2 2, Phil 2 13 (twice).

or accomplish, to result from." Weymouth gives six meanings
in the eleven occurrences, "to work or be at work, to create, to
be able to do, to display (might), to produce (an effect), to carry
out (a plan)." Moffatt presents seven meanings, "to work, to
equip, to enable, to achieve or effect, to exert (might), to carry
out (a plan), to be active." Goodspeed carries eight renderings,
"to be endowed, to be working (powers), to actuate, to be at
work or to act, to exert (strength), to produce (effects), to carry
out (a plan)." This increasing diversity reflects the difficulty in
the traditional understanding of the word, which is apparently
based upon the simple equation, ἐνεργεῖν = to work. Armitage
Robinson, a generation ago, observed that "the meaning of
ἐνεργεῖν—has been so variously understood."[2]

Both the inadequate, colorless translation, and the increasing
variety of renderings may be avoided with a phrase that presents
a vigorous imagery at home in the first century Christian movement and which fits the several contexts with surprising consistency. We observe that ἐνεργέω in our eleven occurrences is
associated twice with δύναμις (once as subject and once as
object), three times with the cognates ἐνέργεια and ἐνέργημα,
and once with the κράτος τῆς ἰσχύος of God. But even when
such terms are not present, ἐνεργέω itself has a supernatural
connotation. Eight times the verb refers to the action of God, and
once to the action of Satan, while the remaining two occurrences
(Mt 14 2 = Mk 6 14, Phil 2 13) clearly relate to supernatural
sources of power. In every case the context bears the atmosphere
of supernatural forces at work, and the action is at home in the
practical dualism of first century thought, where so much of
the conduct of daily life was explained as the operation of good
or evil spirits from outside the human realm. Men were subject
to both these forces and must be allied with the (personified)
Power of good in order to combat the Power of evil. It is in
this atmosphere that we find the action of ἐνεργέω in the New
Testament. Eight times its meaning appears to be "to infuse
with supernatural spirit" (i. e., spirit-possession). In the other

[2] J. Armitage Robinson, *St. Paul's Epistle to the Ephesians* (London, 1904[2]),
241–7.

three occurrences the possession has already taken place, and the verb refers to the operations of the inhabiting spirit.

To illustrate the aptness of this interpretation, we turn first to the synoptic doublet Mk 6 14=Mt 14 2 διὰ τοῦτο αἱ δυνάμεις ἐνεργοῦσιν (Mk, transpose) ἐν αὐτῷ. After repeated miracles of healing and exorcism the fame of Jesus the wonder-worker reaches the ears of Herod Antipas. While others explain this supernatural figure as a messianic Elijah or spirit-filled prophet, Herod explains him by identifying him with the beheaded John Baptist now risen ἀπὸ τῶν νεκρῶν, and there-fore—because of this association with the realm of supernatural spirits—do these δυνάμεις operate in him. While the context is so clearly one of supernaturalism that some of the translators have caught this element, none have gone far enough to catch the realistic imagery of spirit-possession. Alexander Bruce comments, in this connection, upon "the powers of the invisible world, vast and vague in the king's imagination."

Take another illustration, in Eph 1 19–20. There we have the embarassing profusion of terms—which is really emphatic, not merely redundant—κατὰ τὴν ἐνέργειαν τοῦ κράτους τῆς ἰσχύος αὐτοῦ. This series is generally telescoped in translation, in some such phrase as "mighty power," "transcendent (or surpassing) greatness of the power." The key word, however, is not clearly understood in these translations. It is ἐνέργεια, cognate of ἐνεργέω, which carries just as clearly as the latter term the meaning "supernatural force" in all eight occurrences in the New Testament.[3] Not only in the New Testament, but in second and third century Greek elsewhere it carries the same connotation, as Moulton and Milligan set forth.[4] With it as the key word, the attendant series is a fitting prelude to the remainder of the statement: ἣν ἐνέργηκεν ἐν τῷ χριστῷ ἐγείρας αὐτὸν ἐκ νεκρῶν. The King James Version sets the style with this translation: "according to the working of his mighty power which he wrought in Christ when he raised him

[3] Eph 1 19, 3 7, 4 16, Phil 3 21, Col 1 29, 2 12, II Thess 2 9, 11.
[4] ἐνέργεια θεοῦ (Aristeas 266, OGIS 262⁴), ἐνέργεια δαίμονος (Poimandres p. 352²³), of magical operation (P. Mag. Par. 1. 159), of cosmic forces (Herm. ap. Stob. 1. 41. 6).

from the dead." Subsequent translations are similar with only the variation of expression. But the imagery of the picture here portrayed is much more vivid and vigorous. After the Pauline manner the writer declares, "I always mention you in my prayers, entreating the God of our Lord Jesus Christ, the Father of the Shekinah,[5] to give you a πνεῦμα of wisdom and an ἀποκάλυψις in which you recognize him, thus lighting up your mental eyes that you may know what hope lies in his summons, what a wealth of illumination attends the divine inheritance among the people who are holy, and how tremendously powerful is his δύναμις in us who believe." Then comes the climax as the writer continues, "This is a manifestation of the same supernatural force (ἐνέργεια) so mighty in him, which he infused in the Christ when he raised him from among the dead, and seated him at his right hand in the heavenly sphere, superior to every ἀρχή, ἐξουσία, δύναμις, κυριότης, and every ὄνομα that can be named for magical purposes not only in this present era but in the coming era as well." Here the canvas is crowded with mystical, supernatural spirits. The picture is an admixture of both Jewish and Hellenistic figures; the result appears as a Judaeo-Hellenistic μυστήριον based upon the common belief in spirit-possession. Ἐνέργεια always in the New Testament refers to the mystic supernatural force of divine or evil spirit, and ἐνεργέω to its infusion or operation in one spirit-possessed.

Again, in a familiar part of Paul's Corinthian correspondence ἐνεργέω occurs twice along with two occurrences of the cognate ἐνέργημα (I Cor 12 6–11). There Paul is explaining to his troublesome Hellenistic converts in Corinth about τὰ πνευματικά. There are various kinds of χαρίσματα, but only one πνεῦμα. These χαρίσματα are not merely human endowments or gifts in the modern sense, but rather supernatural abilities granted by the one πνεῦμα, who possesses men. Further, writes Paul, there are various ἐνεργήματα, but only one θεός. The ἐνεργήματα are specific supernatural powers, distinguished from ἐνέργεια as general supernatural force, and all have their source in God, ὁ ἐνεργῶν τὰ πάντα ἐν πᾶσιν, i. e. "who infuses

5 Cf. I Cor 15 40 ff.

all these specific supernatural powers in all so gifted." Then
after listing the several powers Paul concludes, πάντα δὲ ταῦτα
ἐνεργεῖ τὸ ἓν καὶ τὸ αὐτὸ πνεῦμα . . . κ. τ. λ. "One and the
same Spirit infuses all these supernatural powers, distributing
them among us as he desires."

II

The occurrences of ἐνεργοῦμαι in the New Testament are
nine in number—seven in Paul, one in Ephesians, and one in
James.[6] Although Lightfoot held that the word is always middle,
"never passive in Paul," we agree with Armitage Robinson to
the contrary that all nine usages are passive. But Professor
Robinson confessed to difficulty in applying the traditional
meaning to the several contexts, and concluded that the active
and passive forms "come nearly to the same thing," viz. "to
be operative" and "to be made operative." The only distinction
he observed was that in the latter case we are reminded "that
the operation is not self-originated." Our suggestion, however,
is that the contexts in which ἐνεργοῦμαι appears are all satisfied
by the passive of the meaning we have already assigned to
ἐνεργέω. "To be infused with supernatural spirit" (or, possessed) is the meaning in two instances; and in the other seven,
"to be made supernaturally operative."

Several heretofore difficult passages are clarified by the application of this interpretation. Begin with the well-known, oft-
quoted statement from Jas 5 16, "the effectual fervent prayer
of a righteous man availeth much" (King James). But
ἐνεργουμένη, the modifier of δέησις, does not mean "effectual
and fervent," nor does the word have reference to the efficacy
of human fervor. Wyclif had translated this verse, "forsothe
the *continuel* preyer of a juste man is muche worthe," for he
found his latin text reading *assidua*. The Old Latin (ff) had read
instead *frequens.* Apparently the difficulty at this point is a
very old one, and it is interesting to see how recent translators
have resolved it. The Revised Versions read: "the supplication

---

[6] Rom. 7 5, II Cor 1 6, 4 12, Gal 5 6, Eph 3 20, Col 1 29, I Thess 2 13,
II Thess 2 7, Jas 5 16.

of a righteous man availeth much *in its working*." The Twentieth
Century version: "great is the power of a good man's *fervent*
prayer." Weymouth: "powerful is the *heartfelt* supplication of a
righteous man." Moffatt: "the prayers of the righteous have a
powerful *effect*." Goodspeed: "an upright man can do a great
deal by prayer *when he tries*." But in all these, we contend, the
real point is missed. By our interpretation, the idea expressed
is, that "the prayer of an upright man is very powerful, when it
is set in operation by supernatural force (ἐνεργουμένη)." It is
not human effort, sincerity, fervor nor persistency that matters,
it is rather that the prayer be ἐνεργουμένη, supernaturally
operative.

A similar expression is found in Paul's Galation letter (5 6),
ἀλλὰ πίστις δι' ἀγάπης ἐνεργουμένη, the usual translation
of which is "faith working through love." But such an English
expression is far from catching all the meaning compressed into
this brief phrase. Paul is in the midst of the argument that any
who submit to circumcision are thereby bound to observe the
whole Jewish Law, and moreover are restricted to that one
method alone whereby they may achieve salvation, that is, they
may be pronounced δίκαιος by God, only on the basis of strict
obedience to the Law. At this point, Paul uses the antonym
καταργοῦμαι, in the aorist passive, of which notice may be
taken here. All of you who seek to be pronounced δίκαιος
through the Law, he says, κατηργήθητε ἀπὸ χριστοῦ, i. e.
"have been deprived of the efficacious spirit of Christ." No
longer is He in you, nor you in Him; you have been exorcised
from him. Next comes a phrase sadly abused and misunderstood,
"fallen from grace" (King James), which obviously here refers
to the forfeit of the opportunity offered through the χάρις of
God to achieve salvation through belief in Christ. You have
fallen away from the faith cult made available by the grace of
God. Such is the argument, which Paul concludes by pointing
out that "neither circumcision nor uncircumcision is powerful"
(to effect salvation), but πίστις ἐνεργουμένη, i. e. belief in
Christ made supernaturally operative, a means afforded to men
δι' ἀγάπης ("because God loves them").

One more illustration may be presented from II Thess. 2 7,

τὸ γὰρ μυστήριον ἤδη ἐνεργεῖται τῆς ἀνομίας. "For the mystery of iniquity (lawlessness) doth already work," the older versions read; while the later versions agree in rendering "wickedness (lawlessness, disobedience) is already at work in secret." Again, we feel that the color has gone out of the picture because the full connotation of ἐνεργοῦμαι has been missed. Here is the picture. The Day of the Lord has not yet come, the writer insists, notwithstanding any report or claim to the contrary. It awaits certain eschatological events, the great rebellion of Satanic hosts, and the ἀποκάλυψις of the Opponent of the Law, who will set himself up over other deities and call himself God, even taking the place of God in the temple. Don't you remember that we told you about this when we were there with you? So now you realize what is causing the delay. But, the writer hastens to add by way of encouragement, the Satanic μυστήριον has already been made supernaturally active (ἐνεργεῖται). Such an interpretation is a long way from the modern concept, that "wickedness is already at work in secret" (Twentieth Century Version). But if fits precisely into the first century mood, and more particularly into its context. Follow the explanation of the correspondent a little further. The only remaining obstacle to the dawning of the Day of the Lord is the preliminary removal of the Satanic agent. Then come the climactic ἀποκάλυψις of Satan himself, whom the Lord Jesus will destroy by merely breathing upon him. Now again, this writer uses the antonym καταργέω: καὶ καταργήσει τῇ ἐπιφανείᾳ τῆς παρουσίας αὐτοῦ. "By the very epiphany attendant upon the Lord's παρουσία he will render powerless (or exorcise) that one whose παρουσία is accomplished by the ἐνέργεια of Satan, attended by δύναμις, σημεῖα, and τέρατα ψεύδους." The παρουσία of the Satanic agent will be "full of wicked deception for men who are going to destruction, because they refuse to love the truth and be saved" (Goodspeed). That is why, he concludes, God is to send ἐνέργειαν πλάνης, so that these men may have faith in ψεῦδος rather than ἀλήθεια. All the way through the correspondent's course of argument the opposing forces of Satan and God, evil and good, falsehood and truth are shown in eschatological imagery. The parallelism of their

respective cosmic action and development is evident from
μυστήριον to ἀποκάλυψις. It is the ἐνέργεια, or supernatural
power, of each that is applied against the other in the hostility
between them. ᾽Ενεργεῖται in v. 7 must be interpreted,
therefore, as a part of this imagery, and connotes that the
Satanic power in the form of a μυστήριον has already been
infused into the human area of the cosmic struggle.

While this heightened meaning of ἐνεργέω and ἐνεργοῦμαι
is not generally found in contemporary Greek outside the New
Testament, it is found in the Apostolic Fathers in all four occurrences of the verb (two active, two passive).[7] The use in Hermas
is particularly interesting, where especially over an extended
dialogue in *Mandates* 5:2:1–6:2:6 the strong term ἐνέργεια
occurs seven times. At the beginning of this section (5:2:1),
ἐνεργέω is used by Hermas' instructor as he explains: "Hear,
then, the ἐνέργεια of Ill-temper—how it destroys the servants
of God by its supernatural power, and how it leads them astray
from righteousness. But it does not lead astray those who are
filled with faith, nor can it possess them (ἐνεργῆσαι) because
my power is with them." Again we have the picture of two
mighty cosmic supernatural forces contending for control, and
in any one man one or the other, but not both simultaneously,
may dwell. Such a usage as has here been illustrated for the
Apostolic Fathers encourages the view that in early Christian
literature as a whole the interpretation here urged is applicable,
but further inquiry has not been made. Of the antonym and
cognates of ἐνεργέω, beyond the occurrences already incidentally
pointed out, a similar argument might be set forth toward
demonstrating that they too all live in the same supernatural
atmosphere and carry the same supernatural connotation, in
the New Testament and Apostolic Fathers. All of which tends
further to support the interpretation we here urge of ἐνεργέω,
generally "to infuse with supernatural spirit," or "to possess,"
while καταργέω means "to render powerless" the opposing
supernatural spirit (which can be done only by a supernatural
spirit), therefore, in effect, "to exorcise."

---

[7] Hermas *Mand.* 5:2:1, I Clem 60 1, Barn 1 7, 2 1.

THE MEANING OF APA

About forty years ago I heard the respected scholar, W. H. P. Hatch, remark in a lecture that the particle αρα had lost any meaning. The remark brought the little particle to special attention and I find that since then in my Greek texts αρα has frequently been encircled. In the course of the years, there has built up an awareness of a consistent sense wherever αρα is found. This sense is not one commonly provided in any lexicon and yet it reflects a distinctive meaning in its context; therefore it is worthy of an effort to explain and to demonstrate this meaning.

It has been stated often that αρα cannot be translated. This statement implies that there is a meaning elusive though it may be, and it further suggests that one may often be perplexed as to the sense, if there be any. Surely clarity and consistency of meaning must be established before satisfactory translation is possible. The traditional and commonplace meaning given is the inferential "then, so, therefore," if it is translated at all. Without necessarily rejecting this sense, it will here be maintained that αρα does possess a primary meaning rarely disclosed in translation and yet consistently in evidence in its every context.

Although my impression of consistent meaning has been cumulative through the years, not until now has the effort been made at a systematic and exhaustive study, which includes the usage of αρα in the Hellenistic papyri, in the Septuagint, in the New Testament, in the Apostolic Fathers and in the early Apologists.[1] Fortunately, an index or concordance has been available in each of these categories to render such a study manageable. In all of these sources I have found a total of approximately 150 occurrences of αρα ranging from the third century B.C. to the third Christian century. In a great majority of the cases (about 130) the texts show the term with an acute accent on the first syllable; whereas only about twenty instances show the circumflex accent. Of course, the accents are not derived from any early non-accenting

---

[1] Lampe's patristic concordance does not list αρα. Sophocles' byzantine lexicon cites only two instances and gives the traditional sense.

manuscripts; but rather the accents have been determined by editors under the influence of the classical rule that ἄρα is the interrogative particle. This distinction is, however, no more than an orthographic formality, especially since it is sometimes difficult to decide whether or not the context is interrogative. Furthermore the interrogative form τίς ἄρα does not employ the circumflex.

One-third (50) of our instances of αρα occur in the New Testament, and half of these are in the Pauline correspondence where the inferential construction is frequent, and in turn half of these are in the form αρα ουν (peculiar to Paul) where the inferential idea is clearly present even without αρα. Nearly one-third (43) of our occurrences of the particle are found in the Septuagint, and half of these instances are concentrated in Job and the Psalms. In the early Christian Apologists we find αρα used twenty-eight times, fifteen occurring in Justin's Dialogue with Trypho. Only thirteen instances have been found in 3000 papyrus texts ranging across five centuries B.C. and A.D. If we now examine a selected series of these occurrences of αρα, it will in a manner recapitulate the cumulative experience of the writer as he has encountered successive contexts of the particle tending to confirm the meaning herein proposed.

Papyri

First, we may note a personal letter on papyrus, written in Egypt about A.D. 200 (OP 2680). Arsinoë writes to her sister that their brother will convey her letter and also a gift. In business-like manner she reports: "If the roads are firm . . . I shall go off immediately to your farmer and ask him for your rents—if he will give them to me (εαν αρα μοι αυτα δοι). You ought to have sent me a letter to him. Or, if you have written in advance to him to give them to me, I shall go off and collect them."

It is to be observed that αρα is here employed in the context of the tentative, of the uncertain, of the unresolved. The farmer's response is not predictable, indeed even the circumstances are unknown and undefined. The equal balancing of opposing prospects and of contrasting possibilities, reflects a state of unresolved circumstances. It is true that all this is discerned in the context, and it is context always that provides the clue to meaning. Initially, at least, the question is here raised as to whether or not αρα consistently appears in this meaning in similar contexts elsewhere.

Once again, we find a speech by an advocate in an Egyptian court, about A.D. 130 (OP 472). He is defending Hermione who is accused of the attempted poisoning of Sarapion. "It was from his own house that he emerged saying that he had been poisoned. When he left Hermione's house he uttered then no complaint to anyone, nor showed any suspicion; rather, it was when he came out of the house where he lives with his son and heir that he then alleged that he had been poisoned. He had indeed reasons for administering poison to himself . . . he was ruined by creditors and mentally disturbed. If there was one who (ει δὲ αρα τις και) did plot against him, the most likely person is his son."

Here, then, is a similar context of the tentative, the uncertain, the unresolved. The evidence does not reveal who might have been the culprit, nor indeed if there was a culprit at all. Not only is there doubt about who may be guilty, but even the premise of any guilt whatever is uncertain.

Let us glance quickly among the papyri at additional contexts of αρα, where even without our further explanation one may readily discern the same element of the tentative, the uncertain, the unresolved alternatives.

"If you should find someone" (ως αρα . . . εαν) OP 1765 (third century)

Appianus to the Emperor: "Who has recalled me . . . Was it (αρα) the senate or you, the arch-pirate?" OP 33 (late second century)

"Please come to me . . . but if not . . ." (εαν δ' αρα μη) OP 1215 (about A.D. 200)

Hermias to his sister: "Am I to be (μη αρα) distracted and oppressed until heaven takes pity on me?" OP 120 (fourth century)

"Do not neglect this, lest indeed (μη αρα ποτε) you choose to hand over the keeping of the whole house to Heraïs" OP 1070 (third century)

LXX

The same connotation of αρα is consistently observed in the translation Greek of the Septuagint contexts, and may be fully exhibited in the frequent usage of the particle.

Sarah laughed and said, "Shall I of a surety (αρα γε αληθως) bear a child, who am old?" Gen. 18.13 ASV

Abimelech to Isaac: "Is she then (αρα γε) your wife? If so, why would you say 'my sister'?" Gen. 26.9

Jacob to Joseph: (αρα γε) "Am I and your mother and brothers to come and bow down to you?" Gen. 37.10

The Book of Job has thirteen instances of this tentative connotation of αρα; one of the best illustrations is the well known exclamation: "Oh that I knew (τις διαρα) where to find him!" Job 23.3 (Moffatt)

Here are examples from the Psalms: (57.2) "Do you really (ει αληθως αρα) speak what is right, gods?" (J. M. P. Smith), and again (57.12 bis): "Whether (ει αρα) there is fruitage for the righteous man ... whether (αρα) there is a god who judges." In the Septuagint version of Daniel 6.21, King Darius calls out: "Daniel, (ει αρα) are you alive or not?"

A span of five centuries of the Greek language ranges from the pre-Christian Septuagint to the post-apostolic papyri, wherein the contextual setting of αρα is consistently tentative, offering unresolved alternatives and uncertain circumstances. In the middle of this period, the New Testament documents comprise the chief literature and exhibit fifty instances of the usage and the sense of αρα. It is therefore incumbent upon us to examine some of these occurrences, with our question in mind: What meaning does αρα have and how may it be expressed in translation?

Mark

In the Gospel of Mark, αρα is used only twice, both times in passages with synoptic parallel. In Mark's account of the Stilling of the Tempest (4.41), Jesus speaks to his companions: "Why are you so terrified? How is it that you have no trust? ... And to one another they said, "Who is this man (τις αρα ουτος εστιν), that wind and wave obey him?" Translations either ignore the αρα or weakly ask, "Who, then, is he?" We may grant that the inferential idea is in the context, with or without αρα. Luke (8.25) repeats the Markan passage verbatim including αρα, but Matthew (8.27) drops the αρα without loss of the inferential logic. But the use of αρα in Mark heightens the wonderment and excitement of unresolved perplexity. The evangelist does have his own answer but he here describes the disciples' state of mind as beyond the limits of reason. The particle αρα bears its own special meaning quite apart from the contextual inference. It conveys the exciting sense of some identification of "this man" beyond normal knowledge or rational solution.

The other use of αρα in Mark occurs in the story of the fig tree
(11.13). Jesus recognized the tree at a distance and he approached
to find out whether or not (ει αρα) it had any figs on it. Did it
or did it not? The answer must wait until he might draw close, and
the answer could be a yes or a no. The sense of the tentative, of
the uncertain, of the unresolved, is again reflected in the particle
αρα. The attitude of inquiry is peculiar to Mark ("to find out whether
or not it had any figs on it"), for the Matthean parallel simply
states that "he saw a fig tree along the road and he came to it
and found no fruit on it." Matthew omits the phrase of inquiry,
and therefore cannot employ αρα. His is a flat description of fact,
whereas Mark holds the reader in suspense for a tentative moment
"whether or not he might find any fruit on it." The particle αρα
adds to the context a sense of alternative possibilities, of opposing
answers.

Matthew

The particle is used more often in Matthew and Luke, often in
synoptic parallel. Following the illustration in Matthew of the
impossibility of a camel passing through a needle's eye, the disciples
draw the inference (19.25): "Then who (τις αρα) could possibly
be saved?" The problem of identifying any person so qualified
implies a completely unresolved conundrum. The tentative, the
uncertain, the impasse, is reflected in the presence of αρα. Of
special interest here is the observation that αρα and its exciting
tension is a Matthean addition to the expression in Mark 10.26
and in Luke 18.26. The little particle is fraught with its own characteristic and consistent sense, beyond the logical inference of
the context. It is the context that conveys the inferential in all
three gospels, whereas alone in Matthew αρα adds the psychological
element of suspense and quandary.

The same sense is illustrated also in Matthew 18.1: "Who (τις
αρα) is the greatest one in the kingdom of heaven?" Who, indeed?
In the question there is implied the same impossibility of identification, the same quandary remaining unresolved in the mind
of inquiring disciples, even after the response of Jesus. Similarly,
in Matthew 19.27, Peter's question is an open question without
a direct answer: "What (τι αρα) will there be for us?"

The particle αρα is used not only in the structure of a question
but also in the declarative form, sometimes in the "apodosis"

of an implied condition. In Capernaum the collectors of the temple-tax asked Peter, "Does not your teacher pay the tax?" Later, Jesus commented: "What do you think, Simon? Do kings take tribute from their subjects or from aliens?" When Peter answered, "Aliens," Jesus urged upon him a conclusion (Matt. 17.26) to the first question: "Would you then reason (αρα γε) that in the case of the temple-tax 'sons' are exempt?" This conclusion by analogy may appear to be correct, and yet traditional practice would challenge that position. Once again the sense of αρα reflects the tentative and the unresolved possibility of opposing positions. Jesus has first appealed to the *opinion* of Peter, and the presence of αρα recognizes dependence upon an element of judgment and persuasion.

The same considerations apply to another well-known context (Matt. 12.28 and Luke 11.20): "If I ... am exorcising demons, (αρα) God's kingdom has come to you" (*jusqu' à vous, zu euch kommen*). Here again is a debatable viewpoint and a questionable logic. The αρα calls for a qualifying phrase such as "Would you agree" or "Is it reasonable to conclude." The consistent function of αρα becomes in its context an important guide to the translator who must not overlook the connotation of the tentative.

Luke-Acts

The usage of Luke likewise reflects the same contextual conditions discussed above. At Jesus' birth, they asked the question (or pondered the inscrutable): "What (τι αρα) will this child be?" They found no clear response in Luke's own comment: "For the hand of the Lord was with him"—which could only increase their wonderment. Again, in the story of the Importunate Widow who finally succeeded in her appeal (Luke 18.2-8), Jesus explains to the disciples: "Will not God vindicate his elect, who cry to him day and night? . . . He will vindicate them promptly. But (he poses the question) when the Son of Man comes, will he find (αρα ευρησει) man trustful of him?" Luke's characteristic πλην reveals the adversative doubt and question which is here reflected also in αρα. The future state of man's trust is unpredictable, and αρα emphasizes that unresolved question.

Another impressive example of the meaning of αρα is found in Luke 22.23. At their common meal Jesus speaks to the disciples: "The hand of my betrayer is with me on the table' . . . and they began to aks each other who (τις αρα) it might be who would do this." The implication is that, in the thought of the disciples, such an action is incredible and to identify a suspect among them would be impossible. The translator, aware of the sequel, represents the disciples themselves as merely discussing "which one" would so act. But the αρα represents them as unbelieving that any one of them might conceivably so act. The very suggestion by Jesus they must consider no more than tentative and uncertain.

Note again the use of αρα by Luke in Acts 12.18. He tells of Peter imprisoned by Herod and miraculously released through the mediation of an angel. Quite mysteriously, Peter makes an appearance at the door of John Mark's mother, and leaves an explanation for James, and then "departed and went to another place." Against all this background of mystery and miracle, the confounded guards wonder "what (τι αρα) had become of Peter!" Once more we find the consistent mood of αρα, in the face of the uncertain, the unresolved quandary. Here the reader is well prepared for this sense of αρα by the careful presentation of the background story of miraculous details and mysterious circumstances. Peter's exciting disappearance eclipsed Herod's failure to find him.

The early incredibility of Gentile salvation gave rise to instances of αρα in Acts 11.18 and 17.27. In the former reference it comes as a conclusion to Paul's persuasion in which he insisted: "The Holy Spirit fell on them just as on us." So he proposes: (αρα γε και) "also to the Gentiles God gave repentance as a means to life." The disciples' acceptance of this assertion, however, depends upon effective persuasion, and that this is so is reflected in αρα which conveys this qualification, "Would you agree" or "Do you see that . . ." One must first accept Paul's testimony and then also acknowledge the logical force of his reasoning. Paul's proposal is not dogmatic, but with αρα is put tentatively and left to the approval of the hearer. The form implies that an element of uncertainty is to be faced and resolved.

In Acts 17.27, Paul is again persuading that *all* men may seek God (ει αρα γε) "on the chance of finding him" (Moffatt). The element of uncertainty here lies in the question whether Gentile seeking can be successful, and the Vulgate version recognized this in its use of *forté*. The use of αρα here again implies the unresolved balance of opposing results, not in the mind of Paul, but recognized by him as resident in the thinking of his hearers.

We may additionally note but briefly a few other occurrences
of αρα in Acts to suggest their relevance to our thesis. The Tribune
speaks (21.38): "Do you know Greek? Might you be (ουκ αρα συ ει)
the Egyptian who recently stirred up a revolt?" Here the use of
αρα modifies the usual interrogative idiom which anticipates "yes"
for an answer, and the question therefore is "Are you or are you
not?" Although the fact is that he is not, the Tribune's question
assumes that either response may be expected. Moffatt and the
NEB translate: "You are not." But the particle αρα gives the
indication of the open question, the unresolved alternatives. In
8.30, Phillip speaks to the Ethiopian official: (αρα γε) "Do you
understand what you are reading?" With αρα, this is an open
question in the mind of Phillip who does not presume to know,
but seeks the answer from the Ethiopian. Evidence is not adequate
for us to discuss the problem of the languages used (by Phillip,
by the Ethiopian, or in the manuscript of Isaiah). We therefore
consider only the Greek report in Acts; and in the Greek idiom
the many consistent contexts of αρα indicate the open question
without biased assumption. In 8.22, Peter advises the calculating
magician, Simon: "Repent of your wickedness and pray the Lord
to forgive you, (ει αρα) if he conceivably may for your heart's
intentions." The αρα implies that Peter finds it difficult to believe
that Simon's heinous sin is forgivable. Either response is open;
God may or he may not fulfill the petition.

Paul

In the Pauline correspondence αρα is used frequently (28 times),
and twelve times it is combined with the inferential ουν. In 1 Cor.
15.15, it appears in the protasis of a condition, where Paul is
discussing the resurrection of Jesus: "How can some of you say
that there is no *anastasis*? If there is not, Christ has not been
raised ... We are even found to be falsely representing God,
because we testified that he raised Christ, whom he did not raise;
that is, if (ειπερ αρα) the dead are not raised." Surely Paul himself
has no doubt that the dead are raised, but the very fact of his
debating both sides reveals his realization that doubt and question
exist. It is quite appropriate for him to use αρα in a protasis whose
acceptance or rejection would divide his readers. So again in our
context αρα shares the quality of the tentative, unresolved alternatives.

In Galatians 2.17, we find αρα in an apodosis. Paul is arguing
the efficacy of faith for the believer's justification, as opposed to
the inefficacy of the Law. He seeks to close off a possible objection:
"If we, seeking our justification in Christ, are found ourselves to
be sinners, is it to be concluded (αρα) that Christ is sin's servant?"
He implies that, on the one hand, some will contend that this is
the logical conclusion; yet, on the other hand, he himself strongly
holds to the opposite view. As Paul puts the proposition, tentatively
with αρα, it is open to either answer.

This is the device of argument often used by Paul: the *reductio
ad absurdum*. We find it again, with αρα, in 1 Cor. 7.14, where
Paul explains that the non-believer in a "mixed" marriage becomes
one of the Christian community through the mate, "otherwise
(επει αρα) their children would be unclean." This again is offered
as the logical proposition and yet Paul affirms the opposite conclusion: "As it is, they are holy." But the proposition is initially,
however tentatively, open-ended and the opposing alternatives
must yet be resolved.

The same form of argument is found once again in 1 Cor. 15.14,
where αρα covers a double apodosis: "If Christ has not been raised,
vain (αρα) is our preaching and vain is your faith." The logic
of this proposition is unwelcome, and the argument works back-
ward: if you hold that the preaching and the faith are not in vain,
then you must revise the premise and acknowledge that Christ
has been raised. The focus of the proposition lies in the αρα apodosis
where the tentative alternatives are yet to be resolved. The particle
αρα is the signal for a decision between the open alternatives.
A few lines further on (15.18), Paul adds an additional apodosis:
(αρα) "so too those who fell asleep in Christ perished"—which
is another logical but unacceptable alternative. In eight lines of
argument (verses 14-18), Paul uses αρα three times, thus creating
a full impression of a delicate weighing of the open alternative.

Another instance of αρα in Paul is in 2 Cor. 5.14: "If one died
in the place of all, then (αρα, would you say that) all died?" Here
is the same tentative approach to Paul's conclusion, not pressed
upon his readers dogmatically but offered for their agreement.
Similarly, we have in Gal. 2.21: "If justification is gained through
the medium of the Law, then (αρα, is it clear to you that) Christ
died needlessly?" And again (Ephesians 2.19): "Since it is true
that Jew and Gentile both have access to the Father in the one

Spirit, (ουν) then it follows (αρα, does it?) that you Gentiles are
no longer aliens." Once again (Gal. 3.29): "If you belong to Christ,
you are descendants of Abraham (αρα, are you not?)." Also, in
I Cor. 5.10: ". . . since you would need to leave the world (αρα,
wouldn't you)." And Hebrews 12.8: "If you go without discipline,
. . . you are as bastards rather than sons (αρα, aren't you?)".
In all of these instances there is the open question, where opposing
responses are considered equally eligible, signaled by αρα which
more often stands first in its clause in the New Testament.

Romans

In Romans alone, Paul uses αρα eleven times, usually in the
form αρα ουν. The case of 5.18 is of special interest, where the
sense of the tentative in αρα covers the entire proposition. Here
it is not the αρα ουν that balances with ουτως και, but rather the
ως that balances with ουτως και, and the function of αρα is to
introduce the entire conception, thus: as this . . . so that (αρα,
would you agree?). The same may be true of Romans 10.17, that
the sense of αρα is applied to the double clause: "So faith comes
from what is heard and what is heard comes from the word of
Christ (αρα, isn't this so?)". In Romans 7.21-8.1, Paul uses αρα
three times within twelve lines of our text in describing his own
ambiguous religious condition. If we apply to this passage the
consistent connotation we have sought to explain, the sense of
the tentative reflects Paul's personal problem even as he testifies
to his conclusions. "If I do what I do not want, it is no longer I
that do it, but sin which dwells within me. I find it (αρα, so I feel)
to be a law . . . So then (αρα, as I see it) it is with my mind that I
serve God's Law whereas with the flesh I serve the law of sin.
There is now (αρα, I hold) no condemnation for those (of us) who
are in Christ Jesus". This celebrated self-debate of Romans 7
is here heavily weighted with the tentative sense of αρα.

Fathers

The Fathers of the second century consistently make use of
αρα with the same connotation of contingency or uncertainty.
Ignatius writes to the Ephesians (8.1): "When no quarrel has
gained a foothold among you, (αρα) you would be living in God's
way." Again, to the Trallians (10.1) he writes of docetic heresy:
"If . . . he suffered only in semblance . . . I die needlessly and

(αρα ουν) would be speaking falsely of the Lord." Hermas often makes quite explicit the sense of contingency in αρα. Vision III (4.3): ". . . who debate in their minds (ει αρα) whether these things are so or not;" and again (7.5): "I asked her (ει αρα) whether all these stones could have a place in this tower." Mandate II (2): "They asked him (τι αρα) what will happen to them." In Similitude 8 (3.3), the angel Michael observes them (ει αρα) "to see whether they have kept the law;" and again in 9 (5.7) the Shepherd asked the maidens "(ει αρα) whether the master of the tower had come." The particle in Diognetus 7.3 is an especially revealing instance: when God sent the Logos to men, "was it, as a man might suppose (αρα γε, ως ανθρωπων αν τις λογισαιτο), in sovereignty and fear and terror?" Another explicit context is found in Justin's Dialogue with Trypho (4.7): ". . . for them (ουδε αρα) there is no benefit from their punishment, (ως εοικεν) as it seems."

We have now reviewed sketchily about fifty instances of the use of αρα, and must resist further temptation to marshal additional illustrations of the consistently tentative context. In all these instances, we have observed the contingency which is open to opposing alternatives and the element of tentativity.

How to Translate

In the light of our discussion above, how might one translate the particle αρα? We have urged that αρα does possess its own meaning, going beyond the traditional sense of the inferential which is usually translated by "then, so, therefore." Not always, but frequently, αρα is found in an inferential context as especially in the argumentation of Job and in the reasoning of Paul where the term αρα ουν is frequent. However, the sense of the inferential is already in the context which does not require the word αρα itself, and also in translation the sense of the inferential is present even when no word stands for αρα, such as "then," "donc," "denn," "igitur," "ergo." It is not surprising, therefore, that some have come to believe that αρα itself conveys no meaning.

It may be necessary to remind ourselves occasionally that meaning is not created by a lexicon nor even by the lexicographer. We are dependent always upon one source and that is the consistent usage of a term in context. We do recognize the inferential context

of αρα in many passages, and yet there are many others passages
where inference plays no part; for example (Matt. 18.1) "Who
(τις αρα) is the greatest . . . ?" or (Matt. 19.27) "What (τι αρα)
will there be for us?" or (Luke 1.66) "What (τι αρα) will this child
be?" or (Acts 12.18) "What (τι αρα) had become of Peter?" In
such passages where the inferential is lacking, it may be supposed
that αρα does not have any meaning.

There *is*, however, a connotation that appears consistently
in αρα contexts, and this is the sense of the tentative, of the contingent, of the suspense between opposing alternatives at that
moment unresolved, of the acknowledgment of uncertain response.

But how is such a meaning to be translated? In some cases
the tentative or contingent may be easily expressed by such terms
as "perhaps," "perchance," "conceivably." "Who perchance is the
greatest?" "What will there be for us, peradventure?" "Who
conceivably is this?" "What might one suppose had become of
Peter?" All such terms suggest alternative possibilities of response
at the moment of speaking, and thus hold the reader's mind in a
state of suspense. This is a psychological quality that overlies the
basic statement. The particle itself, having lost its post-positive
habit, more often is found first in its clause and serves as a signal
of the quandary to be set forth. Already in existing translations,
here and there αρα is represented by an appropriate qualifying
term. From the Hebrew text, Meek in the American translation
(1927) did translate Genesis 18.3: "If perchance (LXX ει αρα) I
find favor with you;" and again Num. 22.11: "Perhaps (LXX ει
αρα) I shall be able to fight against them" (followed by the RSV
also). In the latter, Moffatt reads "maybe," whereas KJ and ASV
both read "peradventure."

In the New Testament also, current translations occasionally
do employ an explicit term which helps to conserve the original
element of suspense in αρα, such as we here cite:

Mark 11.13 (Vg.): "venit siquid forté inveniret in ea."
Luke 1.66 (Luther): "Was, meinest du, will aus dem Kindlein werben?"
Luke 18.8 (Vg.): ". . . veniens, putas, inveniet fidem in terra?"
Acts 8.30 (Moffatt): "Do you really understand what you are reading?"
Acts 12.18 (Weymouth): "What could possibly have become of Peter?"
Acts 17.27 (Vg.): "si forté attractent eum" and similarly (KJ ASV)
    "haply" and (Weymouth and Goodspeed) "perhaps". Compare
    (Phillips, RSV) "in the hope that" and (Moffatt) "on the chance
    of."

1 Cor. 15.15 (Weymouth): "If in reality . . ." Compare "s'il est vrai," followed by Goodspeed, Phillips, RSV.
Galatians 5.11 (Twentieth Century): "It seems that the cross has ceased to be an obstacle."
2 Cor. 1.17 (Phillips): "Does it mean that we are fickle?"
2 Cor. 5.14 (Phillips): ". . . in a sense they all died."
2 Clem. 8.6, 14.3 (Lake): "He seems to mean this . . ."

All of these touches serve to convey the tentative sense of αρα.

The only source that supplies a meaning consonant with our explanation is the modern Greek dictionary. J. T. Pring (*Oxford Dictionary of Modern Greek*, 1965) defines αρα and αραγε in the tentative sense of "can it be, I wonder if," and as an adverb, "is it." Carroll H. Brown (*Greek Dictionary*, 1928[3]) gives the same meanings for αραγε. A. Kyriakides (*Modern Greek-English Dictionary*, 1909[2]) agrees with Pring as to αραγε although he defines αρα separately by the inferential "so, thus, therefore, consequently." It is of great significance that the tentative sense has survived in the Greek of our own day, thus standing in confirmation that this sense is properly applicable to the literature of earlier days.

It is often said that αρα cannot be easily translated explicitly, and this is understandable because its meaning is not explicit but is rather implied by the context. However, the tentative sense of αρα can well be brought out by the use of an appropriate phrase. We have seen that Justin used αρα with just such a phrase of his own ("as it seems") and that Diognetus also had his own phrase ("as a man might suppose"). In similar vein, the Vulgate translated Mark 4.41: "Quis, putas, est ille?" and also Luke 8.25: "Quis, putas, hic est?" In our own translating today we too must find the suitable phrase for each context of αρα. That the translation of αρα may be difficult is indeed true, especially because each instance requires its own phrase, carefully formulated. The criterion for the suitability of a phrase is that it will serve to keep open, to hold in suspense, the tentative alternatives of response. A variety of suitable forms may here be suggested, in illustration of the quality of αρα.

> "If I . . . am exorcising demons, (αρα) would you accept this as evidence that God's kingdom has come to you?" Matt. 12.28; Luke 11.20
> "Then the sons are exempt, (αρα γε) would you say?" Matt. 17.26
> "(αρα γε) Would you agree that you recognize the worth of trees by the quality of their fruit?" Matt. 7.20

"Who (τις αρα) is the faithful and wise servant, would you say?"
Matt. 24.45 Luke 12.42
"(τις αρα) Can we believe that it is possible for anyone to be saved?"
Matt. 19.25
"(ουκ αρα) Might you be that Egyptian who recently raised a revolt?"
Acts 21.38
"So then (αρα ουν) would you agree with this: that as one man's
trespass led to condemnation for all men, so one man's righteous
act leads to acquittal and life for all men?" Rom. 5.18
Here the full statement comprises three verses (17-19) and the
tentative sense of αρα casts its suspense over the whole.

Many another New Testament passage could well have been
expressed by its author with the use of αρα; for example, John
4.29: "(μητι) You are not the Messiah, are you?" where the negative
response is indicated. If, however, αρα had here been used, we
should then translate "Would you be" or "I wonder if you are
the Messiah." Acts 15.9 is the kind of context in which αρα would
have added the element of suspense: "God made no distinction
between us and them, but cleansed their hearts by faith." If αρα
had been used here by Paul, as in Galatians 3.7 and 3.29, this
would have required a prefatory phrase such as "Do you see that..."
It is obvious that αρα is not a required idiom in every such context,
but where it does appear it adds its own distinctive and consistent
meaning, the sense of the tentative in suspense.

Wherever αρα is present it serves as a guide to the translator
to express the tentative and contingent sense within its context.
This would have guarded against erroneous translation in many a
passage hitherto. In 1901, the ASV translated Job 38.21: "(αρα)
Doubtless thou knowest," and so influenced the Moffatt version:
"Surely." But the very essence of an αρα context is doubt and
uncertainty. Here it calls for a tentative form: "Might one suppose
that thou knowest, for you were born when the earth was made?"
In the American Translation, Gordon translated Jeremiah 4.10
(LXX αρα γε): "Thou hast certainly deceived this people," after
the ASV "surely." But this αρα passage calls instead for something
like this: "It seems that you have deceived this people." Weymouth
(1903) translated Romans 7.3: "(αρα ουν) This accounts for the
fact that ..." and 9.18: "(αρα ουν) Which is a proof of ..." Yet
the very presence of αρα advises us that we deal not with fact and
proof, but rather with tentative and uncertain circumstance.

Finally, we may make a double observation about the meaning

of αρα. The first part is negative: does αρα in the literature really mean "then, so, therefore?" Close analysis would suggest that the inferential idea is expressed by the context itself, whether or not the particle αρα is present. The second part is positive: has it here been demonstrated in the numerous contexts examined that αρα does indeed have its own meaning and that its meaning lies in its expression of the tentative state of mind and of the suspense between open alternatives? If so, we may here conclude with an αρα proposal: "Can it be, I wonder, that this meaning should be adopted in any future Greek lexicon?"

THE MEANING OF [KATA] KYRIEYEIN

The reason for dealing with this term may at the outset be made clear by quoting key passages from the King James Version and the Revised Standard Version. In the Synoptic parallels of Mark 10:42 and Matthew 20:25 and Luke 22:25 the KJV reads :

Mk : ... they which are accounted to rule over the Gentiles exercise lordship over them ...
Mt : ... the princes of the Gentiles exercise dominion over them ...
Lk : ... the kings of the Gentiles exercise lordship over them ...
    The RSV, however, reads thus :
Mk : ... those who are supposed to rule over the Gentiles lord it over them...
Mt : ... the rulers of the Gentiles lord it over them ...
Lk : ... the kings of the Gentiles exercise lordship over them ...

Why does the RSV translate Mk and Mt differently from Lk? Why does the RSV change the KJV in Mk and Mt, and translate instead "lord it over"? What change of meaning is thus introduced? Is the RSV justified in representing that the Evangelists described Gentile princes and rulers as "lording it over" their subjects? This idiom in modern English conveys a sense of arrogance and oppression and an abuse of power. Does the KJV or the RSV do better justice to the Greek as originally composed?

Such questions concerning the proper translation all point to the need to understand the terms κυριεύειν (as in Lk) and the compound κατακυριεύειν (as in Mk and Mt). It is therefore proposed here to review the usage of these terms, in the literature extant from the Hellenistic-Roman era, in which the New Testament writings had their literary setting.

First of all, consider the Septuagint, with the aid of Hatch and Redpath.[1] The simple form κυριεύειν is reported in sixty instances, but not once has it been construed to mean "to lord it over". It is

---

[1] *Concordance to the Septuagint* (Oxford Clarendon, 1897) vol. 2.

equated at times with ἄρχειν or with βασιλεύειν, and occasionally with the synonym δεσπόζειν with no heightened sense. The consistent interpretation is simply "to rule, to have dominion". The compound κατακυριεύειν appears less often in the Septuagint, seventeen times. It too is usually translated "to rule, to have dominion", and sometimes "to subdue". Both forms of the verb are used in the same sense and appear to be quite interchangeable. Absolute dominion may be exercised strictly and yet legally. Any intensification by the prefix κατα is not apparent anywhere in LXX usage. The conclusion one may surely draw is that in the LXX version κυριεύειν and κατακυριεύειν are the equivalent of one another, and that both plainly mean "to have or to exercise dominion, to subdue or control, to rule or to be a ruler". Never is any intimation of arrogance discerned in the LXX, and there is no instance of "lording it over".

Secondly, let us consider the papyri surviving from the Hellenistic-Roman era. For this purpose, we have examined the references in forty volumes of the Oxyrhynchus Papyri[2] and a few additional sources, all of which amount to about 3,000 papyrus documents, ranging in date from 73 B.C. to A.D. 316. In this massive collection one finds that κατακυριεύειν is *never* used, and that κυριεύειν occurs about fifty times. The most frequent context is a Lease of Land and the same legal form is always found repeatedly, in the sense "to be the owner, or lord of". In *OP* II (273.24) we find a typical Cession of Land contemporary with the Christian Gospels : "Julia Heracla ... has ceded to her daughter Gaia ... 15 arourae ... Gaia ... shall therefore possess and own the land" (κρατεῖν οὖν καὶ κυριεύειν τὴν Γαίαν ...). Again, in A.D. 130 (*OP* IV 730.19) "Serapion ... leased to Valerius ... 5 arourae ... The lessor shall be the owner of the crop until" full payment has been made. (ὃν καὶ κυριεύειν τῶν καρπῶν ἕως ...). These are typical samples of a repeated context. All these business transactions are authentic and legal, and ownership and control are quite legitimate. The constant sense of κυριεύειν is "to be the owner, or lord of". Nowhere in all the papyri is there an instance where κυριεύειν has been or should be translated "to lord it over".

Next, let us look into the Apostolic Fathers, contemporary with the New Testament books. Goodspeed's Index[3] shows no usage of [κατα]κυριεύειν in I Clem, II Clem, Ign, or the Didaché. In Barnabas

---

[2] Grenfell and Hunt, *OP* I to XL (London : Egypt Exploration Fund, 1898-1972).
[3] Edgar J. Goosdpeed, *Index Patristicus* (Leipzig : Heinrichs, 1907).

there are five instances of the verb, two of which have the compound form. The meaning is sometimes related to ἄρχειν and ἐξουσιάζειν.

vi.13 κατακυριεύσατε rule over (the land)

vi.17 κατακυριεύοντες shall possess (the earth)

vi.18 κυριεύσῃ have domination over (created life)

vii.11 κυριεῦσαι possess it (through suffering)

xxi.5 κυριεύων May God who is Lord over (the world)

Nowhere does the usage in Barnabas convey the sense "to lord it over".

The Shepherd of Hermas finds our verb useful, especially in the Mandates (particularly Mandate XII), usually in the sense "to master, to overcome". The compound form is employed thirteen times and the simple form only twice, with the same meaning for both forms: "to master, to have power, to be lord over, to rule over, to possess, to dominate". The meaning of mastery or dominance is itself elative and is not subject to further degree or intensity. There is no instance in Hermas where the verb is translatable as "to lord it over".

We have further examined early Christian Apologists, with the aid once more of Goodspeed.[4] Aristides uses the compound form only, three times, in the sense "to rule, to control" the earth, water and fire. Justin Martyr employs the simple form four times and the compound form six times; nine instances in the Dialogue and one in his Apology. Six of these passages derive from the LXX (Gen, Deut, Isa, and three forms from Psalms 71 and 109). In Justin, the simple and compound forms share the same meanings without distinction, chiefly "to rule over, to subdue". κατακυριεύσατε is once paired with ἀρχέτωσαν "to have dominion". Other translations of κυριεύειν are "to be Lord" of all, "to have power" over His soul. Once again, the Apologists show that both forms of the verb convey the same sense. Never is either form used in the sense of "to lord it over".

With the aid of Lampe,[5] we have examined instances of our terms in other patristic writings, where we find the meaning to be consistent with the findings above: "to rule, to control, to hold sway, to subdue, to be master of, to be lord over, to dominate". We have further consulted additional passages from the Sophocles lexicon[6] and have found both forms of the verb to mean simply "to rule over, to master", but never "to lord it over".

---

4 Edgar J. Goodspeed, *Index Apologeticus* (Leipzig: Heinrichs, 1912).

5 G. W. H. Lampe, *A Patristic Greek Lexicon* (Oxford: Clarendon, 1961-68).

6 E. A. Sophocles, *Greek Lexicon of the Roman and Byzantine Periods* (from B.C. 146 to A.D. 1100), (New York: Scribners, 1900).

A variety of cognate forms also are found in the patristic writings :

ἡ κυρίευσις — possession, control, domination

τὸ κυρίευμα — control, dominion

κυριευτικός — possessing lordship, superior

These cognates bear a sense harmonious with all the testimony on the basic verb itself.

In so inclusive a sweep of the literature, from Septuagint to Byzantium, in private documents on papyrus and in formal essays, both secular and religious, we find the meaning of [κατα]κυριεύειν to be consistent, "to rule over, to be lord over," with shades of meaning influenced by the context. There is no suggestion anywhere of the meaning "to lord it over", a translation that appears uniquely in the New Testament. Such a sense is provided in none of the lexicons — except one, and that is the Arndt-Gingrich lexicon for the New Testament,[7] which includes this meaning for both forms of the verb. Although this lexicon is adapted from Walter Bauer's fourth edition,[8] at this point the Arndt-Gingrich revision adds the meaning "to lord it over" which was not found in Bauer's fourth edition — nor was it later added in his fifth. Obviously, the meaning "to lord it over" reflects the idiom as found in many an English translation of the New Testament, and the Arndt-Gingrich applies it specifically to II Cor 1:24 ("not that we exercise control over your faith").

Let us, finally, examine the occurrences of [κατα]κυριεύειν in the New Testament. There are eleven occurrences including four in Romans (6:9, 14; 7:1; 14:9) and a Synoptic trio (Mk 10:42, Mt 20:25, Lk 22:25).[9] In the earliest form of this Gospel episode, Jesus says "those who are supposed to rule over (ἄρχειν) the Gentiles exercise lordship (κατακυριεύουσιν) over them and their great men have authority (κατεξουσιάζουσιν) over them, but this is not the case among you. If anyone among you wishes to be a great person, he shall be one who serves. If anyone among you wants to be foremost he shall be as a slave". The Christian virtue is service to his fellows rather than political preëminence and power over them. This contrast has no reference to "lording it over" and there is here no suggestion of arrogance

---

[7] W. F. Arndt and F. W. Gingrich, A Greek-English Lexicon of the New Testament (Chicago : University Press, 1957).

[8] Walter Bauer, Griechisch-Deutsches Wörterbuch .... (Berlin : Töpelmann, 1952⁴ and 1958⁵).

[9] The other four passages are Acts 19:16, II Cor 1:24, I Tim 6:15, I Pet 5:3.

and oppression on the part of Gentile rulers. The Matthean passage is quite similar, and Luke but little different : "The Gentile kings rule (κυριεύουσιν) over them, and those in authority have the epithet Euergetes. This isn't your way, but rather let your great man be as a young man and your leader as a serving man". Again, the contrast here has no reference to "lording it over" and the two forms of the verb have the same meaning.

It is of significance to note that the idiom "to lord it over" never appeared in any English translation before the eighteenth century. Wyclif, Tyndale, Coverdale, the Great Bible, the Geneva New Testament, the Bishops' Bible, the Roman Catholic Rheims New Testament, and the King James Bible — all translated [κατα] κυριεύειν] "to be a lord, to exercise lordship, to reign, to rule, to have power". The same thing is true of the numerous private translations made before the eighteenth century. When Father Quesnel of Paris published an English translation in 1719 he too adhered to the traditional interpretation; however, it was in his commentary that he portrayed the Gentile rulers as absolute masters, imperious, harsh, severe, haughty, men of pride and pomp in contrast to Christian humility and charity. In that same year another Roman Catholic translator, Cornelius Nary of Dublin, was the first to translate κατακυριεύειν in Mk and Mt with the idiom "to lord it over", and in II Cor and I Pet to translate "to domineer". From that date onward it became habitual to use the idiom "to lord it over". Almost all the influential translators today have accepted this idiom (e.g. Moffatt, Goodspeed, Phillips, RSV, NEB, NAB). The few translators who have not succumbed to this fashion stand forth prominently : Anthony Purver of London (1764), Julia Smith of Hartford (1876), and Robert Bratcher of the American Bible Society (1966).

There is reason to suspect that when Nary in 1719 first translated "to lord it over", this idiom did not have the connotation it bears today. When Wyclif translated by the verb lordeschipen (to lordship) he clearly meant "to exercise lordship". About 1550, John Cheke translated κατακυριεύειν in Mt 10:25 "to overmaster, to overrule". In 1582, the Roman Catholic Rheims New Testament also used "to overrule", and in 1812 W. Williams of London also used "to overmaster". These earlier terms must have meant "to rule over, to have mastery over". By analogy, "to lord it over" may then have meant simply "to be lord over, to exercice lordship over". The formal idiom introduced in 1719 has persisted and even spread to New Testament

instances other than the Synoptics; but meanwhile the meaning of
the idiom for us has changed. Similarly, the meanings of "despot"
and "tyrant" have changed, so as to describe an oppressive ruler.
Whether or not such a supposition deserves acceptance, our major
concern here has been to rescue [κατα] κυριεύειν from a common
misinterpretation, especially in its Synoptic occurrences; and to restore
to the New Testament a correct translation of [κατα] κυριεύειν ("to
rule over, to exercise lordship over, to be lord of, to master, to have
dominion over"). There is no place in the New Testament, nor in the
wider expanse of Greek literature, for the translation "to lord it over".

GENERAL-INDEX

INDEX OF PASSAGES

A. OLD TESTAMENT

B. NEW TESTAMENT

C. EARLY CHRISTIAN, JEWISH, AND CLASSICAL

WORD INDEX

παρουσία 190
ἡ παρουσία τοῦ κυρίου ἤγγικεν 51
ὁ πειράζων 6
πίστις ἐνεργουμένη 189
πνεῦμα 187
πνευματικά 187
πολυτέλειας 42
πολυτελείας πλούτου 42
πονηρίας 38
ὁ πονηρός 6
προέφθασεν 57 n*
קָרַב 49 n 1
ῥαββουνεί 7
σατανᾶς 6
σημεῖα 190

τὸ σπέρμα 36, 37, 37 n 18
σπλαγχνισθείς 109
σύμβιος 37
[σωτ]ήριον 96
tephillîn (Syr. Peshitta) 6
ṭoṭaphōth 6
ταλειθά κούμ 7
τὰ τέκνα 36, 37, 37 n 18
τέρατα ψεύδους 190
φθάνειν 48, 55-62, 64
φραγέλλιος 109
φυλακτήρια 6
ψυχαγαγῶν 41
χάρις 112, 189
χαρίσματα 187